Teaching the Drama
in Secondary Schools

Part I: A History of the Teaching of the Drama in Secondary Schools

Part II: Teaching the One-Act Play

by

Joseph Mersand, Ph.D.

The Scarecrow Press, Inc.
Metuchen, N. J.   1969

Introduction

A History of the Teaching of the Drama in Secondary Schools 1880-1937 represents, to the best of my knowledge, the first attempt to record historically the various ways in which the drama was taught in American secondary schools, as suggested in books on methodology. It is a project which has long interested me as I have endeavored to engage my students in an interest in and a love for the drama. Whenever I have been successful I would ask myself, whether I was being original and creative; or simply following suggestions which had been made decades ago. Whenever I have failed, I would similarly ask myself whether I had been using methods which had long been discarded. These questions have been asked by teachers for a long time; and such a study as this, fragmentary as it is, may be of some help.

This book is only the first part of a three-part study of the history of the teaching of the drama in American secondary schools. Part II will carry the historical record from 1937 to the present time. More textbooks on English methodology have been written in the past thirty years than in the first third of our century. It seemed wise not to attempt to put too much into a single volume. Hence the second volume in the series will carry on the story to our own times, showing what is traditional and what is new. The third part of my study will deal with the enormous magazine literature on the subject of teaching the drama ever since the first articles began appearing in the various pedagogical journals. Such periodicals as the English Journal, Educational Theatre Journal, The Speech Teacher, The High School Journal, and many others have during the past fifty or sixty years carried numerous articles by successful teachers describing their experiences. It would be a pity, it seems to me, if these many valuable suggestions were not traced in historical fashion to show the various tendencies that have persisted, those which have been discarded because experience has taught us better, and those which are still in advance of most of our practices.

Section II--Teaching the One-Act Play is a natural

iii

87455

concomitant of such a historical study. Out of the best of the suggestions which have been made in the text-books and in the professional literature and the personal experiences of teaching and directing the drama for almost four decades have come certain convictions and practices which have met with some modicum of success. This, too, will be followed by two other volumes. The second will deal with suggestions for teaching the full-length play; and the final volume will deal with the all-important problem of how to deal with the plays of Shakespeare. Thus the users of these volumes will have not only a historical review of the suggestions of teaching these three forms of drama; but at the same time they will have a positive approach to their teaching problems based on much experience, almost fifty years of playgoing in New York City and elsewhere, and wide reading for over four decades. The bibliographies will be, I trust, particularly valuable to teachers, librarians, students of the drama, and drama-lovers generally. In some respects, they are among the most complete bibliographies of their kind. They have been assembled over a long period of time and will, I hope, save the reader endless time in searching through card catalogues looking for this or that book to answer one question or another. Of course, some errors will be found. When hundreds of books are listed, it is not likely that human error will not intervene. I trust that all such errors will be brought to my attention for correction in later editions.

The author of a book of this kind is indebted to many persons professional and non-professional. They range all the way from my earliest teachers in high school in Boys High School, Brooklyn, to my advisors in New York University's Graduate School of Arts and Sciences. My editor of the Scarecrow Press, Dr. Ralph R. Shaw, and his excellent staff have done a magnificent job of organizing and arranging a mass of factual and bibliographical material and preparing the valuable Index. My students in Methods of Teaching English in Secondary Schools in the following colleges and universities have listened patiently to many of the ideas expressed herein and have stimulated me to further inquiry. Many of them will recognize their own good ideas in my classes in: Cornell University, Queens College, Hunter College in the City of New York, Syracuse University, Teachers College, Columbia University, North Texas State University, University of Colorado, Johns Hopkins University, and New York University, my Alma Mater.

Last but not least, my patient wife, Estelle J. Mersand, has helped this project from its very inception with her good advice, her careful work in verifying references, and many other chores which have by now become familiar to the wife of a scholar-teacher. To her and those listed above I wish to express my deepest thanks for all their assistance.

Joseph Mersand

Jamaica High School, New York City

Part I

A History of the Teaching of the Drama
in Secondary Schools 1880-1937

Table of Contents

I.   The history of the Teaching of the Drama in American Schools 1880-1917

II.   Teaching One-Act Plays in the 1920's

III.   Teaching the Modern Drama

IV.   Teaching the Drama in the 1930's

Chapter I

The History of the Teaching of the Drama
in American Secondary Schools - 1880-1917

The teacher of English or Speech in the secondary school
who has the responsibility of teaching the drama (whether
short or long; Shakespearean or modern) would do well to
become acquainted with some of the traditions. In this way,
he will understand some of the practices which were in use
when he was a student, even though they did little to develop his love for the drama or instill a love for reading or
seeing plays. Also, he will understand why certain procedures are in use today, and why some of them succeed and
others fail.

Drama in the 1880's

When principles for the teaching of drama in American secondary schools were first formulated in print it is
difficult to say; but we do have Professor Brainerd Kellogg's
Plan of Study for 'Perfect Possession' in his edition of
Shakespeare's Tempest published in 1882. [1]

The student ought, first of all, to read the play as
pleasure; then read it over again, with his mind upon the
characters and the plot; and lastly, to read it for meanings,
grammar, etc.

With the help of the scheme, he can easily draw for
himself short examination papers (1) on each scene, (2) on
each act, (3) on the whole play.

1.   The Plot and Story of the Play.
      (a) The general plot
      (b) The special incidents

2.   The Characters. Ability to give a connected account
      of all that is done and most of what is said by each
      character in the play.

7

3.   The Influence and Interplay of the Characters Upon
      each other.
      (a) Relation of A to B and of B to A.
      (b) Relation of A to C and D

4.   Complete Possession of the Language.
      (a) Meanings of words
      (b) Use of old words, or of words in an old meaning.
      (c) Grammar
      (d) Ability to quote lines to illustrate a grammatical
          point.

5.   Power to Reproduce, or Quote
      (a) What was said by A or B on a particular occa-
          sion
      (b) What was said by A in reply to B
      (c) What argument was used by C at a particular
          juncture
      (d) To quote a line in instance of an idiom or of a
          peculiar meaning

6.   Power to Locate
      (a) To attribute a line or statement to a certain per-
          son on a certain occasion
      (b) To cap a line
      (c) To fill in the right word or epithet

It is worth noting that of the 120 titles listed in The
English Classics Series of Maynard, Merrill & Co. in 1882,
the following were plays.

No. 14 Shakespeare's Merchant of Venice (Selections)
No. 21 Shakespeare's As You Like It   (Selections)
No. 22 Shakespeare's King John and King Richard II
       (Selections)
No. 23 Shakespeare's King Henry IV
                     King Henry V (Selections)
                     King Henry VI
No. 62 Alcestis of Euripides.   English Version by Rev.
       R. Potter
No. 63 Antigone of Sophocles.   English Version by Thomas
       Francklin
No. 92 Addison's Cato
No. 101 Marlowe's The Jew of Malta
No. 110-111 Milton's Samson Agonistes

Such a listing is revealing.   No play later than Addi-

son's <u>Cato</u> was studied.   No short plays were studied, which
was understandable.   The one-act play was hardly in existence in 1882.

The Plan of Study as expressed by Professor Kellogg
was obviously for the student who read.   Nothing is said
about the student as interpreter or as a member of an audience seeing a play.   Obviously, nothing is said about the
use of audio-visual aids to enhance appreciation and to increase comprehension, since such aids were not in existence in 1882.

Teaching Shakespeare in 1902

Twenty years later Percival Chubb published his
<u>The Teaching of English in the Elementary and Secondary</u>
<u>School.</u> [2]   Outlining the course in literature in the first year
in high school, he gives an extended explanation of how
<u>Julius Caesar</u> should be taught.   Since this book was used
by thousands of high school English teachers as the methodological Bible for over thirty years, his suggestions are
given in full.   This is how the freshman in high school in
1902 was to be taught to appreciate <u>Julius Caesar.</u>

Let the teacher read it through, with a minimum
of comment, to the class; and it will pay to have
spared no pains to become proficient in the
task. . .

The first reading of <u>Julius Caesar</u> by the teacher
should have left upon his students a deep and lasting impression of the play in its totality, with the parts in true
perspective, of its essentially dramatic and rhythmic features (its rise and fall of emotional emphasis), and of its
poetic power.   This will provide a basis for the development work that is to follow.   First, we shall call for an
outline or synopsis of the scenes to reveal the plot.   This
must be done with utmost brevity in terms of what happens,
in terms of action.   So we shall develop insight into the
first essential of dramatic art: that it is concerned with
what men do under the stress of temptation, struggle, op-
portunity.   And so we may bring out the differential of the
drama as compared with the epic, the novel, the short
story.

Our second reading, by the class, calling for memorizing and presentation of selected scenes by the students,

will be an exercise in interpretation, and will involve the
clearing up of such difficulties in metrics, in words, in
constructions and in allusions, as stand in the way of such
oral rendering and interpretation.   This should be our
practical test: Do we understand?   The teacher may introduce the subject by explaining to the class that the language
of Shakespeare's time, while (as they will have noticed)
very much like our own, yet had its peculiarities, which
sometimes stand in our way (obsolete words and idioms)
and sometimes mislead us (changes in meaning and pronunciation).   This is obvious in the opening of the first scene.
The class may point out, the words, - "mechanical," "ought
not walk," "laboring day," "profession," "cobbles," (for the
pun), "naughty," "knave," "vulgar," etc. - an excellent
crop.   Well, we must be sure, as we go, that we are not
being tripped up in our attempt to decipher what Shakespeare
means.   The teacher will not press the matter far, but will
let the niceties alone.   The feeling for Shakespearean English must grow gradually from year to year.   The students
may tabulate in their notebook twenty salient examples
culled from the text.   When this second circumspect and interpretative reading is done, we may review the ground
covered and round off our studies in language by working
out a few parallelisms (of the teacher's selection) between
Shakespeare's English and Bible English--a first step toward
a literary study of the Bible.

The talk on the metrics--with perhaps a short exercise or two--may come when the first difficulties occur, as
they will in the first and second scenes: as e. g. , the
transition from the prose of the "base mechanicals" to the
verse of the dignified tribunes, the short lines, the free
movement of the verse, the differences of pronunciation
(touched, spirit, construe), the presence of rhyme, etc. The
motive of such work, we repeat, must be the desire to deliver the lines effectively.   One good exercise to test appreciation of rhythm is to require students to divide into
lines passages written on the board in lineless prose form.
At this time, too, we may test familiarity with the play by
short class exercises, asking by whom certain important
lines were spoken.

Now the way is clear for character-study, leading
on into the deeper study of the plot, with which it is to
some extent involved.   This may be by means of problems,
or in question form.   For example, we may ask: "what
mistakes did Brutus make?   And what light do they throw

upon his character?" Or we may call for a tabular presentation of Caesar's character (data for a composition) thus:

Qualities				Evidence
of				
Character	Act	Scene	Line	Words or Incident used

Or we may ask for a comparative study, in similar form,
of Calpurnia and Portia, or a contrast between Brutus and
Caesar.

Lastly, returning to plot again, we may try to master
its logic. Here are some questions we may put: - - -
7 questions. Or, if our class is equal to it, we can enu-
merate (in table) Shakespeare's departures from Plutarch,
and try to discover the reason for them."

In addition to the instructions given above, Chubb
recommends composition topics based on the play, and some
information about the life of Shakespeare. The discussion
of ethics of the play should be incidental. Sometimes the
problems posed by the ethical discussions can be turned over to the debating class. In connection with the work in
public speaking and argument, the class would deal with the
speeches of Brutus and Antony.

A summary of the main points in teaching Julius
Caesar in 9th grade, as recommended by Chubb, are:

1.   First reading entirely by teacher, with outline or
        synopses by students of scenes to reveal the plot.

2.   Second reading in the form of memorizing and pre-
        sentation of selected scenes by students.

3.   Brief talk on metrics by teacher early in the play.

4.   Character-study by means of problems or in ques-
        tion form.

5.   Mastery of the logic of the plot through questions
        and answers.

6.   Discussion of the ethics of the play should be inci-
       dental.

7.   Speeches of Brutus and Antony can be studied in con-
       nection with work in public speaking and argument.

8.   Use of composition exercises to help the imaginative
       grasp of the circumstances and setting of the play.

9.   A few facts of Shakespeare's life should be mastered
       in the 9th year.

How Macbeth Was Taught in 1903

Franklin T. Baker, founder of the Department of the
Teaching of English at Teachers College, Columbia University, and organizer of one of the first comprehensive courses
on the teaching of English in an American college, wrote the
chapter on Literature in the Secondary Schools in The Teaching of English in the Elementary and the Secondary School,
published in 1903.[3]

His suggestions for teaching the drama are centered
around the teaching of Macbeth. He begins by saying that,

A drama is more difficult to read than a story.
Action, description, and motive are usually given
directly in narrative writing; in the drama they are
given indirectly or left to the reader's inference.

The form, broken into scenes and acts, is harder
to imagine as a unified whole than the more con-
tinuous form of narrative. In general, the teacher
will have to see to it that the pupil understands the
characters in their relation to the action, and the
separate scenes in their relation to the whole play.

For illustration of these and other things to be considered in the drama, the following are chosen from Macbeth:

1.   The source of the story, its original form, and its
       modification in Shakespeare's hands.

2.   The opening scenes, giving in their natural environ-
       ment and in the introduction to the Witches a sort of
       keynote to the play.

3.   The position of Macbeth, the promises of the Witches,

the fulfilment of a part of these promises, and the stirring of more ambitious hopes in him.

4. The evidence for and against the belief that Macbeth had conceived the murder before he met the Witches; the nature and degree of his responsibility.

5. Lady Macbeth's part in inciting him to the crime; her methods and her motives.

6. The descriptive elements attending the crime; means of arousing terror, such as the sounds that Macbeth hears in the murder scene and the knocking at the gate.

7. Macbeth's character: his fears of the uncertain or unknown, his excitable imagination, the nature of his scruples, his motives; how these are employed later in leading him to his destruction.

8. The part of Banquo in the first and second acts.

9. The change in Macbeth's motives, terror added to ambition; the recklessness with which he plunges into crime on his own initiative.

10. The change in Lady Macbeth.

11. The banquet scene: how prepared for in preceding scenes, how made effective, its part in determining the future of Macbeth.

12. Macduff as the leader of the avenging force. Where he first appears in this light, and his actions in succeeding scenes.

13. Lady Macbeth's diminishing prominence in the play: her break-down; the sleep-walking scene, how made effective.

14. The irony or Nemesis in the play: how it is shown that Macbeth's hopes are disappointed, his deeds react upon himself, and his troubles spring ultimately from what was in himself at the beginning of the play.

15. Macbeth as a tragic hero: how far he satisfies the accepted canons of dramatic criticism.

Free discussion, taking in all parts of the play, should
be encouraged. It is essential that pupils should read carefully, know clearly the meanings of the sentences, and learn
to bring to the interpretation of one part of the play what they
have found in another. In the drama as in other forms of
poetry, the beauties of individual passages should be noted.
Some of the speeches of Macbeth are proverbial for their high
order of imaginative beauty. [4]

In discussing methodology, Baker believes that

in all his teaching of literature the problem of the
teacher begins, not with questions of method, but
with matters of fact and interpretation. If he knows
his literature well, critically and in its historical
relations, and if he has an alert and sympathetic
type of mind, he has the best equipment for teaching it.

Nevertheless, Baker does feel that certain questions
of method must be considered. "The principal point of doubt
seems to be with regard to the amount of discussion and
analytic work." In the 1890's there was considerable discussion about ways to teach literature effectively. The theories
ranged from one extreme which advocated merely reading the
literature aloud in the classroom, as advocated by Hiram
Corson of Cornell University, [5] to the advocacy of minute and
searching questions upon every detail of the work as promul-
gated by L. A. Sherman of the University of Nebraska. [6]

The first theory proclaimed that literature appeals
through the ear to the emotions, and that any intellectual
treatment, analytic or otherwise, kills the enjoyment. We
shall see that there are advocates of this method of teaching
today.

The proponents of the second method "assume that every
piece of good literature is a perfect work, a mosaic in which
every word and idea have a definite and inevitable function
which analysis will reveal." [7] The heavily annotated texts of
the classics of the 1890's and later exemplify this tendency to
overburden the text with footnotes so that not a single difficult word or allusion is left unexplained.

Baker could not accept either of the extreme views.
He did not believe that in "mere reading" the best of a work
could be apprehended. Nor did he believe that intellectual

activities necessarily killed emotion and destroyed aesthetic
pleasure. He was of the firm opinion that analysis when not
carried to extremes could heighten emotional effect.

Baker, however, felt that some kinds of analytic treatment did go too far, and he cautions against it. The general
principle he advocates is:

> The analysis that reveals to the pupil new meanings
> within his power of comprehension, and new beau-
> ties within his power of appreciation, while keeping
> true to the spirit and tenor of the literature as it
> is known to scholars, --such analysis is not only
> safe, but of the very essence of good teaching. [8]

In 1908 Gilbert Sykes Blakely, an instructor in English
at Morris High School, New York City, published his Teacher's
Outlines for Studies in English. [9] While paying his respect to
Carpenter, Baker, and Scott and to Chubb for their valuable
books on the teaching of English, he had a different aim. His
book was not a discussion of the principles of teaching but
"the application of certain principles to the teaching of some
of the books required for admission to college." [10] The book
has an additional interest for teachers of English in secondary
schools because it was apparently the first methods book in
English literature written by a classroom teacher.

Blakely, in addition to a general statement about the
teaching of the drama, supplied outlines for the study of
Shakespeare's The Merchant of Venice, As You Like It,
Julius Caesar, Macbeth, and Milton's Comus.

Apparently in 1908, several methods were employed
to teach Shakespeare. Blakely says

> One teacher lays great stress on reading the play
> with little or no comment; another, with painful
> slowness, works line by line to bring out the de-
> tails of the thought; while a third lays the greatest
> stress on the structure of the play, following mi-
> nutely the steps from exposition to climax and from
> climax to conclusion.

His own methods are outlined below:

I. Preparation

The presentation of a few matters to arouse interest
and to anticipate some of the difficulties of a first reading.

II. First Reading

The aim of the first reading is to familiarize the pupil with the main facts of the play. General questions may
be asked to guide the student, or directions given to note the
progress of each scene in the development of the play. He
should not be hindered, however, from as rapid a reading as
he can make intelligently.

III. Second Reading

This careful reading will have for its purpose the interpretation of the author's thought. Other matters, however
interesting to a Shakespearean scholar, should, for the most
part, be avoided. After thorough study, many of the matters treated under the next topic will naturally come up for
discussion.

IV. Study of the Play as a Whole

Here it will be possible to sum up the work already
done and to correlate it with new work in some such order
as the following:

A. Content
   1. Setting
   2. Plot
   3. Characters

B. Form
   1. Meter
   2. Style

C. The Life and Character of the Author.

Since Baker's suggestive questions for teaching Macbeth
have been listed earlier, it might be of value to compare and
contrast Blakely's approach five years later.

I. Preparation

A review of the facts about Shakespeare's work and
the development of his art previously studied; a short explanation of the meaning and purpose of tragedy; and an ac-

count of the general belief in witchcraft in the early seventeenth century, will help to give the class the right attitude toward the play.

II. Reading and Study

The purpose of the first and second readings is the same as that already stated in the general plan.

The large number of puzzling passages in Macbeth makes the second reading unusually important.

III. Study of the Play as a Whole

SETTING--Where and between whom were the battles fought in the beginning of the play? Where are Inverness and Scone? About how long a time is involved in the entire play? Which scenes follow one another without loss of time, and which do not?

From the various hints given, what impression do you get of the conditions of life in Scotland at the time of the play?
(I, 2, 20-24; I, 4, 37-38; III, 2, 22-26.)

How is external nature used to heighten the effect made by the witches?

In what other instances is nature used to heighten the effect?
(I, 5; II, I, etc.)

PLOT--What is the purpose of the introductory scene? Compare it with the opening scene in each of the other plays you have studied.

At what point is the introduction of the plot, or the "exposition" complete?

What evidence is there that Macbeth had planned before the opening of the play for the murder of Duncan? (I, 3, 51-52; I, 7, 47-53)

What three incidents help to his success? (I, 4, 42-43; II, 3, 112-113; II, 4, 25-26.)

By what means does Shakespeare make the murder of

Duncan very effective in moving the audience even though the actual deed is committed off the stage?

What facts necessary for the reader to know are brought out in the last scene of Act II? What leads Macbeth to the murder of Banquo? (III, I, 48-72). Where does Macduff first come in as a force in the action? (III, 4, 128-129.)

What hints of his part have we had before? (II, 3, 113; II, 4, 36-38.)

What double purpose had the author in having Macduff's family slain?

To what extent does Lady Macbeth influence the action of the play? The weird sisters? Macduff? Banquo? Macbeth?

Note the steps by which Macbeth rose to fame.

What was the source of Shakespeare's material? Account for the most important changes that he made.

CHARACTERS--What sort of man have we reason to believe Macbeth was at the opening of the play from the position that he held; from what his wife said of him; from what others said of him; and from his attitude in the face of his first crime?

What two contrasts are drawn between Macbeth and Duncan in scenes 2 and 4 of Act I? Is it strange that Macbeth had often wished that he might be King in place of Duncan? Why? Show how the prophecies of the witches became his temptations. From his soliloquies in Act I, scenes 3 and 4, what do you judge of his moral sense? What decision has he reached, if any, before he returns to his wife? In his soliloquy in Act I, scene 7, what two considerations are keeping him from the murder? What arguments of Lady Macbeth were effective in bringing him to a decision? How do you account for the fact that he is extremely vacillating in Act I and fearful in the first part of Act II while in the battle with the rebels he was the personification of bravery and decision? What is his state of mind as soon as the act is committed? What change takes place as soon as it is discovered? Is his fear of Banquo a reasonable one? What effect of his crime is apparent in Act III, scene 2? What, if any, further decline do you note in Act III, scene 4? In Act V how does

Shakespeare contrive to represent Macbeth in a condition of
brutality and yet to arouse a decided human interest in him,
and even some sympathy for him? In Macbeth's several soliloquies throughout the play what mental characteristic is
most prominent? Give examples. To what extent may Macbeth be taken as a type of ambition? To what extent the
type of a noble soul led downward to destruction? What great
truth does his life illustrate, a truth that we may call, the
central idea of the play?

What mental qualities does Lady Macbeth show in Act
I, scene 5? Why does she not discuss with herself the pros
and cons of the act to be committed? What fundamental difference does this illustrate between herself and her husband?
Do you think Lady Macbeth's motive for the murder of Duncan
was selfish or unselfish? Give reasons. What sort of woman
do you suppose she was before the play opens? Why? What
light does Act III, scene 2, throw on her character? Does
her calmness and tenderness with her husband after the guests
have left the banquet indicate her wisdom in dealing with him,
or the pathetic weakening of her strong character, or a natural
tenderness? Give reasons. What makes the sleep-walking
scene so pathetic? How has the dramatist prepared us for
her breakdown? What, if anything, do you find in her to
admire?

Are we to regard Banquo as strong and noble, or
blamelessly weak, or criminally negligent? Why? Compare
Banquo and Macduff in order to bring out the chief characteristics of each. What striking contrast is drawn between Macbeth and Edward the Confessor?

FORM--Illustrate the normal line and the chief variations
from it in Macbeth. How does the number of incomplete
lines compare with the number in the other plays that you
have studied?

Find several highly imaginative passages (like II, 1,
49-60); several that express pathos (like V, 1, 22-86); several that are very condensed (like III, 2, 13-22).

Which of these passages are most characteristic of
this play?[12]

Blakely was a classroom teacher of English in New
York City. Charles Swain Thomas was Head of the Department of English in the Newton High School in Massachusetts

when he published How to Teach English Classics. Just as
Blakely's book referred to the Gateway Editions of the Classics published by the American Book Company; so, Thomas'
volume gave page references to the Riverside Literature
Series published by Houghton Mifflin, beginning with the 1880's.
It is interesting to note, as we trace the different methods of
teaching drama, the late date at which American secondary
schools began to deal with drama more recent than Shakespeare. Thus in 1910, when Thomas' book appeared, the following plays of Shakespeare had appeared in the Riverside
Literature series:

No.   55   The Merchant of Venice
       67   Julius Caesar
       93   As You Like It
      106   Macbeth
      116   Hamlet
      149   Twelfth Night
      153   A Midsummer Night's Dream
      154   Tempest
      163   Henry V
      184   King Lear
      212   Romeo and Juliet
       Of plays other than Shakespeare, the series of 1910
contained

        3   Dramatization of Miles Standish
      181   Goldsmith's The Good-Natured Man
      182   Goldsmith's She Stoops to Conquer
      191   The Second Shepherd's Play
      196   Sheridan's Rivals
      206   Goethe's Faust, Part I
      216   Ralph Roister Doister
      217   Gorboduc

    We note, then, that by 1910, some 18th century plays,
one 19th century play, and some of the early English plays
had been added to Shakespeare for study in secondary schools.

    Thomas, like Baker and others before him believed
that "the keenest enjoyment and appreciation of a Shakespearean play will come with its study."[13] He, too, believed that
the first reading should be "hasty but attentive reading of the
play entire." He continues:

        The time necessary for this in the case of Macbeth
        is short. The average pupil will probably need less

than two hours and a half. The reading will be followed by a mastery of the lines and close attention
to the structure. The dramatic function of each
scene should be thoroughly understood. Along with
this will naturally come a clear conception of each
character phase. The critical notes...should be
carefully read but the pupil should never allow himself to become enslaved to any editor's opinion; he
should learn to rely upon his own judgment, and
this judgment he should always be ready to defend
by appropriate citations. [14]

Thomas supplies twenty-four pages of questions for
teachers to ask their students. Some are questions of fact;
others stimulate thought. For example, Thomas' questions
about Act I, scene 1 are:

Comment upon the appropriateness of the first scene.
Is it apparent at once that the play is a tragedy?
What evidence of supernatural power is revealed in
this scene? Is it better that this scene be brief?
Why? [15]

Composition in the Teaching of Shakespeare

The close relationship between the study of Shakespeare
and composition activities had already been mentioned by
Chubb in 1902. He wrote:

While the many opportunities the play presents for
work in Narration, Description, and Exposition will
be utilized in connection with the course in Composition, we must use these exercises to help the i-
maginative grasp of the circumstances and setting
of the play. What sort of man was Caesar to outward view, as Shakespeare presents him is an instance. Or we have given as a general topic 'A
Street Scene in Rome,' asking each student to describe as he sees it, vividly in his mental eye, any
one street scene in which the populace of Rome
share, that mob whose presence is felt, whose mur-
mur is heard, so continually throughout the play.
Various moments of the play will be selected. [16]

Thomas's theme assignments, suggested in 1910, are
more stimulating to the creative imagination and have a contemporary methodological flavor, even though they were pub-

lished more than fifty years ago. He was interested not only
in helping students to visualize the streets of Rome (to use
Chubb's topic), but in arousing creative reconstruction of
scenes which Shakespeare did not write. Some examples
follow. Writing of Macbeth's letter to his wife (Act I, Scene
5), Thomas suggests:

> It is of course obvious that this portion of the let-
> ter read is the end, and that the beginning is omit-
> ted. Write this portion as you imagine it.[17] Sup-
> pose that the dramatist wished to have Lady Mac-
> beth reply to this letter. Write out in full what
> you think he might appropriately have her say.[18]

For many years teachers have been asking students to
write newspaper accounts of events in novels and plays read
by their students in class. Thomas suggested this activity
in his little manual in 1910:

> Write an account of the murder of Macbeth as it
> might be prepared for a carefully edited, conserva-
> tive modern newspaper. Write headlines, date,
> and all such necessary details as are brought out.[19]

Class newspapers based on the literature read are frequently found today. Thomas suggested this activity:

> An interesting exercise would be the editing of a
> class newspaper which would publish in successive
> issues the events which are chronologically brought
> out in the play. The first number of the paper could,
> for example, describe the battle and report the ex-
> perience of Macbeth and Banquo.[20]

Many teachers ask students to put themselves in the
place of a character in a novel or a play and speak or write
as he or she would. In 1910 Thomas made this suggestion:
"Putting yourself in the place of the doctor, write such an
account of his experience as you imagine he might write in
a letter to an intimate friend."[21]

A similar vicarious writing assignment is: "Write
out Lady Macbeth's confession as you imagine it spoken to a
priest just before her death."[22]

In addition to composition assignments which construct
original letters, class newspapers, confessions, and the like,

Thomas recommended, like Chubb in 1902, argumentative compositions. For example: "Write an argument disproving the assertion that Macbeth was the third murderer."

Description was also included in the compositions recommended, but with the addition that the student would describe a scene as if he were a part of it. "Describe the banquet scene. Imagine yourself to have been present as one of the guests, wholly mystified by the action of Macbeth."

Even paraphrase was suggested by Thomas: "Take one of the longer speeches of the play, and write it out in the clearest and best prose that you can command."

A third volume prepared to assist teachers using the Standard English Classics published by Ginn and Company and the New Hudson Shakespeare was An Introduction to the English Classics by William P. Trent, Charles L. Hanson, and William T. Brewster. This appeared in 1911 and was revised in 1916. All the plays studied were by Shakespeare except Milton's Comus. [23]

In the section on How to Study a Shakespeare Play, the authors make the following suggestion, already made by earlier authors:

1. The pupil should begin by reading the play through for outline of the story, so that on taking up the play in detail, he may be able to appreciate the dramatic value of each part. (See also Blakely, Thomas, and Chubb who, however, suggested that the teacher read the play rapidly to the class).

2. Familiarity with Shakespeare's text should precede any study of the Introduction or of the notes at the bottom of the page.

3. The Introduction need not be studied as a whole but may well be fitted in as needed to supplement the pupil's slender knowledge of sixteenth-century drama, language, and customs.

4. Recognizing that the aims of teachers vary widely and that abilities of pupils show a wide range, the plan of the New Hudson Shakespeare (published by Ginn) has been to provide equipment to meet the needs of all high school classes.

5.   Pupils should memorize favorite passages of the text
      for oral recitation, and should be encouraged to act
      simple scenes in class. (This suggestion Chubb made
      in 1902). If real histrionic talent is revealed the play
      or parts may be done before the entire school.

The authors recognized that there were several major
emphases which the individual teacher might prefer, and they
suggested different ways to use the Introduction and footnotes.
Such emphases might be:

a)   The play as a piece of dramatic literature.
b)   The place of Shakespeare in the history of English
     literature.
c)   The interpretation of the social and political England
     of Elizabeth.
d)   The changing character of the English language.

The plays discussed by Trent, Hanson, and Brewster
are Macbeth, As You Like It, Julius Caesar, Twelfth Night,
King Henry V, The Merchant of Venice, A Midsummer Night's
Dream, and Comus.

Since we have compared the methods suggested for
teaching Macbeth by Baker (1903), Blakely (1908), and Thomas
(1910), it may be profitable to note similarities and differences
in this volume of 1916.

First, they think that it is desirable, especially with
Macbeth, to study the play aloud in class. Thus the preliminary silent reading by students may be omitted because
Macbeth is short and because in no other play by Shakespeare
is his suggestiveness more compelling.

The authors recommend omission of some scenes if
lack of time prevents close study of every line. Questions
to be asked would lead students to make comparisons with
other characters of Shakespeare; to make comparisons with
the settings in other Shakespearean plays; to compare the
supernatural atmosphere in Macbeth with that in A Midsummer
Night's Dream.

Oral talks and written themes are suggested on such
subjects as:

1.   The costume of the Scotch Highlanders.

2.   Life in an ancient Scotch castle.

3.   The localities named in Macbeth.

4.   History of the stone of Scone.

5.   The witchcraft superstition.

Plotting the Action of a Play

Plotting the action of a play graphically and with such terms as rising action, falling action, exciting force, etc. goes back to Gustav Freytag's Technique of the Drama, published originally in German in 1863 and translated into English by MacEwan. In 1898 Elizabeth Woodbridge published her The Drama: Its Law and Its Technique, which was an adaptation and modification of Freytag to make it suitable for college students. [24]

By 1910, plotting of the incidents of a play had become quite common, and Thomas included such a graph in his volume. [25] Trent, Hanson, and Brewster give a detailed analysis of the plot of Macbeth in terms of the technical language utilized by Freytag and Woodbridge; enumerating the position of the various acts and the scenes in terms of Freytag's structural design of a play.

Questions to be asked by the teacher were to stimulate class discussion and/or more formal debate. Such questions, asked by other writers of teachers' manuals, are:

1.   Was Lady Macbeth's swoon only a pretense?

2.   Was Macbeth the third murderer?

3.   Should the ghost of Banquo actually appear on the stage?

In addition to recommending questions, oral talks, written reports, discussions, and debates on one or more aspects of the Setting and the Story, the authors had suggestions for the Characters, the Construction and Style, and Shakespeare's Life and Work.

The Characters in Macbeth

Comparisons were to be made; for example between Macbeth and Hamlet; with Caesar and Napoleon. Lady Macbeth was to be compared with Regan and Goneril.

The influence of character upon character was to be

understood by formulating answers to such questions as:

1. Would Macbeth have murdered Duncan without the in-
    stigation of the witches?

2. Would Macbeth have murdered Duncan without pressure
    from Lady Macbeth?

3. Did Lady Macbeth urge her husband to the crime solely
    from personal ambition to be queen?

Questions on the construction and style of Macbeth concerned themselves with the use of prose in the Porter scene,
in the sleep-walking scene, and in Lady MacDuff's conversation with her son. How does the verse used by the witches
differ from blank verse? What portions of the play seem to
be by hands other than Shakespeare's? Shakespeare's language,
the changes in our own time, his imagery are also subjects
of discussion.

For class discussion or for more ambitious themes by
specially qualified pupils (the beginning of a term paper?) the
following topics are recommended:

1. A comparison of Shakespeare's Macbeth and The Witch.

2. Shakespeare's treatment of the historical sources of
    the plot of Macbeth.

3. Is the porter scene unworthy of Shakespeare?

Shakespeare's Life and Work

As far back as 1902, Chubb had recommended some instruction in the life and work of Shakespeare as early as the
9th year. Rather than concentrate on remembering many
trivial details of the life of Shakespeare, students, at the time
when they were capable of studying Macbeth should discuss
such questions as:

1. How did the influences of the age of Elizabeth lead
    Shakespeare's genius toward the drama rather than
    some other form of literary expression?

2. What influences of Shakespeare's life caused him to be
    the poet of nature and human nature alike?

3. Into what periods are the plays of Shakespeare grouped?

Vocabulary and Allusions

llusions must be explained before the student
he meaning of a passage. Furthermore,
eare's words have a different meaning from
ave. Shakespeare's use of such words as
doubt, practice, invent, exhibition have some-
meanings today. Many allusions in Shakes-
were quite familiar to the audience of his time
sions in the Porter scene in Macbeth) are now
less they are explained either by the teacher
s. How detailed such analysis of allusions
depend upon the knowledge of the teacher and
the class. The caution expressed by Thomas in
s just as valid in the 1960's, is that the study
"so minute as to endanger a loss of the beauty
ficance of the whole design."

How to Achieve the Poetic Appeal

e some students may perceive poetic excellence
are's plays, the majority of our students need to
attention directed to the passages of marked ex-
An assignment might be to select the most "poeti-
e" in a given scene or act. On the following day
s read their favorite passage aloud and comments
by the class. Shakespeare's plays contain hundreds
passages, many of which have become part of the
eritage of the world.

emory Assignment and Dramatic Presentation

hubb, in his discussion of the teaching of Julius Cae-
1902, recommended that the second reading by the
e first reading was to be done by the teacher) cal-
memorizing and presentation of selected scenes.
, in 1917, continued this tradition and urged the tea-
demand a good deal of memory work in connection
e study of the drama. He felt that such memorization

offers the student excellent mental drill, unconscious
develops poetic taste, and at the same time increase
his working vocabulary and secures the retention of
poetical imagery.

Following a contention of Matthew Arnold, Thomas be-
d that these memorized passages would give the student

4. Into what classes are Shakespeare's plays divided according to their dramatic type?

By 1917 Charles Swain Thomas was a Lecturer on the Teaching of English in Harvard University and his second book on methods appeared. The Teaching of English in the Secondary School[26] was no longer a handbook for The Riverside Literature Series, but a more inclusive compendium of many suggestions on procedures. Chapter X was on The Teaching of the Drama, with Particular Reference to Shakespeare.[27]

Thomas repeats the view he expressed in 1910 that the entire play should be assigned for rapid reading, in a single sitting in the case of a play like Macbeth. For the first time in the literature, he recommends that the play be seen if it happens to be playing in the area.

This viewing might be substituted for the first rapid reading so as to provide for the student "new dramatic possibilities and provide many valuable points for future discussions. The idea is to get a perspective view of the entire action--a conception vitally important for the intelligent mastery of the later details."[28]

Since the paramount aim is to stimulate interest, how is the teacher to stimulate his students to want to read Macbeth through in a single sitting (in the days of social distractions, moving pictures, and automobiles of 1917). His suggestions for stimulating interest are:

1. Macbeth is usually voted by seniors as the most popular play in the high-school course. It is interesting that this opinion, from 1917, was confirmed in 1964 in a poll conducted by Scholastic Teacher in connection with its special issue in quadricentennial celebration of Shakespeare's birth.[29]

2. Thomas referred to the character Hugh Paret in Winston Churchill's novel A Far Country on whom Macbeth made an indelible impression while Paret was a student in Harvard. Contemporary teachers might select more recent examples of outstanding persons who were affected permanently by their school or college study of Macbeth.

3. A third suggestion for stimulating interest by Thomas is to read Malcolm's last speech and read the line that

speaks of Macbeth and Lady Macbeth as "this dead butcher and his fiendlike queen." Students will answer after they had read the play through rapidly whether this was a fair characterization of Lady Macbeth. Other questions which students might consider deal with Lady Macbeth's death and the murderer of Banquo.

Thomas was too experienced a master-teacher to think that the interest of all students could be aroused by the means listed above--even in the "good old days" of 1917. He realized that some classes need more mandatory assignments (and some even welcome it). For these students a short-answer test after the first rapid reading is to be announced.

This short-answer test is to be dictated by the teacher, the papers will be exchanged and graded by the students, and correct answers given.

Such a short-answer quiz might contain the following questions:

1. With whom was Duncan at war?

2. Who tells Duncan of Macbeth's bravery in the recent battle?

3. Who are especially praised for their bravery?

4. Of whose traitorous action does Ross bring news?

5. Who is with Macbeth when he meets the witches?

6. By what title do the witches first address Macbeth?

7. With what title does Duncan invest Malcolm?

8. How does Lady Macbeth get news of the weird sisters' salutations?

9. Who is Banquo's son?

10. After the murder where did Malcolm go?

11. Who discovers the murder?

12. Who supplies the humor interest in the play?

13. How ma

14. Who is t

15. To what

16. What Than
    design?

17. Who escapes

18. In what castl

19. What is the m

20. Who kills Macb

Methods o

After the interest
play has been read "once
given on the contents, the
should be included in furth

1. Visualization
2. Vocabulary and a
3. Poetic appeal
4. Memory assignme
5. Humor in drama
6. Plot structure
7. Character study

Many of these had appea
sed above. The newer items w
detail.

How to Visualize

Students should be helped to
questions about the relative stage-p
their personal appearance, the soun
similar questions that emphasize ser
acter differentiations. Many lines in
fusing unless students can visualize w
located when they speak, particularly
a soliloquy while others are in conver
of the stage.

Certain a
can understand
many of Shakes
what they now
presently, still
what different
peare which
(e.g., the allu
meaningless u
or by footnote
should be will
the nature of
1917, which
should not be
and the signi

Whil
in Shakespe
have their
cellence.
cal passag
the studen
are made
of poetica
cultural h

sar, in
class (t
led for
Thomas
cher to
with th

lieve

selected norms which would direct him toward a more accurate judgment of things aesthetic and things spiritual. Prose
as well as verse should be memorized. Thomas believed
that "wisely selected prose passages thoroughly memorized
may secure a ready response in the learner's style." Memorized passages, in Thomas' opinion, can give students
standards of moral and social judgment and thus can contribute to character development.

Humor In Drama

Since Shakespeare sometimes introduced humor even
in his sternest tragedies, students should perceive and enjoy
it. The Porter's scene in Macbeth, the actions of Lancelot
Gobbo in The Merchant of Venice, the drunken scene of
Stephano, Trinculo, and Caliban in The Tempest, the artisans
in A Midsummer Night's Dream performing Pyramus and
Thisbe, are some examples of scenes which can easily be
performed in the classroom with good effect.

How to Study the Plot Structure

In the earlier years of high school, plot should be
thought of as story and technical terms should be avoided.
In the more advanced classes, if the teacher thinks it wise,
the five divisions named by Gustav Freytag may be studied:

1. Introduction
2. Rising Action
3. Turning-point (Climax)
4. Falling action
5. Catastrophe

Since these terms are fully explained in Freytag and
Woodbridge and in most books on drama appreciation, we
need not repeat them here. Thomas shows how the plot of
Macbeth can be divided conveniently into these parts.

How to Study Character

Thomas believed that the deepest impression made upon students as they studied plays was made by their study of
the characters. The character of a person is portrayed in
four ways:

1. By what the person says or fails to say
2. By what the person does or fails to do

3. By what is said about the person
4. By what the person causes others to do

Any character in a play can be selected, and students can point out passages which illustrate these four methods of revealing character. Another method is to divide the class into four groups, each of which will concentrate on studying the same character but by one method only.

Like other writers before him, Thomas warns against over-minute analysis of character and recommends that the study be confined to the more obvious and the more salient points.

In daily life, the effect of one character upon another fascinates us and the same should be true of character analysis in the drama. What effect had Lady Macbeth upon Macbeth? What influence does Cleopatra exert upon Antony?

A great dramatist works through character contrasts, and Shakespeare's plays are full of such contrasts. Brutus vs. Mark Antony; Shylock vs. Antonio; Hamlet vs. Fortinbras.

The development of character is another important phase of study. Macbeth interests us not so much because of what he is at the beginning of the play, but because of what a brute he becomes as a result of his inordinate ambition. Mark Antony in Julius Caesar is another good example of development of character, but in this instance he grows in stature.

Thomas is concerned with the ethical significance of tragic flaws in character.

> The objective protrayal of tragic results almost inevitably weaves its subtle impression into the character of the young reader. And this is the best result of the drama in the schools. [31]

Once again Thomas cautions against over-analysis, as he concludes his chapter on the teaching of the drama:

> No teacher will wish, in this study of drama, to go so minutely into the analysis of plot or character as to detract from the aesthetic enjoyment of the selected play.

Up to 1917, few of the books on methodology mentioned
a contemporary dramatist. The discussion of method was
confined almost exclusively to Shakespeare. However, in a
footnote to his discussion of ways to reveal character, Thomas
refers to Bernard Shaw's long and elaborate stage directions.[32]

Another teacher's manual to accompany a series of
English classics was written by George L. Marsh for the
Lake English Classics, published by Scott, Foresman. This
appeared originally in 1912 and was revised in 1921.[33]
Among the plays discussed were:

First Year
The Merchant of Venice
A Midsummer Night's Dream

Second Year
As You Like It
Henry V
Julius Caesar
Twelfth Night
The Tempest
Romeo and Juliet

Fourth Year
Macbeth
Hamlet

Since we have discussed the treatment of Macbeth by
Baker (1903), Blakely (1908), Thomas (1910 and 1917), let us
see what suggestions were made by Marsh, who was an associate professor of English at the University of Chicago.
Marsh's aids to study consisted of three types: Questions,
Theme Subjects, and Selections for Class Reading. The
questions were General, The Plot, and the Characters.

A typical General Question was: When was Macbeth
first printed? What is the probable date of its first production?

A typical question about the Plot was: Is it more effective not to have the murder of Duncan take place before
our eyes? Why?

A typical question on the Characters was: In how
many ways in Act I is Macbeth shown to be worthy of being
King?

Among the theme subjects were the following:

Write an account of the finding of Duncan's body, using modern newspaper style. Since a similar theme assignment had been suggested by Thomas in 1910, it may have become the fashion at that time to suggest this type of theme.

Other theme topics ranged from the Changes in Macbeth's Character, a Defence of Lady Macbeth, the Figurative Language of the Play, to a summary of the play.

The suggestions by Marsh concluded with selections for class reading. Since this is the first of the teacher's manuals to make such recommendations, they are listed below. They represent what one teacher of methods thought to be playable scenes:

1. The weird sisters

2. Lady Macbeth's ambition is stirred

3. Macbeth's hesitation is overcome

4. Macbeth and the phantom dagger

5. After the murder

6. The murder is discovered

7. The murder of Banquo is planned

8. The banquet scene

9. Macbeth and the witches

10. The sleep-walking scene

11. Macbeth before the battle

12. The battle

It is interesting to know the scenes recommended for class reading in 1912 because this seems the first time that such scenes have been specifically indicated. Chubb recommended classroom presentation in 1902 but did not specify the scenes to be read.

Emma Miller Bolenius was an instructor in English in

a Newark, New Jersey High School and in 1915 published
Teaching Literature in the Grammar Grades and High School.[34]
Chapter VII is devoted to teaching the drama, and ends with
suggestions for teaching The Merchant of Venice and Julius
Caesar.

Miss Bolenius added a new note in the history of
methodology of the drama--a history of the dramatic instinct
and a brief history of the drama.[35] Bolenius appears to be
the first author on methods who refers to the drama later
than Shakespeare as worthy of reading. She says:

> The modern drama is interesting reading. Shaw,
> Rostand, Synge, Maeterlinck, Ibsen, and others
> are popular on the library shelf and run their season
> at the theater.[36]

Teaching the Technique of the Drama

Although Bolenius felt that young people could not appreciate an elaborate discussion of technique, she felt that
they could understand a division into acts, each of which contributed to the whole.

> A play must be introduced--we must know the
> characters, place, time, and certain facts upon
> which the plot rests. This naturally takes place
> in Act I. As we said before, a plot is a clash
> of forces. These forces must develop. In Act II,
> therefore, we find the complicating forces (tying-
> up forces) at work. These reach a climax some-
> where in the middle of the play, Act III, when af-
> fairs for the hero are at the tottering point. Will
> he win or will he lose? That is the climax. The
> action turns, one way or the other. Sometimes
> a seemingly unimportant action may bring about
> the turning. Act IV brings in the resolving forces,
> those that will lead to the untying of the knot. The
> last act witnesses the conclusion: in a tragedy,
> death or ruin; in a comedy, happiness or success.
> Children will enjoy working out crudely the pyramidal
> development of a play.[37]

Such analysis of the structure of a play appears early
in the methodology, and was probably used by many English
teachers after Woodbridge's book on the technique of the
drama appeared in 1898.

The Underlying Structure of the Play

Elementary blackboard diagram showing every well-constructed tragedy or comedy

Climax or Turning Point

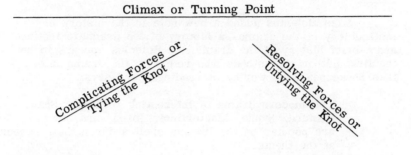

Introduction   Conclusions

(Reproduced from Bolenius: Teaching Literature in the Grammar Grades and High School. Boston: Houghton Mifflin, 1915, p. 159).

The diagram from Bolenius's book was used, in one form or another, by many teachers for decades to represent a play's structure graphically.

Her description of the elements of an ideal play, written half a century ago, makes good sense today:

> Various elements combine to make the ideal play.
> Stage scenery portrays the setting. Costumes cheat
> us into believing that the actors are the real char-
> acters, and the present age another. Incidents of
> the plot hang together by cause and effect. A plot
> must not have in it any incident that does not con-
> tribute vitally to the action; for plot is a chain of
> events, each event depending on one before and pro-
> ducing one to come. There must be no unlikely or
> forced coincidences. Emotion must be sincere.
> Characters must act in keeping with the qualities
> given them and no character ought to change unless
> something has had a chance to affect it. Costumes
> must suit the times portrayed. Settings must be
> historically correct. Actors must enunciate so
> that they can be heard well; they must forget them-
> selves in the parts they portray; they must suit
> these parts physically, and temperamentally. No

play dare lag; suspense must carry it on.[38]

Bolenius gives some general suggestions for teaching Shakespeare, and then specific suggestions for teaching As You Like It, Twelfth Night, Macbeth, Hamlet, The Merchant of Venice, and Julius Caesar. She is the first of the writers on methodology to write even briefly on how to teach Goldsmith's, She Stoops to Conquer.

Among her general suggestions are:

1. Teachers must be careful not to make the reading of a Shakespearean play a lesson in etymology, but they must clarify the text.

2. The reading of parts will sometimes help to achieve such strong interest that the pupil will of his own volition conquer the strangeness of diction (which, Bolenius thinks, is the greatest obstacle to appreciation).

3. Reports may be given on the characters.

4. A trip to the theatre may be promised (This was in 1915).

Since various analyses have already been given of the suggestions for teaching Macbeth beginning with Franklin T. Baker's in 1903, it will be valuable to see what Emma Miller Bolenius, a classroom teacher in a large city (Newark, New Jersey), suggested in 1915.

> Macbeth is a tragedy, wonderful in structure. The witches are supernatural beings, usually interpreted, as personifications of Macbeth's own desires. The drama is strong meat for young people, but there are some striking and vital lessons: the power of suggestion, danger of vacillation, wicked associations, peril of opportunity, sin its own punishment, how and why sin accumulates, etc.

A teacher, absorbed by the gigantic struggles of forces in this drama, can make boys and girls thrill with the soliloquies of Macbeth, with Lady Macbeth's arguments, with the weird trappings of the witches, the temptation, the murder, the banquet, and the sleep-walking scenes. The plot runs its upward path well for Macbeth, fulfilling the first prophecies. The plot runs its downward course with the working-out of the

second set of prophecies, which Macbeth's inordinate ambition has demanded. The escape of Fleance at the time Banquo
was murdered is the turning point in the play.[39]

Bolenius seems to be the first to recommend a play
later than Shakespeare for high school use, Goldsmith's,
She Stoops to Conquer. By using pictures and by assigning
outside reading the teacher can help students visualize life in
the eighteenth century.

Another first for Bolenius is her recommendation of
exercises in the dramatic form, both in prose and verse.
For example:

1.   A ballad like Lowell's Singing Leaves or Abou Ben
      Adhem can be written in dialogue, so that two pupils
      can give it.

2.   Writing a monologue by devising what a person would
      say under certain circumstances is an excellent first
      exercise in originality.

3.   Actual dialogues between characters the students know.

4.   Stories may be dramatized. In Miss Bolenius's clas-
      ses Hawthorne's, Snow Image and Irving's, Legend of
      Sleepy Hollow and Rip Van Winkle were dramatized.

Committee work, about which so much has been written in recent years, was done by Miss Bolenius in 1915 and
earlier. Thus if a longer piece is to be dramatized, the
class should plan first what scenes are to be dramatized.
Then committees of students work together on a single scene.
Among the longer works which, in Bolenius's opinion, can be
so dramatized are: The Lady of the Lake, Ivanhoe, The
Princess, Silas Marner, A Tale of Two Cities.

Bolenius also recommends impromptu dramatization
as a good way to test the pupils' knowledge of a story.

Original plays are suggested, as well as motion picture
scenarios and scripts.

Most valuable for the student of the historical study
of the drama are Bolenius's two extensive series of lesson
plans for The Merchant of Venice and Julius Caesar. Since
the methodology of the former has not yet been discussed, it

will be explained here.

Making the person and time of Shakespeare real

Before beginning the study of a Shakespearean play,
Bolenius would use visual aids to enable students to see what
Shakespeare looked like and what his environment was. These
aids would include pictures, simple drawings on the chalk-
board, maps, and even a poem written on the board, such as
Thomas Bailey Aldrich's "Shakespeare--The King."

Students are assigned readings about Shakespeare and
his times and report to the class in the form of a club pre-
sided over by one of their students. It is significant that
fifty years ago Bolenius cautioned against too much telling by
the teacher and more participation by the class. There were
some things which teachers might tell better; such as:

> ...The giving of a graphic picture of Elizabethan
> days and ideals, --the spirit of adventure stealing
> out across the seas, the rise of the middle class,
> the freedom of life and thought, the demand for
> action, the versatility of the times, the boyish en-
> thusiasm, the ardent imagination, the coming of new
> things, the seething of new ideas... [40]

Reading the Play

In teaching the play, Bolenius follows most of her predecessors in suggesting that

> the ideal way is to read the play rapidly at first to
> get the story, then to read it carefully the second
> time to study characters, development of plot,
> descriptions, and fine lines.

Making a Chart of the Plot

Bolenius, who earlier had referred to studying the
structure of a play, suggests that teacher and class should
work out a chart showing the various threads of the plot, and
on p. 177, gives an example of a student's plot chart for The
Merchant of Venice.

Studying Characterization in Shakespeare

There are basically four ways of getting an unbiased

view of a character:

1.   By observing how he acts

2.   By observing how he speaks and what he says

3.   By observing how other people treat him

4.   By observing what other characters say about him

Students select a character and then find data in the play to reveal his or her individuality. Such a character for analysis may be chosen before the play is read. Then, as the student reads the play, he accumulates data for building up his concept of the character.

Questions at the end of the study

Such questions, as suggested by Bolenius for The Merchant of Venice, are:

Which characters do you like best? Why? What scene have you enjoyed most? Why? What lines in the play do you like best? Why? Quote examples of punning, of brilliant wit, of intense feeling, of character description, of observation of nature, of humor, of pathos, of beauty of allusion, of terse common sense, of customs of the day.[41]

Acting out the Parts

Bolenius repeats what several other authorities, beginning with Chubb in 1902 have said about the value of student dramatizations of selected scenes.

Notes

1.   New York: Maynard, Merrill and Co., 1882, p. vii-ix.

2.   New York: Macmillian, 1902.

3.   Carpenter, George R., Baker, Franklin T., and Scott, Fred N. New York: Longmans, Green, 1903.

4.   Op. cit., p. 276-78.

5. See his The Aims of Literary Study. New York: Macmillan, 1894.

6. See his Analytics of Literature: A Manual for the Objective Study of English Prose and Poetry. Boston: Ginn, 1893. In Chapters xiii and xiv, p. 144-89 he analyses in detail Macbeth and other Shakespearean tragedies.

7. Baker, op. cit., p. 278.

8. Ibid, p. 281.

9. New York: American Book Company.

10. Op. cit., p. 4.

11. Ibid., p. 63.

12. Ibid. p. 79-83.

13. Thomas, Charles Swain How to Teach English Classics Boston: Houghton Mifflin, 1910, p. 40.

14. Ibid.

15. Ibid.

16. Chubb, op. cit., p. 293.

17. Thomas, op. cit., p. 65.

18. Ibid.

19. Ibid.

20. Ibid.

21. Ibid.

22. Ibid.

23. Trent, William P., Hanson, Charles L., and Brewster, William T. An Introduction to the English Classics. Boston: Ginn, 1916.

24. Woodridge, Elizabeth The Drama: Its Law and Its Tech-

nique. Boston and Chicago: Allyn and Bacon, 1898.

25. Thomas, op. cit., p. 62.

26. Thomas, Charles Swain The Teaching of English in the Secondary School Boston: Houghton Mifflin, 1917.

27. Ibid., p. 198-223.

28. Ibid., p. 198.

29. See "What Is Happening in the Study of Shakespeare in American Secondary Schools," Scholastic Teacher, Feb. 21, 1964.

30. Thomas, The Teaching of English in the Secondary School, p. 201.

31. Ibid., p. 222.

32. Ibid., p. 218, footnote 1.

33. Marsh, George L. A Teacher's Manual for the Study of English Classics Chicago: Scott, Foresman, 1912, 1921.

34. Bolenius, Emma Miller Teaching Literature in the Grammar Grades and High School. Boston: Houghton Mifflin, 1914, p. 153-186.

35. Ibid., p. 153-58.

36. Ibid., p. 157-58.

37. Ibid., p. 158-59.

38. Ibid. p. 159.

39. Ibid. p. 162-63.

40. Ibid., p. 172.

41. Ibid. p. 178-79.

Chapter II

Teaching One-Act Plays in the 1920's

From the beginning of the teaching of drama in American secondary schools, Shakespeare's plays were almost the only plays taught. As was mentioned in Chapter I, Emma Miller Bolenius in 1915 had recommended Oliver Goldsmith's She Stoops to Conquer. Beginning with the 1920's two new developments came:

1. An interest in teaching modern drama.

2. An interest in teaching one-act plays.

The rapidity with which books of one-act plays for school use appeared can be traced in the following chronology:

1920 Alice M. Smith, Teacher of English at the Franklin High School, Minneapolis, Minnesota, edited Short Plays by Representative Authors (New York: Macmillan).

In 1921 three (!) additional collections appeared. They were:

1. Helen Louise Cohen, Chairman of the English Department of Washington Irving High School, New York City, edited One-Act Plays by Modern Authors (New York: Harcourt, Brace).

2. Sterling Andrus Leonard, of the University of Wisconsin and the Wisconsin High School edited The Atlantic Book of Modern Plays (Boston: Little, Brown).

3. Edwin Van B. Knickerbocker, Chairman of the English Department of George Washington High School, New York City, edited Plays for Classroom Interpretation (New York: Henry Holt).

Throughout the 1920's and ever since, edited collections of one-act plays for high school use have appeared

regularly. Methods books in their discussion of the teaching
of the drama now ordinarily have a section on teaching Shakespeare, a section on teaching modern drama, and one on teaching one-act plays. In developing a methodology for the two
later forms, the authorities frequently went back to the tried
and true suggestions which have been enumerated in Chapter
I of this historical survey of methodology but they also added
new principles and procedures.

Helen Louise Cohen was a pioneer in introducing contemporary drama in general, as well as one-act plays into
the high school curriculum. Speaking from her own teaching
experience, she explained that:

> When one is young, it is easier to enjoy literature
> written from a point of view nearer to one's own
> life and times. Reading good contemporary litera-
> ture is likely also to pave the way for a deeper ap-
> preciation of the great masterpieces of all time.[1]

Not only did she speak in general terms about appreciating the classics through an earlier appreciation of the contemporary; but Cohen was deeply interested in arousing permanent interest in the drama in particular.

> For this book was planned to encourage an under-
> standing attitude towards the theatre, to deepen the
> love that is latent in the majority of us for what is
> beautiful and uplifting in the drama, and to make
> playgoing a less expensive, more regular, and more
> intelligent diversion for the generation that is grow-
> ing up.[2]

Whereas Bolenius held out the promise of a trip to the
theater as a way to arouse interest in the study of a Shakespearean play, Cohen encouraged regular playgoing. It should
be remembered that the American theatre in the 1920's was
entering into a flourishing period and that the proximity of
her school to the theatre district make it comparatively easy
to recommend worthy plays to her students.

Aside from an extended historical introduction to the
new dramatic art of the 1920's, Cohen's first collection of
one-act plays made a major contribution to methodology in
her section on how to teach the writing of one-act plays (p.
xxxiv-1). Cohen felt that her collection of short plays could
be acted by students as well as being read by students.

Apparently Cohen's volume found favor with many teachers because in 1923 she published The Junior Play Book (New York: Harcourt, Brace); in 1927, More One-Act Plays by Modern Authors (New York: Harcourt, Brace); and in 1934, a revision of her first book.

In the section for teachers, in The Junior Play Book, Cohen states that this is the "first collection of plays that has been made especially for use in the ninth year of the school course." She also suggests:

1.   Of the eleven plays in her collection, not more than a half dozen should be taken up in class. The remainder should be read at home for recreative reading.

2.   Plays that require building up of a background should be studied and discussed in class in the same way that other pieces of literature, classic modern, or contemporary, are handled.

3.   Books of plays are not to be confined to the public speaking or elocution department only; but are to be used in the study of English just as volumes of short stories, of essays, or of speeches are used.

4.   The aims for studying plays, classic or modern are:

        a. interesting young people in good plays;
        b. helping them make connection between drama and healthful community recreation;
        c. adding to their general culture;
        d. giving them an added zest in the printed play and in the theatre.

For specific procedures we must turn to the introductions to each of the plays in The Junior Play Book. One of the plays included is Booth Tarkington's The Trysting Place, a favorite in many collections. By examining her suggestions for study, we may perceive how Cohen handled this play with her students and her suggestions for fellow-teachers.

Each play in any of Cohen's collections is prefaced by a helpful introduction designed to interest the young reader. If there are difficult words, these are explained before the play begins. Books and articles for supplementary reading are recommended. Finally there are Suggestions for Study. For The Trysting Place they are:

1.   What is the significance to the plot of the play of The
      Young Woman's (Mrs. Curtis's) fourth speech?

2.   Why is Mrs. Briggs in such a hurry to have her daugh-
      ter leave "the trysting place?"

3.   Why does Mr. Tarkington call this play a farce and
      not a comedy?

4.   How do you feel towards Lancelot at the close of the
      play? Do you think of him in the end as tragic or
      absurd?

5.   Compare Lancelot Briggs with the hero of Seventeen;
      with the other boys of his age in Mr. Tarkington's
      other plays and novels.

6.   Which is generally considered to be Booth Tarkington's
      more significant work, his novels or his plays?

        Questions of fact alternate with questions of judgment.
Literary terms are expected to be known. The play is to
be compared with other works by the author. Students are
expected to react to the characters and to exercise their
judgment about them (even as early as Grade 9).

        In her introduction to the 9th grade readers for whom
the Junior Play Book was intended, Cohen expresses her hopes
that in addition to enjoying the plays, they will notice how the
effects were achieved; and that they will be interested in
writing plays themselves.

        Because this book appeared in 1923, a very exciting
year in the history of American drama, when many experi-
ments in production, lighting, and stagecraft were going on,
Cohen wanted the 9th graders to become aware of all these
innovations. For the first time in the literature of methodology in drama we read:

            These questions (i.e. the Suggestions for Study) are
            put so that you may begin thinking about the best
            way of producing plays, may watch the newspapers
            and magazines for accounts of novel and artistic
            methods of setting and lighting the stage, and may
            see the close relationship between the kind of play
            and the kind of design which that play demands for
            a background. [3]

In 1927 Helen Louise Cohen published More One-Act
Plays by Modern Authors, and continued her interest in en-
couraging students to go beyond the confines of the text-book.
Ever since her first book in 1921 she had emphasized the exciting activities in all phases of the current American and
world theatre. Now in her third volume of short plays for
high school students she urges students not only to see current plays but to read about them.

> When a text like More One-Act Plays by Modern
> Authors is being used, the class group will want to
> keep in touch with new books on the theatre and
> with the periodical literature that deals with the sub-
> ject. It is suggested that files of Drama, of Thea-
> tre Magazine, and Theatre Arts Monthly be kept
> on reference, and that portfolios and bulletin boards
> show evidence of the collection of all kinds of ma-
> terial bearing on the drama and the theatre. [4]

Another innovation is the interest in independent research through the study of current book and periodical literature on the drama.

Correlation among departments is also recommended.
Says Cohen:

> The various arts and sciences can be made to sup-
> plement the study of modern plays. Costumes, the
> dance, incidental music, settings, and lights can
> be undertaken as a piece of cooperation between the
> department of English and the other departments of
> the school. The construction of models is a pro-
> cedure that always gives life to the printed page. [5]

An examination of Helen Louise Cohen's, Study Questions on Paul Green's The Last of the Lowries will reveal
some of the things upon which she placed emphasis:

Questions of background

1. What is a Croatan?

2. What are some of the aspects of life in North Carolina in the historic past and at the present time that
have furnished dramatic material to Paul Green?

4. Make a list of the dialect words in the play and write

their meanings.

Questions pertaining to plot structure

3.   Show by means of some simple diagram the parallel
      incidents in Synge's Riders to the Sea and Green's
      Last of the Lowries.

8.   What moment in the play do you consider the turning
      point?

11.   How might the principle of contrast be applied in the
      production of The Last of the Lowries?

Questions pertaining to the characters

5.   Which of the characters stands out most clearly?

6.   Is Mayno the wife of one of the dead outlaws or of
      Henry Berry?

Questions relating to similar works

7.   What characteristics of folk drama has this play?

10.   What are the titles of some of the collections of tra-
      ditional English ballads surviving in various Southern
      states?

12.   Give other examples of the literature of outlawry;
      e. g., in the Bible, in ballads, in Shakespeare.

13.   Make a list of recent plays the scene of which is laid
      in remote corners of the South.

Additional activities included writing a review of Paul
Green's, The Lord's Will and a study of the then (1927)
flourishing Bureau of Community Drama at the University of
North Carolina under Frederick H. Koch.

Even a cursory examination of these study questions
will reveal the many purposes, other than recalling the details of the play, that Cohen had in mind.

The Contributions of Edwin Van B. Knickerbocker
to the Teaching of the One-act Play

Contemporary with Helen Louise Cohen in his propaganda for the one-act play was another New York City School supervisor, Edwin Van B. Knickerbocker, Chairman of the English Department of George Washington High School. Four of his collections were published and they achieved wide circulation.

1.   Plays for Classroom Interpretation. New York: Henry Holt, 1921.

2.   Twelve Plays. New York: Henry Holt, 1924.

3.   Short Plays. New York: Henry Holt, 1931.

4.   Short Plays: Revised. New York: Henry Holt, 1949.

Knickerbocker published over a period of three decades and his suggestions for using one-act plays in classrooms were followed (and probably still are) by many teachers.

Some of Knickerbocker's views, although expressed over forty years ago seem very contemporary in their emphases. Thus, in describing the method for using his first book, Plays for Classroom Interpretation (1920), he states:

> In such work the plays are acted out in the classroom with expressive oral rendering of the lines, and with complete action, gesticulations, and facial expression. The lines are read from the text, no stage is required, and no stage equipment or costuming is necessary, although some simple provision for these is desirable. The interpretation of a play is highly motivated and socialized project work, providing numerous problems of genuine interest and value.

> Because the work is group work, it is desirable that something of the spirit of the studio should prevail rather than the atmosphere of the more formal classroom. [6]

The Outcomes of Properly Directed Work in Dramatics

Teachers of both English, Speech, and Dramatics will recognize many of these outcomes listed by Knickerbocker in 1921:

Properly directed work in dramatics

1.   Develops the student's power of self-expression through
        its training in the coordination of mind and body.

2.   Makes for social efficiency, both in the development
        of the spirit of team-work and in the inculcation of a
        knowledge of social usages.

3.   Quickens the powers of visualization and auditization.

4.   Tends to deepen the student's knowledge of human
        nature.

5.   Provides highly motivated and socialized project work.

6.   Affords unusual opportunities for speech improvement
        and develops in the student an ability to read aloud ef-
        fectively.

7.   Stimulates interest in related fields of art and history.

8.   Provides occasion for real co-operation between de-
        partments in the school.

9.   Work with the modern short play tends to develop in
        the students a proper taste in an important phase of
        present day literature.[7]

The Method

Since, in Knickerbocker's opinion, "no method of procedure (i.e., in classroom interpretation of short plays) has
before this been presented in text-book form," it is necessary
at this point to outline his method in some detail:

1.   The students read at home the play to be studied. An
        idea of the plays they were expected to read in 1921
        can be obtained from the seven plays in this volume.

        a. "The Golden Doom"--Lord Dunsany
        b. "Two Crooks and a Lady"--Eugene Pillot
        c. "Will o' The Wisp"--Doris F. Halman
        d. "Spreading The News"--Lady Gregory
        e. "The Turtle Dove"--Margaret Scott Oliver
        f. "Allison's Lad"--Beulah Marie Dix
        g. "Ulysses" (Scene 2, Act III)--Stephen Phillips

2.   Students do preliminary work.

3.   They take up the detailed presentation.

Opportunities are provided for oral and written composition. For proper interpretation there are opportunities
for special investigations and committee work.

Following the reading of the play at home, students are
then assigned preliminary study at home, followed by discussions in class. The six aspects to be studied and discussed
are: Plot, Theme, Atmosphere, Setting, Preliminary Characterization, Music.

One method of division of labors is to divide the class
into as many groups as there are problems for consideration,
and assign to each group the special task of making an intensive study of one problem. When a particular problem is
discussed in class, the "special interest" group leads the discussion while the other students give their own opinions.

One or more problems may be discussed in a single
period, depending upon the importance of the topic under discussion and the intensity of treatment the topic merits.

If the committee approach is not feasible, then every
member of the class studies the problem or problems assigned for a given day.

Informality should be encouraged. The interpretation
of the play is a project and the entire class should be concerned with every phase of it. If the classroom is kept in-
formal, says Knickerbocker, and mutual respect is engendered,
then many valuable ideas will be forthcoming which a more
formal atmosphere might stifle.

Written composition need not be neglected. For example, students may write out their solutions to the various
problems of the preliminary study. Some of these reports
may be read in class to start the discussions. After a day
of discussion, students may be asked to summarize in writing the main arguments pro and con.

In addition to these expository or argumentative compositions, which may vary from a paragraph or two to several pages, other writing opportunities exist. For example:
letters for information, advice, or loan of materials.

Cooperation may take place with other departments in

the preparation of sets, designs, models, simple settings, scores for music.

The third stage in the dramatic interpretation of short plays is the actual presentation of selected scenes. Committees may be assigned the performance of one scene. Other students will prepare properties and set the stage. On occasion several committees may prepare the same scene or play. Discussion follows each performance. A final performance may include those actors considered best in their roles by the class.

This, in brief compass, is the method of classroom interpretation of short plays developed by Knickerbocker when he was a teacher of English at Evander Childs High School and later when he became Head of the English Department at George Washington High School.

In 1924 Knickerbocker published his second collection, Twelve Plays (New York: Henry Holt). In this book he did not confine himself to classroom acting. He now saw a three-fold use for short plays:

1.   To be read in English classes as literature.

2.   To be acted out in the classroom.

3.   To be produced in public.

If a short play is to be considered as part of the literature course, it should have one or more of several values:

1.   It may be worth while as a portrayal.

2.   It may possess elements of beauty.

3.   It may be sheer entertainment. [8]

However, in addition to the general value as explained above, students reading a short play as literature must also consider it critically. "To do this, we must be able to judge the effectiveness of its several elements and to determine their relative importance and value."[9]

The elements, most of which Knickerbocker had listed and discussed in his first book are: theme, atmosphere, plot, situations, characters, dialogue, action, and setting. Recog-

nition of the elements that make up a play should lead to
greater understanding and appreciation and to development of
a set of critical criteria by which to approach new plays,
short or long.

Since the principles of classroom interpretation in
Twelve Plays are quite similar to those already summarized
from Plays for Classroom Interpretation it will not be necessary to repeat them here.

A third aspect of play study described in Twelve Plays
is the possibility of public performance. Many of the obvious activities, ranging from publicity, ticket-printing, stage-
managing, etc. are explained.

In 1931 Knickerbocker issued his third collection,
Short Plays (New York: Henry Holt). Many of the suggestions mentioned in his two previous volumes are incorporated
and brought up to date in this one. His three aims for
studying short plays have now been increased to four:

1.   Plays may be read and studied as class work in much
       the same way that short stories are read and studied.

2.   Plays may be given an interpretative oral reading in
       the classroom, with the students reading the lines
       from the texts in character.

3.   Plays may be acted informally in the classroom with
       makeshift properties or none at all, and with the lines
       read from the book rather than given from memory.

4.   Plays may be produced for public performance with
       full attention to costuming, properties, lighting, and
       scenery. [10]

Throughout the 1920's, 1930's, 1940's new collections
of one-act plays appeared, each with suggestions for teaching.

In addition to the early one-act play collections described above, the following were, for a time, popular for
one reason or another:

B. Roland Lewis, Contemporary One-Act Plays. New York:
       Charles Scribner's Sons, 1922.
James Plaisted Webber and Hart Hanson Webber, One-Act
       Plays. Boston: Houghton Mifflin, 1923.

Frederick Houk Law, Modern Plays--Short and Long. New
    York: Century, 1924.
Milton M. Smith, Short Plays of Various Types: New York:
    Charles E. Merrill, 1924.
James Plaisted Webber and Hart Hanson Webber, Short Plays
    for Junior and Senior High School. Boston: Houghton
    Mifflin, 1925.
George A. Goldstone, One-Act Plays. Boston: Allyn and Ba-
    con, 1926.
Barrett H. Clark and Thomas R. Cook, One-Act Plays.
    Boston: D. C. Heath, 1929.
S. Marion Tucker, One-Act Plays for Study and Production.
    Boston: Ginn, 1929.
Virginia Church, Curtain. New York: Harpers, 1931.
Sterling Andrus Leonard, The Atlantic Book of Modern Plays.
    Revised Edition. Boston: Little, Brown, 1934.
Helen Louise Cohen, One-Act Plays by Modern Authors: Re-
    vised Edition. New York: Harcourt, Brace, 1934.
Charles Swain Thomas, The Atlantic Book of Junior Plays:
    Revised Edition. Boston: Little, Brown, 1936.
Francis Griffith and Joseph Mersand, One-Act Plays For To-
    day. New York: Globe Book Co., 1945.
Francis Griffith and Joseph Mersand, Modern One-Act Plays.
    New York: Harcourt, Brace, 1950.
Richard G. Decker, Plays for Our Time. New York: Oxford
    Book Co., 1959.
Marcus Konick, Plays for Modern Youth. New York: Globe
    Book Co., 1961.
Paul Kozelka, 15 American One-Act Plays. New York: Wash-
    ington Square Press, 1961.
Marjorie Wescott Barrows, Drama I. New York: MacMillan,
    1962.
M. Jerry Weiss, 10 Short Plays. New York: Dell, 1963.
John C. Schweitzer, A Variety of Plays. New York: Charles
    Scribners' Sons 1966.
John Gassner and Frederick H. Little. Reading and Staging
    the Play. New York: Holt, Rinehart and Winston,
    1967.

Notes

1.   Cohen, Helen Louise One-Act Plays by Modern Authors.
     New York: Harcourt, Brace, 1921, p. vii.

2.   Ibid., p. viii.

3.   Cohen, Helen Louise The Junior Play Book. New York:
     Harcourt, Brace, 1923, p. xiii.

4.   Cohen, Helen Louise More One-Act Plays by Modern
     Authors. New York: Harcourt, Brace, 1927, xiii.

5. Ibid, p. xiv.

6. Knickerbocker, Edwin Van B. Plays for Classroom Inter-
    pretation. New York: Henry Holt, 1921, p. vii.

7. Ibid. p. viii.

8. Knickerbocker, Edwin Van B. Twelve Plays. New York:
    Henry Holt, 1924, p. 279.

9. Ibid. p. 280.

10. Knickerbocker, Edwin Van B. Short Plays. New York:
    Henry Holt, 1931, p. xi-xii.

Chapter III

Teaching the Modern Drama

As recently as 1915, the only play later than Shakespeare's day which was discussed as a subject for high school
use was Oliver Goldsmith's She Stoops to Conquer.[1] Charles
Swain Thomas two years later showed awareness of the plays
of Bernard Shaw by mentioning in a footnote:

> The only exception to this is seen in the long and
> elaborate stage directions sometimes seen in the
> works of the more recent writers, notably Bernard
> Shaw.[2]

In the introduction to his Plays for Classroom Interpretation, in 1921, Knickerbocker complained:

> But teachers know that textbooks for the most sat-
> isfactory kind of dramatic work have not been avail-
> able. There are school editions of Shakespeare,
> and there are on authorized school lists certain
> other dramatic classics like She Stoops to Conquer.[3]

Although collections of modern plays, such as those by
Thomas H. Dickinson had begun to appear in 1915, these
were not designed for high school use. Once again, Helen
Louise Cohen, who had pioneered with One-Act Plays by
Modern Authors in 1921, in 1922 published Longer Plays by
Modern Authors (American),[4] which, in her opinion, was
probably the first to be selected for high schools. In her
preface, Miss Cohen mentions that two modern plays had been
included in the latest reading list of the College Entrance Examination Board. From this date on (1922) any discussions
of teaching the drama may no longer be confined to Shakespeare, Comus, and She Stoops to Conquer but must include
discussion of modern plays--both long and short, as well.

Clarence Stratton, Director of English in the Cleveland
High Schools, wrote his The Teaching of English in the High

56

School in 1921. He devoted Chapter V to Drama.[5] He begins by asserting that "next to the highest form of lyric
poetry, drama is the most difficult kind of literature to teach
in high school."

The difficulties in teaching drama are several:

1.   It is a highly specialized form.

2.   Time and place are restricted.

3.   The pupil has difficulty in making the play become
      alive.

4.   The imagination must be awakened.

Overcoming the Difficulties in Teaching the Drama

First, both teacher and students must know something
about the nature of the stage, its traditions, methods of production, schools of acting, differences in interpretation.[6]

Second,the teacher must be more important than the
editorial material. Excessive footnoting can defeat the purpose of elucidating the text; and merely parades the pedantry
of the editor.

Third, skillful questioning is necessary. A question
on an irrelevant footnote is a waste of time. Many questions
in the realm of ethics and philosophy are "potential boomerangs."
A play should be studied for its vision of life, not as an ethical treatise on myths.

How Does the Teacher Prepare to Teach?

Stratton makes specific suggestions for the teacher,
some of them for the first time in the literature. These may
be summarized:

1.   About a week before the study of a play is to begin,
      the teacher should read the complete play through, not
      in an annotated school edition, but in a regular book.

2.   He should master the entire drama as a literary pro-
      duction intended for the stage.

3.   Immediately upon completion, he should go back to the

beginning and carefully study the first unit, act, or
scene, in the light of all the information contained in
the Variorum Shapespeare edited by Horace Howard
Furness [if a play by Shakespeare is being studied].

4.   With a clear idea of what there is to know about the
       play, a definite idea of the help needed by the pupils,
       a clearly outlined series of objects to be attained, he
       should be able to direct their attention, awaken their
       interests, enlarge their sympathies and draw out their
       opinions by wisely selecting the additional material to
       explain and supplement the text. [7]

By examining some of Stratton's general hints to teachers of Shakespeare, one can easily imagine some of the errors
that were being made in the early 1920's.

1.   Avoid the tendency to excessive philological analysis;
       simply define the difficult word and let it go at that.

2.   Teach the historical plays as plays, not as history.
       For example, Julius Caesar is not Roman history, and
       Henry V is not English history. Both are exciting
       dramas and should be taught as such.

3.   Enrich the study of the plays by recordings of Eliza-
       bethan music or compositions inspired by the works
       such as Mendelssohn's A Midsummer Night's Dream.

4.   Encourage students to attend Shakespearean plays when
       they are available.

5.   Pictures and sketches for stage settings should be wel-
       comed and shown to the class; but they do not neces-
       sarily represent literary appreciation.

6.   Although teachers should encourage students to consult
       newspapers and magazines for materials pertaining to
       the drama in general and to Shakespeare in particular,
       such materials do not take the place of a recitation
       on assigned reading.

7.   Making a model of a Shakespearean stage should not
       be the reason for a passing grade in the English course.

8.   With each successive year, the student should be ex-
       pected to recall a modicum of the Shakespearean plays

he learned earlier, as well as the facts about Shakespeare's life and times. In other words, the learning
should be cumulative not merely repetitious.   There
is not much value in starting the new play of Shakespeare as if the class had never heard of the Bard of
Avon.

All these general suggestions make good sense.   The
fact that some of the abuses Stratton ridicules in 1923 still
are found in classrooms in the 1960's shows how long poor
habits of teaching can persist.

How to Begin the Study of Shakespeare in Class

Stratton was quite specific about the proper procedure
for teaching Shakespeare. He would begin the study of the
play in class according to the following procedure:

1.   Satisfy the students' curiosity concerning the title of
        the play.
        Incidentally, some idea of the later-than-Shakespeare
        plays which were read in high school in 1923 can be
        gotten from his reference to the following: The School
        for Scandal, She Stoops to Conquer, The Good Natured
        Man, The Piper, Milestones. Thus we see that three
        18th century plays and two early 20th century plays had
        crept into the curriculum!

2.   Explain the cast of characters, at least the leading
        ones. This means not only teaching the correct pro-
        nunciation but the relationships of the leading persons.

3.   Discuss the place or places of action. Help students
        to visualize the setting even before the dialogue is
        read.   Students should be asked to describe each scene.

4.   Characters should be described, in their initial ap-
        pearance and in their later development.

5.   After this preliminary explanation by the teacher,
        Stratton would have the students begin to read the
        speeches in turn as they occur.   The teacher may oc-
        casionally interrupt with a comment or explanation, but
        in general the students should read with little inter-
        ruption.

Stratton realizes that the speeches of a single charac-

ter may be given several different interpretations when read
by several students at sight, but he is not concerned. In
fact, students can profit from observing the differences. At
the end of this first period, an assignment, say to read Act I,
may be given.

This approach is somewhat different from that of
Thomas and others who suggested that the entire play should
be read at one sitting before the intensive study is begun.
Stratton, on the other hand, says, "The Study of a play should
be begun in class."[8]

What to Do in the Second Class Period?

This is what has become now the traditional recitation
consisting of questions and answers. As Stratton explains:

> At this time (i.e., the second period), with books
> closed, the pupils should tell interestingly and cor-
> rectly and proportionally the events of the story so
> far. Then should ensue skillful questioning by the
> teacher to amplify the knowledge already exhibited.
> Some details will have to be explained, some mini-
> mized, others enlarged, the significance of some
> pointed out, the incompleteness of others. Such
> general discussion--for from it, since all have
> studied the same material, none should be omitted--
> will lead inevitably and naturally to mention of sus-
> pense, contrast, and rise of interest.[9]

The paragraph above is almost the classic exposition
of the typical recitation on literature as it was practiced in
the early 1920's and as it has continued today.

Should Plot Be Taught?

As was noted in the discussion of Bolenius and her
predecessors, study of plot construction entered early in the
methodology of teaching the drama. Stratton would teach,
even in the lowest grade where drama is taken up, the difference between the exposition and the beginning of the action.

However, Stratton goes beyond his predecessors in de-
crying the tendency of teachers of "forcing the play into the
Procrustean model prescribed by Freytag and his mechanistic
followers." Although a knowledge of such terms as climax,
tragic suspense, catastrophe, falling action, and happy ending

is useful, he considers as false the statement that "all plays
can be analyzed according to a predetermined diagram."
Furthermore, "the attempt to force modern original plots into
such frames will result disastrously for the analytical study,
and not contribute much to appreciation."

Students should be lead to perceive the broad differences
between tragedies, comedies, and tragicomedies.

Audio-Visual Aids in Teaching Drama

Several earlier authorities had suggested enrichment
of the study of the play by all kinds of visual aids. Both
students and teacher should be on the alert for such materials
in books, magazines, and newspapers. A bulletin board
should be kept alive with such illustrations. It is not enough
that illustrations should be brought in and explained by the
students. These should be of real assistance to the pupils.
Many illustrations may be quaint but of little value.

Teaching the Relation of Blank Verse to Drama

Sooner or later the student will perceive that Shakespeare's plays are written in blank verse. Explanations should
be found for its universal acceptance by Elizabethan dramatists. Students can report on the Earl of Surrey, Tottel's
Miscellany, and Marlowe's mighty line. Students should be
led to realize that blank verse is suitable to expression of all
man's thoughts and emotions.

For every recitation, students should be made respon-
sible for a certain portion of the play. At first the recita-
tions will be in the form of questions on the play. Later will
come such items as:

> ...reports on the stage settings, the stage group-
> ings, the meanings of the printed stage directions,
> the action suggested by the lines themselves where
> author's directions are lacking, the manner of de-
> livering speeches, the significance of voice and
> gesture in connection with words, or apart from
> them, the revelation or concealment of character,
> the things lines mean in addition to what they say,
> the effect upon the audience. [10]

Interpretation of the play should follow comprehension
when obtained by the methods listed above. Characters

should be assigned and pupils should assume positions before
the class to interpret the roles they depict.

How should roles be assigned? Educationally there is
good reason for assigning to each student the part for which
he or she is temperamentally and physically fit. However,
an equally good case can be made for assigning roles to bring
out the opposite traits which the student generally demonstrates.
Thus the shy boy may occasionally be given the part of the
braggart; the forward girl may play the part of a retired
young lady.

Should Every Play Be Studied Line by Line?

This will depend upon the play. Some plays can be
read mostly at home; others, like Hamlet and Macbeth merit
more careful study. Occasionally entire scenes may be summarized.

As a culmination for the study of a play every student
should present some portion memorized. It would be ad-
visable for groups to get together to do scenes in sequences
so that the entire play can thus be reviewed.

By 1923, when Stratton's book appeared, modern plays
and one-act plays had entered the high school curriculum, and
Stratton makes a plea for their judicious use. Among the
modern plays which he lists are: John Drinkwater's, Abraham Lincoln, John Galsworthy's, Justice, Maurice Maeter-
lincks's, The Blue Bird, Josephine Preston Peabody's, The
Piper, and Arnold Bennett's and Edward Knoblock's, Milestones.

In 1924, Russell A. Sharp, a teacher at Northeast
High School, Kansas City, Missouri, published Teaching English in High Schools, one of the Riverside Educational Mono-
graphs.[11] Chapter IV, Problems in Teaching the Classics,
has many valuable suggestions.

The proper assignment in teaching the drama is just
as important as the proper assignment in any other phase of
English. Sharp says,

> The assignment must serve as a guide to show the
> student the way he is to go; at the same time it
> must be a goad to lash his mind to reflective
> thinking.

An example of a bad assignment in Julius Caesar is:

> For to-morrow, study Julius Caesar to page 17.
> The average freshman has never before in his life
> studied poetic drama; he hasn't the faintest idea
> how to attack the problem. Almost invariably he
> thinks when he has run through the words two or
> three times that he has prepared the lesson. Prob-
> ably he cannot even retell the story of those few
> pages, but at least he has followed the teacher's
> mandate to read to page 17. What more could you
> expect him to do, little untrained child that he is.[12]

How should the assignments in a classic be organized?
Sharp's suggestions given in 1924 are still found in many
English classrooms today.

1. The daily lesson, whenever possible, should constitute
   a natural division in the classic.

2. The assignment should include a few carefully chosen
   thought-provoking questions which point to the important thoughts to be gained from the lesson.

3. The questions should not be too numerous.

4. The information obtained should not be "mere bits of
   information which are apparent to all who read."

5. It is best to write the questions on the board before
   the class hour rather than to trust to dictation.

As examples of his own assignments, Sharp gives the
following for Macbeth:

> Assignment: Study Act I, Scenes 6, 7. Questions,
> Sc. 6: Purpose of opening speeches of Duncan and
> Banquo? Tragic irony in this scene? Sc. 7:
> Study carefully Macbeth's opening soliloquy. What
> is the nature of his fear? Does he understand him-
> self? Why does Lady Macbeth speak so harshly to
> him? Have they previously discussed the murder?
> Who is the leader in making plans? Why?

One of the seminal volumes on the principles of teaching literature in the early 1920's was Sterling Andrus Leonard's,
Essential Principles of Teaching Reading and Literature, which

appeared in 1922.[14] Leonard has a great deal to say about
Educational Dramatization and Dramatic Reading, in Chapter
X. Since so many later writers on methodology in teaching
literature quote Leonard, it is worth examining his ideas on
teaching through dramatization.

Leonard, like his predecessors going as far back as
Chubb in 1902, believed that dramatic reading "is a most excellent aid to the school room study of literature in all grades
and high school years." Such reading, in his opinion, furnished useful motivation for reading aloud clearly and expres-
sively. "It requires of each pupil careful preparation, not
alone of the part he wants to try, but of the entire story of
play."[15] Among the scenes from high school literature recommended by Leonard are the tavern scene and the dance at
Squire Cass' house in Silas Marner and Antony's speech in
Julius Caesar.

In addition to dramatizing of scenes from novels and
plays, Leonard in his work with students, first at the Lincoln
School, then associated with Columbia University and later at
the University of Wisconsin High School, tried to get his students to write their own little plays or settings for famous
speeches. For example, he explains the various steps his
seventh grade class went through in writing an original setting for the Gettysburg Address as part of a Lincoln's Birthday program.[16]

Dramatizing Hawthorne's "Feathertop" in Ninth Grade

One step beyond the preparation of dramatic settings
for famous speeches is the dramatization of stories read in
class. The illustration Leonard gives is his own experience
with a ninth grade class that had read Hawthorne's "Feathertop,"which traces all steps from the teacher's reading of the
story and his suggestion that they try dramatizing it, to the
final script as it was performed.[17]

Leonard summarizes the values of dramatic reading
and original dramatization--views which are just as valid
forty years later.

Naturally the one gain that stands out as most important in the teaching of literature is the power of
realizing what is read. No one who has helped in
dramatizing a play like"Feathertop"or Silas Marner
or Dickens' Christmas Carol can ever again read

a similar story without increased power of seeing it happen before him. No one who has gone through the labor of developing a play of The Return of Odysseus, or who even has seen the thing done with appreciation, can consider classics remote and ineffectual. [18]

In 1926 three college professors of English pooled their views to produce a provocative volume entitled The Teaching of Literature. Charles Carpenter Fries and James Holly Hanford taught at The University of Michigan and Harrison Ross Steeves at Columbia University. [19] Hanford, who subsequently became a distinguished Milton scholar and President of the Modern Language Association, wrote Chapter I, The English Teacher at Work, and Chapter VI, Our Literary Heritage and the Survey Course. Some of his views on the teaching of Shakespeare in the secondary schools merit our attention.

Fries, who later became an outstanding linguist, wrote Chapter II, Literature as a Subject of Study in the Schools; Chapter III, Objectives in the Teaching of Literature; Chapter IV, Some Principles Underlying the Teaching of Literature; Chapter V, The Organization of a Course in Literature. Professor Steeves discussed such topics as Contemporary Literature in the Schools, Literature As an Art Form: The Study of Types; and The Relation between the High School and the College Course in Literature.

The book is more a statement of general principles and philosophy than a manual of instructions in how to teach specific books. Some of the general principles expressed in 1926 are quite valid today. For example, every teacher of literature would like his students to experience keenly the work being studied.

Fries expresses it this way:

> Success in teaching any bit of literature is to be measured by the keenness with which the experience there set forth is realized by the pupils. Are you teaching The Merchant of Venice? How keenly do your pupils actually realize all that Shylock must have felt during the trial? or what Bassanio must have felt, after his success in winning Portia, upon the arrival of the messenger with the news that his friend's life must be the price of that success? [20]

Continuing on the subject of experiencing literature,
Fries lists the following as one of the ways:

> One may enter into the feelings of persons in a
> critical situation. This aspect of literary approach
> has been illustrated above in connection with The
> Merchant of Venice. To appreciate all that Shylock
> must have felt in the trial scene of that play or, in
> Romeo and Juliet what Juliet must have felt during
> the time she hesitates before drinking the sleeping
> potion, is to realize important literary aspects of
> these plays.[21]

Professor Steeves in his chapter on Contemporary Literature explains why so many students who were subjected
to an intensive analytical study of Shakespeare developed an
antipathy toward him.

> When we look for some show of stimulated interest
> in Milton, in Edmund Burke, even in Shakespeare,
> we find an attitude of weary resistance. The reason
> is simple; we have cluttered up the real purpose
> of literary study--a better vision of life--with what
> is precise, but incidental; weighty, but only in an
> academic sense.[22]

Other cogent comments are made by the authors on
such topics as widening the cultural horizons of the students
by means of Shakespeare;[23] comparing the structures of two
or more Shakespearean plays;[24] the value of seeing a performance of Shakespeare in modern dress;[25] and the realiza-
tion of Shakespeare as the culmination of The Renaissance
man and the Elizabethan man.[26] Too many neophytes fresh
from a course in Shakespeare in college feel that they are
ready to conquer the world of the classroom with such knowledge, and in this respect, Fries, in his first chapter, wisely
remarks:

> He finds, for example, that it is not his knowledge
> of the technique of drama which will best aid him
> in interesting his class in Shakespeare but his
> personal fund of wit and of wisdom, imagination,
> feeling, and experience of life.[27]

In the 1920's the literary anthology for high schools
came into existence. One of the first series was Literature
and Life, edited by Edwin Greenlaw, Head of the English De-

partment of Johns Hopkins University, and Dudley Miles,
Head of the English Department of Evander Childs High School,
New York City. In 1926 they published a handbook for use
with their four-volume series, Teaching Literature.[28] This
was the forerunner of many other teacher guide-books which
have accompanied the various anthologies that have appeared
since that time.

The authors emphasize the necessity for visualizing
a play. They recommend that students be taken to see productions. Since Shakespearean productions may be few and
far between in some areas (and they were much fewer in
1926 than they are today) the solution must reside in dramatization by the students. Like Leonard in 1922, these authors
endorse the idea of having the students, through proper committees, make the selection of the scenes to be dramatized.

Dramatization may range from unrehearsed reading of
the lines after some study the night before to careful productions before the entire school. To understand setting, a
good device is to make a miniature setting. To understand
character, one of the best ways is to act out the role. Too
detailed analysis of character may become deadly, a warning
issued to teachers time and time again. Short plays as well
as Shakespeare and contemporary dramatists are included in
this series and specific study aids are given for each type.

Charles Swain Thomas Ten Years Later

In 1927 Charles Swain Thomas, then of The Graduate
School of Education of Harvard University, revised his The
Teaching of English in the Secondary School.[29] Except for
the addition of a section at the end of the chapter on Questions and Interpretive Comments and a Bibliography, the 1927
chapter on The Teaching of Shakespeare is practically the
same as it was in 1917.

Some of the suggestions made by Thomas in his section on Questions and Interpretative Comments to increase
interest in Shakespearean study are:

1.   Students with mechanical ability should build a model
     Elizabethan stage. Girls might dress dolls in costumes
     of the Elizabethan period.

2.   Pupils make riddles which can be answered by quo-
     tations from the plays studied.

Example:
What is a good definition of a high school?
Answer: "Where none will sweat save for promotion."

3.   A class newspaper contemporaneous with the action of
      the play.   Example: The Arden Gazette in connection
      with As You Like It.

4.   In connection with the study of Macbeth, students will
      read Alice Duer Miller's modernization of the plot in
      Instruments of Darkness.

      In 1929 Percival Chubb revised The Teaching of Eng-
lish, [30] which had originally appeared in 1902, and which has
already been discussed.   Basically, his approach to the teaching of Shakespeare, as exemplified by his treatment of Julius
Caesar had not changed.   Chubb still believed that the first
reading should be done entirely by the teacher, and all his
other suggestions have been covered in the discussion of the
1902 edition.

      However in the time between the two editions, the one-
act play had entered the curriculum and so had the modern
drama.   Although he does not recommend any particular one-
act plays, he does believe that they should be "taken up in the
same way that the short story will have been considered in
relation to the full-length novel."[31]

      The modern (in 1929) playwrights whom he lists as
worthy of consideration are Barrie, Maeterlinck, Stephen
Phillips, MacKaye, and possibly O'Neill in his less gruesome
plays.   He establishes the relationship between the study of
Shakespeare and study of the drama of our own times in
this fashion:

      We shall provide a four-year course in Shakespeare,
      which will connect us with the drama of today and
      affect for good, we hope, our pupils' patronage of
      the theatre.[32]

      Summarizing the advances in the teaching of the drama
in the 1920's we note the following:

1.   Introduction of the study of the one-act play.

2.   Introduction of the study of modern drama.

3.   Greater emphasis on dramatization by students.

4.   Greater concern for the contemporary theater by
        fostering student attendance as well as their reading
        of book, magazine and newspaper accounts of theatre
        happenings.

5.   Greater emphasis on the teacher's preparation for
        teaching drama.

6.   The introduction of audio aids, such as recordings of
        Elizabethan music and some of the great music in-
        spired by Shakespeare (in Mendelssohn, Verdi, Gounod,
        etc.).

7.   Greater emphasis on the proper homework assignment.

Notes

1. Bolenius, Emma Miller Teaching Literature in the Gram-
    mar Grades and High School Boston: Houghton Mifflin,
    1915, p. 163-64.

2. Thomas, Charles Swain The Teaching of English in the
    Secondary School Boston: Houghton Mifflin, 1917, p.
    218, note 1.

3. Knickerbocker, Edwin Van B. Plays for Classroom
    Interpretation New York: Henry Holt, 1921, p. viii.

4. Cohen, Helen Louise Longer Plays by Modern Authors
    (American). New York: Harcourt, Brace, 1922.

5. Stratton, Clarence The Teaching of English in the High
    School. New York: Harcourt, Brace, 1923, p. 103-26.

6. Stratton, op. cit., p. 105.

7. Ibid., p. 109-10.

8. Ibid., p. 112.

9. Ibid., p. 114.

10. Ibid., p. 117.

11. Sharp, Russell A. Teaching English in High Schools.

Boston: Houghton Mifflin, 1924.

12. Ibid., p. 46.

13. Ibid., p. 48-49.

14. Leonard, Sterling Andrus Essential Principles of Teaching Reading and Literature. Philadelphia: J. B. Lippincott, 1922.

15. Ibid., p. 301.

16. Ibid., p. 307-312.

17. Ibid., p. 313-31.

18. Ibid., p. 332.

19. Fries, Charles Carpenter, Hanford, James Holly, and Steeves, Harrison Ross The Teaching of Literature.

20. Ibid., p. 60

21. Ibid., p. 70.

22. Ibid., p. 129.

23. Ibid., p. 103.

24. Ibid., p. 146.

25. Ibid., p. 101.

26. Ibid., p. 111-12.

27. Ibid., p. 2.

28. Greenlaw, Edwin and Miles, Dudley Teaching Literature. Chicago: Scott, Foresman, 1926, p. 33-35.

29. Thomas, Charles Swain The Teaching of English in the Secondary School. Revised Edition. Boston: Houghton Mifflin, 1927, p. 282-312.

30. Chubb, Percival The Teaching of English: Revised and Largely Rewritten. New York: Macmillan, 1929.

31. Ibid., p. 377.

32. Ibid., p. 572.

Chapter IV

Teaching the Drama in the 1930's

Ways to Teach English was the title of the book by
Thomas C. Blaisdell of State Teachers College, Slippery
Rock, Pa., which appeared in 1930.[1] It was the first of
several important methods books to appear in the 1930's,
each of which had a substantial chapter on how to teach the
drama.

Blaisdell devotes two chapters to the drama: Chapter
37 on Teaching the Drama; Chapter 38 on Dramatizing in
the Classroom. Some of Blaisdell's suggestions are in the
tradition already described. Occasionally he adds something
to that tradition. Thus, what Thomas listed as his first
requirement of good teaching of Shakespeare--Visualization--
Blaisdell calls Helping students to See and Hear.[2] The class
..."in imagination must be guided to the place in which the
action of the drama is occurring." Blaisdell himself edited
several plays of Shakespeare and had written detailed descriptions of each scene to help his readers to visualize them.

Reading Aloud

Like Chubb in 1902, Blaisdell in 1930 felt strongly
that in junior high school and in early senior high school the
teacher should read the entire play aloud to the class. Later,
the teacher may designate pupils to read the lines of given
characters before the class. But students should read only
the scenes which the teacher had read previously.

Clarifying the Language

All editors of Shakespeare's plays are aware of the
need to explain language differences, whether it be the edition
by Hudson in 1879 or the latest paperback edition. Methods
teachers have frowned on excessive explanation and on philological expeditions. Blaisdell suggests that the teacher substitute current synonyms for difficult Shakespeare words as
he is reading aloud. In this way the students absorb the

72

Elizabethan as they hear the modern equivalent.

Work by Students

If the teacher is to read the entire Shakespearean play before the 11th grade, what do the students have to do? Blaisdell suggests that as homework they be given books to read adapted to their grade. Once a week each student will talk for 2-3 minutes on his book. A daily completion test or true-false test may be given on the reading.

The Place of Written Questions

Questions for guiding the study of Macbeth were included by Franklin T. Baker in 1903 and have been included for this play as well as for others. Blaisdell, too, feels that written questions to direct the thinking of the student are a help to the study of Shakespeare or any other piece of literature. Some questions are better than none at all; but such questions must never be permitted to interfere with interest in the play, especially in junior high school or the first year in senior high school.

Character Study

Just as Thomas in his book of 1917 had a substantial section on character study, so Blaisdell believes that

character portrayal and development is probably the most important thing to receive attention. The student should be taught to evaluate every act of every person in the play. Each thing done by Shakespeare's men and women is done either to reveal character or to reveal feeling. [3]

Structure of a Play

Blaisdell states that in Shakespeare's plays each scene has a specific artistic purpose; and students must be lead to understand this purpose. The middle of the third act is of particular importance since it shows that the end is inevitable. Blaisdell designates as fateful scenes the recognition by Macbeth of Banquo's ghost, Marc Antony's oration over Caesar's body, and the play within the play in Hamlet.

What Can Be Omitted

Since Blaisdell's purpose is to develop in students a

love for Shakespeare, rather than scholarship, he feels that
the following can be omitted:

1.   Sources of Shakespeare's plots, before the 12th grade.

2.   Below the 12th grade avoid the study of Shakespeare's
        critics and commentators.

3.   The date of publication or order in which the plays
        were written are not important to any student who is
        trying to learn to love Shakespeare.

4.   Excessive annotations of strong grammatical construc-
        tions.

How Much Memory Work?

There have been two schools of thought about memory
work.   One school, represented by Thomas, would "demand
a good deal of memory work in connection with this study of
the drama."[4]   Blaisdell, on the other hand, would never require it.   It should be encouraged, but never required.

The Modern Drama

By 1930, the modern drama had been studied in our
high schools for a decade.   Blaisdell agrees that study of
modern drama is desirable.   The teacher should read much
in class; students should read at home and before the class.
If some students seem to prefer modern drama to Shakespeare, Blaisdell is not concerned.   Eventually the taste of
the students will be developed so that they will appreciate
Shakespeare.

Virginia J. Craig's The Teaching of High School
English also appeared in 1930.[5]   Her chapter on the teaching of drama shows her deep interest in the modern drama
as well as Shakespeare.   The following forty modern plays
she would recommend for home reading, to be followed by
short, objective oral or written tests.   These plays are recommended because they are entertaining and because they
have enduring values.   Some of them have subjects that lead
to consideration of pressing social problems:

1.   Ibsen, The Pillars of Society

2.   Ibsen, Ghosts

3.   Ibsen, A Doll's House

4.   Echegaray, The Great Galeoto

5.   Chekhov, The Sea Gull

6.   Hervieu, The Torch Race

7.   Bjornsen, The Gauntlet

8.   Pinero, The Second Mrs. Tanqueray

9.   Fitch, The Girl with the Green Eyes

10. Wilde, Lady Windermere's Fan

11. Strindberg, The Father

12. Rostand, Cyrano de Bergerac

13. Synge, Riders to the Sea

14. Barker, The Voysey Inheritance

15. Suderman, Magda

16. Hauptmann, Rose Bernd

17. Maeterlinck, Pelleas and Melisande

18. Maeterlinck, Monna Vanna

19. Shaw, Candida

20. Shaw, The Devil's Disciple

21. Brieux, The Three Daughters of M. Dupont

22. Brieux, The Red Robe

23. Andreyev, He Who Gets Slapped

24. D'Annunzio, Giaconda

25. Yeats, The Land of Heart's Desire

26. Barrie, The Admirable Crichton

27.   Barrie, What Every Woman Knows

28.   Barrie, Quality Street

29.   Galsworthy, Justice

30.   Galsworthy, The Eldest Son

31.   Galsworthy, The Silver Box

32.   Dane, A Bill of Divorcement

33.   Glaspell, Inheritors

34.   Masefield, The Tragedy of Nan

35.   St. John Irvine, John Ferguson

36.   Dunsany, The Tents of the Arabs

37.   Milne, The Lucky One

38.   Kelly, The Show-Off

39.   O'Neill, Anna Christie

40.   O'Neill, Marco Millions

Craig was prophetic when she wrote, "an innovation that should and will come in the near future is the more extensive use of serious or tragic modern drama."[6] Although she speaks in behalf of the modern drama, she recommends one play of Shakespeare for each year of high school.

Dramatization

Following the tradition, Craig also recommends class dramatization of parts of a Shakespeare play as an excellent training to supplement the class discussion of plot, characters, and setting.[7] Each student should be given one part in one scene and these parts should be memorized. As for the best scenes for dramatization, they are:

1.   Where feeling is intense and movement and gesticulations are the natural result.

2.   Where repartee is rapid and sparkling. As You Like

It has many such scenes.

In the actual presentation, Craig suggests two per-
formances. After a scene is presented first, it should be
criticized by the class. The second time, it should be an
attempt at finished performance.

As a final comment on the views of Virginia J. Craig,
we may conclude with her reason for students' preference of
tragedies to comedies. Tragic conflicts and impending dis-
asters are powerful sources of excitement and suspense.

Lou La Brant wrote The Teaching of Literature in the
Secondary School in 1931 and devoted Chapter V to How to
Read a Play.[8] Although novels are more generally read than
plays, she feels that many characteristics make the play
ideal reading for leisure:

> ...it is short and may be considered at one sitting;
> it presents a clear-cut problem or situation or
> character study; it appeals to the imagination, to
> a liking for romance, color, beauty; it is associa-
> ted with ideas of recreation; and since it is in-
> tended for interpretation, its whole structure tends
> to draw the reader out of himself into the people
> of the play.[9]

Since the emphasis throughout the chapter is in training students in reading a play, La Brant takes a step forward.
Most of her predecessors have spent so much time in empha-
sizing the effective initial reading by the teacher that they
have de-emphasized the importance of training students in
reading plays on their own when their teacher is no longer
available.

How to Teach the Reading of The Merchant of Venice
in the Ninth Grade

The problem of the beginning:

Before the play is begun, let the class discuss the difference between a play and a novel. A play is all conversation with the speaker's name at the lefthand margin. Some
time can be spent discussing the Elizabethan stage; and for
this discussion a model of a theatre may help.

Students have to learn what the cast of characters

means.   On the stage this list causes no problem because
characters are easily identified by costume, appearance, and
voice.   But to the inexperienced 9th grader, who is reading
a play, the cast is just a list of names.   The characters in
a contemporary play are listed on the program in their order
of appearance.   In Shakespeare's day, the teacher must point
out, they were listed in social order, with royalty first, and
humble people (like the Porter in <u>Macbeth</u>) toward the end,
and the women in the cast at the end.

After the explanation of the cast, the division of Acts
and scenes needs clarification.

Problem of the setting:

Many writers already discussed have stressed the need
to visualize the setting.   La Brant, too, realizes the need to
do this for young readers.   They are accustomed in fiction
to extensive descriptions.   In <u>The Merchant of Venice,</u> the
only description is:

Venice.   A street, Enter Antonio, Salarino, and Salanio.   Various authorities have suggested different ways to
help students visualize the setting.   Blaisdell (1930) wrote
lengthy expansions in his editions of Shakespeare.   Most
methodologists would have the teacher give this explanation.
Lou La Brant cautions teachers of the danger of accustoming
their students to getting these explanations entirely from the
teacher.   It may be quite acceptable to give all the background
for the first play, but good teaching consists in enabling the
student to find this setting, the background, for himself in
plays that he reads later.   The student must learn to read
the play for answers to many questions that puzzle him.   For
example:

"How old is Antonio?"
"What has to be on the stage for furniture?"
"How do the characters look?"
"What are their expressions?"

In other words, the students learn to read not only
for the action but also for the "ability to sense time and
place through conversation."

Students have to be shown that the opening lines in a
play may be in the middle of a conversation.   Thus the opening line--"In sooth I know not why I am so sad" is really

Antonio's answer to the question of either Salanio or Salarino as to the reason for his sadness.

Finally, students reading their first play should be told that the opening speeches are especially designed to make the situation clear. Hence the characters may say things which may appear obvious to other characters on the stage, but not so obvious to the reader or listener.

The problem of characterization:

Thomas (1917) went to considerable lengths to enable teachers to help students understand characterizations. Practically all writers on methodology realize that the appreciation of the characterizations is one of the most lasting benefits of studying drama.

In a novel, the author tells the reader many things about a character: What they really think; why they feel as they do; what their true motives are. But in a play, says La Brant, you can judge characters the way one does in real life--from what people do and say. Sometimes the information comes from what other people think and say about a character. For example, the reader judges Shylock's character from what he does and says. He also gets a view of Shylock as given by Antonio. But Antonio's judgment of Shylock must be evaluated in the light of his own character as it is revealed by his own deeds and words, and by the opinions of Antonio's friends and of Shylock. Hence the teacher must train his students to study the characters in all their relationships.

To answer that so and so has such traits is not enough. What is the evidence? Is it what the character himself says or does? Is it what his friends or his enemies say about him? How trustworthy are such opinions? Such training helps to break the student's tendency to give the most obvious answer that comes to mind.

The problem of the structure:

La Brant has no use for that type of study of structure of a play "which ingenuity has devised for changing a live play into a dull diagram resembling as nearly as possible a problem in mathematics or the even less popular grammar diagram."[10] Yet a student should know something about the structure of a play which differentiates it from a novel.

For example, since a play lasts about 2 1/2 hours, things must be told rapidly on the stage--there is no time to see them happen. In the beginning of a play a speaker may relate an event which would be difficult to project on the stage.

Finally, La Brant makes a suggestion about utilizing talking films which is most apropos today. Just as teachers in 1931 were being urged to use talking films to help students appreciate the plays studied in class, so teachers today are being urged to use television drama. [11]

Reed Smith was co-editor of a high school literature series, Good Reading for High Schools originally published in 1931. [12]

In 1935, in Chapter **XV** of The Teaching of Literature in the High School [13] he expressed his views on teaching of Literature.

Admitting that Shakespeare is difficult for high school students because of the plot, the language, the blank verse, etc., he offers the following suggestions for removing these difficulties.

1. Obtain a Good Teacher's Edition

In addition to the edition used by the class, the teacher should have accessible the Furness Variorum Edition, and for more frequent reference the more detailed Rolfe edition published by the American Book Company or the Hudson edition published by Ginn. No one knows what interesting questions will arise which can be answered only by the teacher's rich knowledge to be obtained from these more complete editions.

2. Setting the Stage

Since a play was meant to be performed on a stage, the teacher, early in his instruction, must explain the physical conditions under which Shakespeare's plays were given and to help his class to visualize these conditions. Like other writers before him Smith recommends the use of a small working model of the Elizabethan stage; or, failing that, plenty of blackboard sketches and pictures of both the inside and outside of an Elizabethan Theatre.

3. As the Play Proceeds

Smith emphasizes the importance of making clear the

probable positions, expressions, and gestures of the actors
at any given moment. What is being done is often more important than what they say. Similar suggestions have been
made by earlier authorities under the term "visualization."

4. Reading Aloud

Smith quotes Blaisdell on the value of having the
teacher read the entire play aloud, especially in the junior
high school years, [14] but he would permit junior high school
students to read it aloud. Among additional suggestions he
makes are:

a. Formation of a drama reading club in school to
read light, lively, modern plays as an adjunct to
the serious work in class.

b. If there is an English Club in the school, the
members might devote several meetings to reading one-act plays or portions of longer plays, at
the time when Shakespeare is being studied in
class.

While the plays are being read aloud, students will
perceive humor which they may never have noticed by themselves. Smith suggests these three questions to ask about the
presence of humor in any scene:

1. Are there any puns in this scene?

2. Is there any funny speech or situation?

3. Is there anything in the scene that Shakespeare's
audience probably thought funny but which we do
not, or the other way around?

In addition to the humorous passages, the more memorable ones should be pointed out as the teacher does his
daily reading.

5. Memorizing

Recognizing that there are two diametrically opposed
schools of thought on the subject of compulsory memorizing,
Smith aligns himself with those who would require memorizing. Short, carefully selected passages should be assigned
for every member of the class to memorize. Sometimes

the class may decide which of several memorable passages
it wishes to memorize.

6.   Shakespeare and Music

Shakespeare's songs in his various plays should either
be performed vocally or instrumentally through the cooperation of the music department or by use of the recordings
available.

7.   The Story of the Play

Because the plot of Shakespeare's plays is so difficult to follow, Smith recommends that the students be given
the story beforehand.   Students may read this in the introductory material of the annotated text; in such summaries
as Lamb's, Tales from Shakespeare; or the teacher may
prefer to tell it in his own words.   Smith believes that
Freytag's pyramidal structure of a typical dramatic plot can
be used with caution to make graphic the events of a play.
As each scene is finished these two questions may be asked:

1.   What do we know now about the plot that we did
not know till this scene was read?

2.   What past scene does this scene link up with and
continue?

8.   The People in the Play

Smith follows most of his predecessors in stressing
the importance of characterization in Shakespeare and the
difficulty high school students generally have in understanding it.   For many young and immature readers the characters in a printed Shakespearean play are so many names.   A
simple suggestion that is a first step toward differentiation
is to ask of the class:

Who is the oldest person in the play?
Who is the youngest?
Which is of the highest rank?
Who are lower in the social scale?
Who is the lowest in rank of all the characters?[15]

Since a play is essentially a struggle, the class should
become aware as soon as possible of the part that the major
characters play in the conflict.   Smith suggests the following

questions which the teacher can use to guide his class:

1. Whose story does the play tell? That is, through whose eye are we meant to see the incidents and the other characters?

2. Who are the three or four most important people?

3. What does the leading person want and work for?

4. Who are on the side of the leading person and who are against him (or her)?

5. What are the relations between these two groups of people (the pros and the cons) as the play opens that helps to start the action moving?

6. Is it a good or an evil desire?[16]

Such simple questions, says Smith, will clarify the plot and plant the seeds for intelligent interpretation of character.

It is because characters are of mixed qualities and because they change and develop that high school students have difficulty in understanding them. The characters in fiction which they have read before they came to Shakespeare are either good or evil, as they are so often in films and on television. Students should be helped to see the many-facets of the characters and their ever changing qualities.

To enable students to understand a character Smith lists the four ways already mentioned by Thomas in 1917. Like La Brant, Smith offers a few words of caution about judging a character in a play by what others say of him. Hamlet would hardly be an unprejudiced commentator on Claudius; Antonio and Bassanio would hardly be objective about Shylock. As Smith expresses it so well, "In Shakespeare, as in life, what people see depends upon what they want to see, and due allowance must always be made for passions and prejudices."[17]

Certain questions, with modifications to fit the particular play may help to elicit an understanding of character. Smith suggests these:

1. Who is the main character?

2. What is the main character's chief need and de-
    sire?

3. Is this struggle against human opponents, hostile
    surroundings, or against his own worse or bet-
    ter self?

4. What people, things, circumstances, or forces
    aid him in his struggle?

5. What people, things, circumstances, or forces
    oppose him in his struggle?

6. Is the main character (or any other character)
    different at the end of the play from what he
    was at the beginning?

7. If so, what influences changed him and what does
    he chiefly do or say that shows this difference?

8. How is the main character chiefly revealed?
    (a) by what he says (b) by what he does? (c)
    by what the other characters say about him?

9. If any of the characters consists of a mixture of
    good and bad traits, be prepared to discuss in-
    formally in class the good side versus the bad
    side, citing specific words and deeds as evi-
    dence. [18]

9. Difficulties of Language

Admitting the difficulties of Shakespeare's language,
Smith offers the following suggestions:

1. As the teacher reads aloud, substitute a simple
    synonym for the difficult word.

2. In the upper years of high school, the teacher
    tells less and elicits more by questions and
    discussion.

Caution must be exercised about the verbal difficulty
in Shakespeare which is caused by the change in meaning of
a particular word from the Elizabethan era to our times.
Only a carefully annotated edition can inform the teacher so
that he can clear up any obstacles to comprehension that may

arise.

Studying the Non-Shakespearean Drama

By 1935, when Smith's book was published, the modern drama and the one-act play had been added to Shakespeare as part of the secondary English literature curriculum. Smith recommends the following for reading or study; the list should be compared with Virginia J. Craig's list above.

Barrie, J. M., *The Admirable Crichton
              Peter Pan
Brown, Alice, Joint Owners in Spain (one-act)
Cohan, George M., The Seven Keys to Baldpate
Drinkwater, John, *Abraham Lincoln
Fitch, Clyde, Beau Brummell
              Nathan Hale
Gale, Zona, The Neighbors (one-act)
Gillette, William H., Secret Service
Ibsen, Henrick, *A Doll's House
Jerome J. Jerome, The Passing of the Third Floor Back
Kennedy, Charles Rann, The Servant in the House
Lytton, Bulwer, Richelieu
MacKaye, Percy W., The Canterbury Pilgrims
                   The Scarecrow
Miller, Alice Duer and Milton, Robert, The Charm School
Noyes, Alfred, Sherwood, or Robin Hood and the Three Kings
Peabody, Josephine Preston, The Piper
Shaw, George Bernard, *Caesar and Cleopatra
Synge, J. M., Riders to the Sea (one-act)
Wilde, Oscar, *Lady Windermere's Fan
Yeats, W. B., *The Land of Heart's Desire

It is of interest that the six starred plays were on the proposed list recommended by the College Entrance Examination Board in 1935.

The One-Act Play

Reed Smith concludes his chapter on the teaching of the drama with a discussion of the growth of interest in the one-act play from 1900 to 1935. Smith recommended serious study of the one-act play in the high school English curriculum, and recommended, also, that students be encouraged to write their own one-act plays. He offers these three steps:

1.   While the class is writing simple narratives, choose

an incident or a situation with humorous or thrilling
possibilities and first assign it to be written as
straightforward narrative.

2.   Correct and criticize the narratives, and return them
       with the direction to retell the story entirely by
       means of what the characters say to each other, with-
       out the aid of any impersonal narrative at all.

3.   The third and last step is to arrange these narrative
       conversations in dramatic form, with stage settings
       (in lieu of the descriptions of the first step) and with
       the names of the characters before their speeches--
       and the thing is done. [19]

Lucia B. Mirrielees

Lucia B. Mirrielees, whose textbooks on methodology
in secondary English served for over twenty-five years in
countless classrooms, wrote a stimulating chapter on the
Teaching of Drama in Teaching Composition and Literature
in Junior and Senior High School (1937). [20]

Like so many other experts in methodology, she emphasizes at the outset: "Remember that a play is a play."

1.   Recognizing the Pupils' Difficulties in Drama Reading

This aspect has been mentioned by every commentator
previously mentioned. To many students the cast of characters consists of names; the stage directions are practically
meaningless, and the setting hard to visualize.

2.   Recreating Stage Directions

Mirrielees would delay discussing the bare Elizabethan
setting but instead would have the teacher present as lavish
a description as possible either from knowledge of a production he has seen of the classic he is teaching or from his
reading of a work such as the Furness Variorum Edition.
In this regard, she is at variance with La Brant and Thomas
who would explain what the Elizabethan stage was.

3.   Converting the Printed Page into Speech

It is by participating in the play, by taking the various
parts, that students can make meaningful the words of the

script, particularly the humor of a Launcelot Gobbo or a Sir
Toby Belch.   Serious scenes, too, like the magnificent trial
scene in The Merchant of Venice can be made to live by the
students.

4.   Teaching Certain Stage Conventions

In our discussion of La Brant's suggestions for teaching students to read The Merchant of Venice, we have noted
how Shakespeare's plays frequently open in the midst of a
conversation.   Students have to be trained to think back before the curtain opened. Mirrielees also stresses this skill.[21]
The Merchant of Venice opens with Antonio's remark: "In
sooth I know not why I am so sad."   In another scene, the
opening lines are: "Shylock: Three thousand ducats.   Well.
Bassanio: Ay, sir, for three months."

In still another scene, we learn that Gobbo has already discussed with Shylock his intention to depart from
his service, when Shylock says: "Well, thou shalt see, thy
eyes shall be thy judge, the difference of old Shylock and
Bassanio."

These three illustrations show that a playwright often
"cuts all preliminary conversation and brings his characters
on in the midst of discussion."

Another convention that is obvious to experienced
teachers, but which must be pointed out to their students, is
that a play does not begin at the beginning of a story but
near its climax.   Referring to The Merchant of Venice again,
we mature playgoers realize that Shylock and Antonio have
met before in business relations; that Antonio has large mari-
time investments; and that Antonio the business man and
Bassanio the romantic lover have been friends for a long
time.

At first, says Mirrielees, the teacher does a good
deal of explaining, ranging from placing the strangely sound-
ing names on the blackboard and pointing out their pronoun-
ciation, to explaining the past of Antonio, Bassanio and Shylock.   But the danger of telling too much has already been
pointed out by La Brant.

As Mirrielees states it:

...All that you tell them has little teaching value.

It is purely a prologue to the far more important
matter of having them deduce from the lines themselves what lies behind. At first much help is
necessary, but by hints and questions you can bring
pupils to build imaginary pictures implied but not
stated by the writer. [22]

Since stage directions in Shakespeare's plays are few,
students must learn to see the gesture and the movement
in the text.

An excellent example in Julius Caesar is Mark Antony's
uncovering of Caesar's slashed body in the course of this
speech:

Kind souls, what, weep you when you but behold
Our Caesar's vesture wounded?   Look you here!
Here is himself, marr'd as you see, with traitors.

Shakespeare's text offers no stage direction, but
Antony's gesture is obvious.

In addition to actions, many of the entrances of new
characters are indicated by remarks of characters already
on the stage.

Not only visualization of actions of single persons and
groups is necessary, but of the scenery as well, as Thomas
had advocated in 1917.   Since Shakespeare's stage had very
little scenery, his audience had to conjure up the various
settings from the language alone.

Mirrielees wants students to imagine stage settings,
just as the Elizabethan audiences did.

5.   Recreating Characters

As with recreating stage settings, actions of characters, and past action, by reading implications into the text,
so too, students must make the characters come alive.   In
other words, the lines portraying character must be read
with imagination.

6.   Progression in Teaching Shakespeare

Mirrielees cautions against trying to do much in the
early years of Shakespeare study.   Not every mythological

reference must be explained in detail. The main thing is to
keep a play a play, not a critical or lexical exegesis. The
obvious progression is first to teach students how to read a
play. Then they can learn how to consider character, plot,
and setting. Finally, they can develop some criteria for
judging the excellence of a play seen or read.

7. The Place of the Modern Drama

Mirrielees also believes that modern drama, both
short and long, should be taught and in 1937, she recommended Drinkwater's, Abraham Lincoln, Peabody's, The
Piper, Barrie's, Peter Pan, and The Admirable Crichton,
Maeterlinck's, The Blue Bird, Rostand's, Chantecleer, Noyes',
Sherwood, most of which were also recommended by Reed
Smith and Virginia J. Craig. She recommends much reading
by mature students of the modern plays discussed in current
magazines and newspapers.

8. How Should the English Teacher Prepare to Teach Drama?

1. Become acquainted with a good number of Shakes-
    peare's plays and the critics.

2. Know a good many of the contemporary English
    and American playwrights.

3. Know the actors who have portrayed great roles
    of the classics. (In 1937, Mirrielees mentioned
    George Arliss and Otis Skinner as Shylock; Helen
    Hayes as Mary of Scotland; Katherine Cornell,
    Jane Cowl, Eva Le Gallienne as Juliet.) In the
    1960's there are, of course, comparable stars
    for these roles.

As the teacher comes across lines which he has heard
interpreted on the stage, he should capitalize on his experience and inform the class. (For example, how did all the
Hamlets he has seen in the past thirty years read the "To
be or not to be" soliloquy, etc.)

Mirrielees concludes her chapter on teaching the drama
with a plea that attention be given to developing discrimination
in motion pictures.

They offer admirable material for oral work, for
written or oral comparison with plays read, for

discussion of such topics as dramatic incidents, well-timed entrances, character contrasts, artistic interpretation, and appropriate setting. [23]

Such advice does not seem necessary in the 1960's but in 1937, it was pioneering.

Dorothy Dakin

A second methods book that appeared in 1937 was Dorothy Dakin's Talks to Beginning Teachers of English. [24] Dakin taught for many years at the State College of Washington in Pullman, and what she has to say about the teaching of drama was based on long experience, beginning in a small high school.

Dakin, like so many before her, emphasizes the importance of teaching a play as a play, rather than a piece of literature to be read or studied. To arouse the imagination of the class, she would introduce the study of any Shakespearean play by reading the first scene or two or by a bit of dramatization. For example:

> A few days before you plan to begin the reading of Macbeth, ... call aside three girls with dramatic ability, and with your help, let them plan and present before the class the witches' scene in which Shakespeare strikes the keynote of the play. [25]

Like many other methodologists, she urges teachers to visualize the setting, the characters, and the action. She, too, urges much oral reading by the teacher, and the preparation of questions for every assignment. Here are some questions which Dakin suggests for Macbeth, Act One, Scene 2.

1.   Who are the king's enemies at the time the play begins?

2.   What do the characters in this scene say about Macbeth?

3.   What impression of Banquo is given?

4.   What sort of man is Duncan? Is he a man of action? Give reasons for your answer.

5.   What are the events of the battle reported in this scene? [26]

Dakin urges intelligent presentation of the first scene of a Shakespearean play because in it Shakespeare often strikes the keynote or suggests the atmosphere. Thus "The eerie chanting of the witches in Macbeth suggests the supernatural nature of the play and the secret depths in the soul of Macbeth. Excitement and fear are indicated in Hamlet by the opening lines."

In the milling crowd presented at the opening of Julius Caesar, we receive an impression both of the fickle nature of the "vulgar" and the conflict between those who venerate the memory of great Pompey and those who follow Caesar. [27]

Class Dramatizations

Dakin, too, believes in class dramatizations. After each act, the teacher should select a significant scene or scenes and assign parts in them to pupils. These parts need not be memorized, but each student should have practiced reading them aloud so that he can read his part easily. Class furniture should provide setting. Action should be introduced, and entrances and exits planned. Simple properties can be used.

Writing as a Means to Visualization

In addition to dramatization as a means to visualization, Dakin suggests writing a paper to describe the setting or costumes of a certain scene or act. Students can derive considerable help from pictures in books, magazines and motion pictures. (In the 1960's television would be included.)

Use of Quotations

Familiar quotations may be typed by the teacher, with sufficient space below each for students to write answers to such questions: when, where, and by whom said.

Memorization

Dakin takes the voluntary approach toward memorization. She quotes Charles Swain Thomas's suggestion about the use of nonsense riddles for review purposes. [28]

Like others before 1937, Dakin suggests, as useful in providing atmosphere, reports on the historical period concerned, projects such as the building of a model of a Shakes-

pearean theatre, dressing dolls in Shakespearean fashion,
papers contrasting two characters.

Setting, Characterization, Plot

Like any other narrative, a play contains setting, character, and plot. Setting should be clarified as to time and
place.

As for characterization, the students' comprehension
will vary with their age. Freshman and sophomores should
know the main attributes and be able to support their claims
by exact references. But older students should be able to
see changes in character and the effect of one character upon
another. Hamlet and Macbeth offer excellent opportunities for
such a study, but Dakin warns that such a development of a
character be confined to only one or two persons.

Plot should be discussed in every year in which Shakespeare is taught. In the first two years, students should be
able to make brief statements of the content of each scene.
After studying the entire play he should make a summary of
the struggle and its results.

In the upper grades, students should be able to outline the Introduction, Rising Action, Turning Point, and Con-
clusion. Dakin prefers such an outline to the more formal
diagram that was formerly recommended.

Understanding the Author's Purpose

After reading the entire play, students should be able
to determine the purpose of the play. In Macbeth, for
example, Shakespeare wished to show the tragic results of inordinate ambition.

Appreciating Shakespeare's Poetry

Students should understand why Elizabethan playwrights
chose to write in poetry and why their audiences delighted in
it. With the younger students, the teacher's own effective
reading may be enough. Older students should understand
something about the characteristics of blank verse. Forceful
reading by the teacher with some explanation of the meter of
blank verse should be sufficient. An interesting exercise
with mature students is to ask them to paraphrase a famous
passage and then read aloud the paraphrase and the original

in blank verse.

Since Shakespeare also uses prose, students should
understand that he usually employs prose to express the work-
aday thoughts of common man: the porter in Macbeth, Launcelot Gobbo in The Merchant of Venice, the clowns in Hamlet.
Sometimes he uses it with more elevated characters when they
are engaged in mundane matters: Macbeth's letter to Lady
Macbeth, Hamlet's letter to Horatio, Hamlet's directions to
the players and his antics with Polonius.

What to Avoid in Teaching Shakespeare

1.   Do little with dating of the play or the source of the
       plot.

2.   Avoid too detailed study, which might ruin the con-
       ception of a play as a play.

3.   Do not overdo etymological research.

How Much Time for Each Play?

Dakin would not spend more than three weeks on any
one play. Each play should be divided, before the instruction is begun, into units that can be assigned each day.
Usually, says Dakin, students can read an act a day. Guiding questions should be provided for each unit. The actual
reading can be done rather quickly, leaving time for discussion of the play as a whole: plot, purpose, characters, significant characters, reports on pertinent topics. For fourth
year students, a suitable project, either before or after the
play, is a brief historical outline of the development of the
drama, a discussion of the characteristics of tragedy and
comedy.

Avoid Veneration

Shakespeare should be taught as a writer who understood human beings and who should be appreciated for this
understanding. To place him on a pedestal, far above human
comprehension will not make students care to read him or
see him performed in later life.

The Place of Modern Drama

Dakin recommends modern drama, either long or short,

in addition to Shakespeare. Modern drama does not need as
much detailed study as Shakespeare. Plot, characters, setting, and purpose should be discussed. Dramas should be
compared and contrasted with other narratives studied. Whatever the play read, it should be presented as an explanation
of life and personality, closely related to the student's life
and his problems.

Notes

1.   Blaisdell, Thomas C. Ways to Teach English. Garden
       City, N. Y.: Doubleday, Doran, 1930.

2.   Ibid., p. 454-57.

3.   Ibid., p. 461.

4.   Thomas, Charles Swain The Teaching of English in Sec-
       ondary Schools. Boston: Houghton Mifflin, 1917, p. 210.

5.   Craig, Virginia J. The Teaching of High School English.
       New York: Longmans Green, 1930.

6.   Ibid., p. 26.

7.   Ibid., p. 84.

8.   La Brant, Lou The Teaching of Literature in the Secondary
       School. New York: Harcourt, Brace, 1931. p. 68-83.

9.   Ibid., p. 68.

10. Ibid., p. 82.

11. See Postman, Neil Television and The Teaching of Eng-
       lish. New York: Appleton-Century-Crofts, 1961.

12. Cross, Tom Peete, Smith, Reed, and Stauffer, Elmer C.
       Editors, Good Reading for High Schools. Boston: Ginn
       and Company, 1931.

13. Smith, Reed The Teaching of Literature in the High School.
       New York: American Book Company, 1935, p. 289-328.

14. See above.

15. Smith, op. cit., p. 307.

16. Ibid., p. 307.

17. Ibid., p. 310.

18. Ibid., p. 310-311.

19. Ibid., p. 318.

20. Mirrielees, Lucia B. Teaching Composition and Litera-
    ture in Junior and Senior High School. New York:
    Harcourt, Brace and Company, 1937, p. 366-86.

21. Ibid., p. 370-74.

22. Ibid., p. 371.

23. Ibid., p. 379-380.

24. Dakin, Dorothy Talks to Beginning Teachers of English.
    Boston: D. C. Heath, 1937, p. 260-79.

25. Ibid., p. 261.

26. Ibid., p. 262. Compare these questions with similar
    questions on Macbeth.

27. Ibid., p. 263.

28. Thomas, Charles Swain The Teaching of English in
    Secondary School: Revised Edition. Boston: Houghton
    Mifflin, 1927, p. 308.

Part II

Teaching the One-Act Play
in Secondary Schools

Table of Contents

Introduction

I. The Meaning of the Appreciation of the Drama

II. How to Know the Best Plays

III. What Makes Great Dramas Great?

IV. Specific Techniques for Teaching the One-Act Play

V. How to Teach The Valiant Creatively, with Text of the Play

VI. Classifying One-Act Plays

VII. The Student Playwright

VIII. General Bibliography

Introduction

Part II--Teaching the One-Act Play in Secondary
Schools will be followed, at a later date, by Part III--Teach-
ing Longer Plays in Secondary Schools, and by Part IV--
Teaching Shakespeare in Secondary Schools.

This volume is designed to be used by:

1. Inexperienced teachers of English or Speech who wish
    to know some of the tried and true techniques for
    teaching the drama in general and the one-act play in
    particular.

2. Experienced teachers who would like some new points
    of view or who would like to pursue certain aspects
    of the teaching of the one-act play in depth. The
    rather extensive bibliographies should prove helpful
    for the latter.

3. For the sophisticated or especially interested student
    who would like to read for himself in certain aspects
    of the drama for which there is not sufficient time in
    class. Any experienced teacher knows that if he teach-
    es a good lesson, it should not end with the end of
    the class period. This book will enable the committed
    student to read and to do research on his own, once
    his curiosity has been aroused in class.

4. The general reader, who may have had no formal in-
    struction in appreciation of the drama, either in sec-
    ondary school or in college, who wishes to increase
    his appreciation of this fascinating art form. When
    one-act plays were not being done on the professional
    stages in America or in Great Britain as frequently
    as they used to be, they were revived in vaudeville.
    One of the author's most unforgettable experiences at
    the legitimate theatre was a performance by the ma-
    tinee idol, Bert Lytell, in The Valiant on the stage of
    the Palace Theatre in New York City, the Mecca of
    all aspirants to stardom in vaudeville in its heyday in

101

the 1920's. Later, such radio dramatists as Norman Corwin and Arch Oboler contributed to the renaissance of the one-act play through its presentation by radio. Countless one-act plays have been made into full-length movies, including The Valiant and such modern classics as The Old Lady Shows Her Medals.

5.   Librarians in school, college, and public libraries who wish to find the sources of particular one-act plays or bibliographies on the various phases of the drama.

6.   Finally, television has inspired a whole new generation of playwrights to feed the insatiable appetites of a new mass audience with short plays. Such writers as Rod Serling, Gore Vidal, Paddy Chayevsky, Robert Alan Aurthur and a host of others have done for the one-act play on television what Eugene O'Neill and his contemporaries did for that art form in the teens and the twenties.

The contemporary drama lover can find in this volume sufficient background material to enable him to get greater pleasure and understanding from plays he may read, see on the stage or adapted on the screen, or watch on television.

This section consists of seven chapters, which may be taught either as they appear in the volume or as the teacher prefers since each is a separate entity.

Chapter I, "The Meaning of the Appreciation of the Drama," endeavors to open wider horizons for the teacher and student, so that the fullest possible enjoyment will be derived from a dramatic performance or from a creative reading.

Chapter II, "How to Know the Best Plays," gives some sources that will make it easier for teacher, student and general reader to select from the vast treasury of plays those which are of most interest to him or her. The Bibliography provides a list of several hundred collections of one-act plays; it gives the title, author, publisher, date of publication and the list of plays in each volume. It is intended to list as completely as possible the one-act plays in print and should save endless hours in searching for the location of individual titles.

Chapter III, "What Makes Great Dramas Great?," tries

to answer a question that was asked by Aristotle over 2, 500 years ago, in his Poetics, and is still being debated by critics and experts in the drama. For those teachers, students or general readers who may be stimulated to further reading, I have provided at the end of the chapter a copious bibliography of interesting books on the topic by outstanding playwrights, critics, and on teachers of the drama in secondary school and college.

Chapter IV, "Specific Techniques for Teaching the One-Act Play," is one teacher's concept of how this art-form can be taught with personal satisfaction and success. It is based on almost forty years of teaching this form in secondary schools. In fact, one of the first books I had to teach when I began my secondary school career in Boys High School, Brooklyn, New York, was Helen Louise Cohen's Modern One-Act Plays (Harcourt, Brace and Company, 1921). Extensive classroom experience, four decades of seeing one-act plays on all kinds of amateur and professional stages, and continued reading of the textbooks and periodical articles have gone into the preparation of this book.

Chapter V, "How to Teach The Valiant Creatively" attempts to provide an extended analysis of the teaching problems, together with suggestions for solving them, of this particular play which has held the attention of audiences for almost half a century. The full text of the play has been included, with the permission of Samuel French. Earlier in the volume one of Thornton Wilder's early one-act plays, The Message and Jehanne has been reprinted with the permission of Brandt and Brandt, current holders of the copyright. These two examples of one-act plays should enable the student to follow the points made by the creative teacher as the instruction proceeds. It is by no means intended that the way to teach The Valiant thus indicated is the only way or the best way. It is one successful way, and if it serves no other purpose than to stimulate the inventive teacher to seek his or her own methods for this play or any other play, then my purpose has been accomplished. Although many inexperienced teachers began their apprenticeships by adopting the methods of experienced teachers, there have always been and will always be teachers whose native endowment or inventiveness will guide them, from the very beginning of their instructional careers. Anyone who has ever had to supervise teachers, as I have had to for the past quarter century, knows the joy of recognizing a natural teacher.

Chapter VI, "Classifying Plays," was written because appreciation cannot be built on inexactitude, misinformation or partial information. I have tried to give simple but accurate definitions of the various types of one-act and of longer plays. The bibliography at the end of the chapter has been chosen from scores of volumes that have treated one or another specific form. The bibliographies in the volumes cited can guide the reader along his own lines of study.

Chapter VII, "The Student Playwright," should prove especially interesting to those teachers who feel that something creative and personal should result from the study of any literary form. There are always students who can write poetry, passable short stories, essays and articles. The one-act play is a bit more difficult for the secondary school student, but the careers of some of the most successful dramatists of modern times reveals that they began writing little plays in their school days. I believe that the student who writes his own play and sees it produced by his classmates or by the school dramatic society will find this to be one of the most rewarding experiences in his entire secondary school career. Here again, an attempt has been made to provide a bibliography at the end of the chapter that should provide the teacher, student and general reader with many valuable hints from the masters.

No book dealing with methods of teaching is written by the author alone. To the many thousands of students whom I have taught in Boys High School, Long Island City High School, and Jamaica High School, my deepest gratitude for many happy hours in teaching and discussing one-act plays. To my scores of colleagues in these schools and to my college students, with whom I have discussed almost every one of the ideas in the book not once but many times, I owe a debt that can hardly be repaid. I have been most fortunate in having as supervisors the late George J. Crane and Samuel Streicher, both master teachers; Abraham H. Lass, now Principal of Abraham Lincoln High School, Brooklyn; and currently Mr. Louis A. Schuker, Principal of Jamaica High School, who have stimulated me to experiment with new methods, who have been generous of their advice and encouragement, and who have provided the atmosphere in which creative teaching of the drama could be practiced.

My wife, Estelle J. Mersand, has assisted both with perceptive comments on the entire text and in preparing the bibliographies and the Index.

Finally, I hope that this book will enable a new generation of teachers and students to appreciate an art form that has given pleasure to so many millions for so many years. If the readers will come away with a better understanding and greater enjoyment of the drama, my efforts will have been well rewarded.

Joseph Mersand

Chapter I

The Meaning of the Appreciation of the Drama

A love for dramatic art seems to be inherent in us.
If we let our natural instincts have their way, we would be
interested in plays without any encouragement from outside
agencies. As far back as recorded history takes us, we
learn that people have created and attended plays. Sometimes, as in the days of the Greeks, plays were associated
with great religious or political festivals. There was an awe
and respect for the Greek tragedies which our contemporaries feel only rarely. [1]

Every civilized, semi-civilized or savage people in
our times has its own drama of varying degrees of artistic
perfection. The war dances and other ceremonial dances in
darkest Africa have dramatic significance. Moving pictures
made in the South Sea Islands and in the land of the Eskimos
testify to the highly developed dramatic feeling of inhabitants
at these opposite poles. [2, 3]

If one admits that all this is true--that almost all
human beings of the past and the present are sensitive to the
magic of dramatic art, the question is naturally asked: "Why
is it necessary to teach young boys and girls how to appreciate and know the better drama?" Many answers can be given
to justify such a course of instruction.

Perhaps an analogy with music might make the matter clear. Rare indeed is the human being who is not affected by some kind of music. One music critic and popular author, Sigmund Spaeth, in his book, Enjoying Music, [4]
has classified all music as either foot-music, heart-music,
or head-music. Those who are sensitive to foot-music are
the people who must react to the rhythm of a musical composition. They cannot help dancing or drumming with their
fingers or tapping their toes when a song with strong rhythm
is played. The type of music they love appeals to almost
all races and nationalities. One does not have to take courses in music appreciation in order to like it.

There is a kind of drama that is a counterpart of foot-music; and there is a type of theater-goer or movie-fan or radio and television-listener who is a dramatic jitter-bug. This person sees all the thrillers, the Westerns, and the gangster pictures. He usually reads the pulp magazines filled with tales of horror, mystery, and violent deaths.

It would not be honest on the part of the writer to condemn this type of literature, drama, and movie without reservation, because it is not entirely worthless. There is a certain stage in the development of the young boy or girl when these emotional forms of entertainment are almost the only variety of art that appeals. That is why such a novel as Ivanhoe is usually recommended in the first year of secondary school. It is exciting, with its tournament, its storming of the castle, its many scenes of action. Homer's, Odyssey, Stevenson's, Treasure Island, and Dickens', A Tale of Two Cities, and similar books are taught in the first two years of high school because they appeal to a perfectly normal love for excitement in literature.

This love for excitement has been explained in many ways. Psychologists, teachers, and other students of the development of human beings have collected considerable data on the subject. They almost all agree that this love for the exciting life among young people is quite normal and is not to be ridiculed or criticized.

Just as it is not necessary to teach anyone to enjoy the latest dance numbers when they are played by the most popular orchestras, so it is not necessary to help children to like this elementary type of dramatic entertainment. That even older folk are susceptible to this art is evident by the popularity of motion pictures and television plays filled with action, whether they be Bonanza or Gunsmoke. People like to watch things in rapid motion whether they be horses, automobiles, airplanes or G-men. The popularity of the film, Ben-Hur, after more than seventy-five years is a perfect example of this. Many generations have thrilled to the chariot race, regardless of the form in which it was presented.

Drama, however, includes much more than rapid locomotion, and there are many more pleasures to be derived from its contemplation than the breathless excitement resulting from watching a race. This brings us to the second type of music mentioned by Dr. Spaeth--heart-music. Heart-

music includes the melodious type of music, the tune-hits
of our days and yesterday.   Included also are the musical
compositions that are programmatic or representational of
actual sounds in nature.   Many of these tunes are associated
with words that tell a story.   These compositions are the
most popular in orchestral and other concerts.   The listeners
who enjoy these selections are made happy or sad--their
"heart" is moved by them.   If one should ask them why they
prefer heart-music they would probably be unable to give any
definite reasons.   These listeners need not know anything
about the art of music, about rhythm, melody, harmony,
counterpoint, chords.   They are the dévotées of the Sunday
afternoon symphony concerts.   They crowd the concert stands
in the parks.   They hum popular songs of the day.

In drama appreciation we have a similar group.   These
playgoers find in a play, motion-picture, or TV drama a
source of relaxation from the cares of the day.   The world
behind the footlights is a strange world, less drab and less
humdrum than the world of daily business or daily homework.
These people find in plays an escape from their own lives.
The story or plot holds their attention so that they forget the
existence of a dull world outside the theatre.   Coleridge, the
author of that colorful, unnatural poem, The Ancient Mariner,
and one of the greatest dramatic critics that ever lived, expressed the relationship between the world of the stage and
the mind of the spectators as "the willing suspension of disbelief."   The audience is willing to stop believing for the
duration of the play that John Jones and Mary Smith are John
Jones and Mary Smith and accept them as Prince Hamlet and
Ophelia.   When Ophelia dies and Hamlet is killed, we feel
poignantly sad because we do not want to remember that they
will repeat the performance on the following night and many
nights thereafter.

Again it is not really necessary to teach young men
and women how to suspend their disbelief and thus enjoy a
play.   Place a troupe of capable actors before any group of
youngsters and in a few moments tha audience will believe in
them.   Sometimes it is not necessary to have words; then we
have pantomime.   Sometimes the words spoken may be in a
language entirely foreign to the audience and yet they will impress an audience.   The story is told that Madame Nazimova
was asked to entertain a certain group of her admirers.   She
offered to recite something in her native language, which was
Russian.   When she was finished, her audience was in tears.
To their great surprise Nazimova informed them that she had

recited the multiplication table in Russian. Such is the
power of the actor over the feelings of others. Sometimes
you hear the expression that something is "good theatre."
Critics who use it seldom define it or even know precisely
what it means. They say that they feel it when it is present.
Such famous one-act plays as The Valiant, The Drums of
Oude, Where the Cross is Made and The Happy Journey
to Trenton and Camden are "good theatre."

One needs merely to attend enough plays in order to
develop a "heart" interest in them. Ask any group of youngsters whether they would prefer in a recreation period a play
acted or a book to be read alone. Most of them would turn
to the former. Children are constantly acting in their own
little plays. Little girls of three or four begin to play house
as soon as they have dolls and toy dishes. Little boys will
play "cops and robbers" or "gangsters and G-men." Very little
encouragement is needed to get children to dramatize stories
which have been read in their own classes.

The element that interests us in a play at this stage
of our development as drama-lovers is the story or plot.
By plot we mean a closely connected series of incidents,
each of which is dependent upon the other, with a definite
outcome. The element of suspense is a powerful agent for
attraction. At this stage, we do not care very much for the
characters or the setting or the ideas in the play. The plot
is all-important.

After a time we discover that the number of plot situations is not unlimited; that many plots resemble each other;
and that our interest in mere story-element wanes. A book
written by George Polti, The Thirty-Six Dramatic Situations[5]
maintains that there are only that number of plot-formulas in
all dramatic literature.

When the playgoer, in addition to his interest in plot,
begins to notice character-development or atmospheric suggestion, then he has advanced to the third stage of drama
appreciation: the head or intellectual stage. Such a person
sees every new performance of Hamlet; he has seen every
available Hedda Gabler. The opera-lovers who subscribe to
the Wagner cycle year after year; the student of the theatre
who spends his Christmas and Easter Vacations seeing as
many plays as he can; the reader of plays--all these show
the highest stage of development in appreciation of drama.
They correspond in music to those idolators of Bach, to

those who attend concerts carrying the scores of their favorite symphonies, to those who understand the technical aspects and the art of music. In the field of the drama we
also have patrons who follow the development of character,
the artistry of the exposition, the subtlety of the indication of
atmosphere, the appropriateness of the direction, the correct-
ness of speech, lighting, decor, and the many other elements
which go into making a perfect play. It is the last type of
appreciation which we must teach and which needs to be
learned by our students. It is well worth the time and effort.
Art is created to give a maximum degree of pleasure to its
dévotées. That pleasure is richest for those who are prepared by training and knowledge to appreciate it. "Art is
long, life is short," said the Romans. Those who derive
from dramatic art only a fraction of the enjoyment that should
be felt are missing one of the most valuable experiences in
life. It is our job as teachers of the drama to show them
the way to go.

Notes

1. Cheney, Sheldon The Theatre--Three Thousand Years of
   Drama, Acting and Stagecraft New York: 1939. p. vii-
   ix.

2. Franklin, Jose Classics of the Silent Screen New York:
   Citadel, 1959. p. 116-117.

3. Ibid., p. 41.

4. Spaeth, Sigmund The Enjoyment of Music New York:
   Random House, 1933. See also his The Common Sense
   of Music New York: Boni and Liveright, 1924 and his
   A Guide to Great Orchestral Music New York: Modern
   Library, 1943.

5. Polti, George The Thirty-Six Dramatic Situations, translated by Lucile Ray Englewood, New Jersey: The Editor
   Company, 1916.

Bibliography

The Art and Pleasures of Playgoing
Agate, James Playgoing--An Essay New York and London:
    Harper and Brothers, 1927.
Brewster, Eugene V. The Art of Judging a Play Los Angeles:

John Murray, 1933.

Brown, John Mason The Art of Playgoing New York: W. W.
   Norton, 1936.

Burton, Richard How to See a Play New York: Macmillan,
   1914.

Cannan, Gilbert The Joy of the Theatre New York: E. P.
   Dutton, 1913.

Downs, Harold Theatregoing London: C. A. Watts, 1951.

Drinkwater, John The Art of Theatre-Going Boston: Little,
   Brown, 1927.

Hopkins, Arthur How's Your Second Act? New York: Alfred A.
   Knopf, 1918.

Morley, Malcolm The Theatre London: Sir Isaac Pitman
   and Sons, 1935.

Munro, C. K. Watching a Play London: Gerald Howe, 1933.

O'Hara, Frank Hurburt and Marguerite Bro. Invitation to the
   Theatre New York: Harper and Brothers, 1951.

Short, Ernest Introducing the Theatre London: Eyre and
   Spottiswoode, 1949.

Strong, L. A. G. Common Sense About Drama New York:
   Alfred A. Knopf, 1937.

Styan, J. L. The Elements of Drama Cambridge, England:
   Cambridge University Press, 1960.

Thompson, Alan Reynolds The Anatomy of Drama Berkeley
   and Los Angeles: University of California Press, 1942.

Wright, Edward A. A Primer for Playgoers Englewood Cliffs,
   New Jersey: Prentice-Hall, 1958.

General Histories of World Drama

Allen, John Masters of European Drama London: Dennis
   Dodson, 1962.

Cheney, Sheldon The Theatre: Three Thousand Years of Drama,
   Acting and Stagecraft New York: Tudor Publishing,
   1939.

Freedley, George and John L. Reeves A History of the
   Theatre New York: Crown Publishers, 1941.

Gassner, John Masters of the Drama 3rd Rev. and Enl. Ed.
   New York: Dover Publications, 1954.

Hughes, Glenn The Story of the Theatre New York and Los
   Angeles: Samuel French, 1928.

Macgowan, Kenneth and William Melnitz The Living Stage--
   A History of the World Theatre Englewood Cliffs,
   New Jersey: Prentice-Hall, 1955.

Roberts, Vera Mowry On Stage--A History of Theatre. New
   York: Harper and Row, 1962.

Chapter II

How to Know the Best Plays

There is no better way for students to develop standards for judging plays than actually seeing or hearing the
masterpieces. Of course, if Richard Burton could perform
his Hamlet in every town and city where high school students
reside; if Katharine Cornell could have contributed her productions of Candida, The Wingless Victory, Saint Joan, and
The Age of Innocence; if Alfred Lunt and Lynn Fontanne could
have toured the country with The Sea Gull, The Taming of the
Shrew, and Elizabeth the Queen; if Helen Hayes could have
played Victoria or Mary of Scotland everywhere; if all of
these leading personalities of the American stage could have
been seen by every student in our secondary schools, a good
portion of the best drama would have been provided.   Since
such good fortune is denied to most of our students, we
must choose substitutes.

On December 6, 1962 several million people watched
Christopher Plummer in an unforgettable television performance of Cyrano de Bergerac. Whether it be Judith Anderson
in Medea, Maurice Evans in The Tempest, Julie Harris in
Pygmalion, Helen Hayes in The Cherry Orchard, or scores
of others, great actresses and actors are appearing in many
masterpieces in this powerful mass medium.   Such handy
reference guides as TV Guide, Cue, or the periodic program
previews issued by CBS and NBC should be available to all
junior and senior high school English teachers so that they
may plan to use these great dramas as they are presented
on the air.

Next to the TV dramas, the widest appeal is made by
motion pictures based on great plays. Fifty million people
attend our cinema-houses weekly. What a vast audience for
the proper vehicles of great dramatic significance! Although
Hollywood has frequently been criticized for poor taste in
selection of its scenarios, even the most carping critics have
admitted the cultural benefits of such moving pictures as A
Midsummer Night's Dream, Romeo and Juliet, Quality Street,

113

Mary of Scotland, What Every Woman Knows and Shaw's
Pygmalion, to mention but a few. [1]

Teachers have many sources of information about
films that have been made or are being made from plays or
novels. For example, Film Reports, published by The Film
Board of National Organizations in New York City gives a
monthly check-list of films in progress and their sources. [2]
It is surprising how many films are based on novels or plays
that are on the reading lists for secondary students. The
season of 1963 produced films based on such successful novels
and plays as Advise and Consent, Anna Karenina (1935 re-
run), Billy Budd, Breakfast at Tiffany's, Voltaire's Candide,
Cat on a Hot Tin Roof (1958), El Cid, Electra (in Greek),
Elmer Gantry, Long Day's Journey into Night, Mutiny on the
Bounty, No Exit (by Jean-Paul Sartre), Playboy of the Western World (by Synge), A Taste of Honey by Shelagh Delaney,
Two for the Seesaw, Waltz of the Toreadors (by Jean Anoulh).

As a third means for knowing the best dramas we
advise the study of several recently published anthologies,
which are relatively inexpensive and remarkably rich in content. One of the best is John Gassner's A Treasury of the
Theatre, (Simon and Schuster). It contains thirty-four un-
expurgated, unabridged plays. Burns Mantle and Garrett P.
Sherwood edited The Best Plays of 1909-1919; these contain
generous excerpts from what they considered the ten best
plays of that period. Burns Mantle and his successors have
done the American drama a great service; since the season
of 1919 they have provided excerpts from the ten best plays
each season. [3] Every high school library should include these
volumes. The Theatre Guild Anthology is valuable as an indication of the type of plays offered by one of the most distinguished producing organizations in the world. Every
serious student of the drama, moreover, should own a one-
volume Shakespeare. The Modern Library has published
several collections of plays. One volume editions of the
plays of Barrie, Galsworthy, Shaw, Noel Coward, O'Neill,
Behrman, and others may be obtained inexpensively. Also
at small cost, one can obtain, in the Modern Library edition,
collections of plays by Chekhov, the French Classic dramatists, and the English Restoration dramatists.

Paperbound Books In Print (published by the R. R.
Bowker and Co.) lists many volumes of plays, either indi-
vidually or in collections. The Fireside Theatre is a book
club which makes available, at a comparatively small price,

a new Broadway play each month. For those who wish to
keep up with the best one-act plays, Margaret Mayorga's
Best One-Act Plays appeared from 1937-1961. Not only does
she supply the complete texts of what, in her opinion, are
the best one-act plays of the year; she also summarizes
many others that have appeared during the year.

One can thus purchase for not too much money a shelf-
ful of collected editions of plays, containing several hundred
acknowledged masterpieces, with critical introductions and
notes, which will supply any eager student with enough reading material for years; material which cannot but increase
his culture, his knowledge of dramatic art and its aesthetics,
and give him sufficient examples upon which to exercise his
growing powers of critical judgment.

To supplement the reading of plays, students will find
reproductions of stage-settings helpful. The Ketterlinus
Company in Philadelphia publishes an inexpensive series of
twelve painted scenes from Shakespeare's plays as selected
by the late George Lyman Kittredge of Harvard University.
These are large enough to be framed and would be a credit-
able adornment to any classroom or home. Theatre Arts
Books, Inc. has published a set of 250 prints of settings,
ranging from the Greek to contemporary drama. These can
be mounted on cards and can serve as excellent motivation
material in classes in the history of dramatic art. Film
strips, although no substitute for the actual play, can give the
spectator or auditor some pleasure and emotional enrichment
offered by the living play. When it is impossible to see
plays, all devices that will assist in visualizing the drama
should be employed. A few of them have been enumerated
above.

There is something which each student can do for himself to gain information of the theatre of the world as it
exists today. Those who live in New York City or in other
large cities with legitimate theatres are naturally at a greater
advantage in this respect than their fellow-students out of
metropolitan areas. With several daily newspapers, each
possessing a dramatic critic, the student can acquaint himself quite readily with the newest plays by reading the reviews.
Thus, if each pupil collects the reviews of one critic, he may
have, at the end of the theatrical season, a complete history
of that season. A practice in the classes of the writer is
the keeping of scrapbooks of the reviews of all the critics
in New York. It is possible at any time to discover the es-

timates made by a half dozen critics of any play that has appeared on Broadway. Thus material is supplied for exercises in comparative dramatic criticism, in critical writing, and for noting the progress of the drama. Many other items of interest appear on the drama pages of the daily newspapers. The Sunday Drama Section of the New York Times should be preserved as a permanent file and systematically indexed.

Those school libraries which can afford to subscribe to New York Theatre Critics' Reviews[4] will have a complete record of each season from the drama critics of several leading newspapers. These have been issued since 1940, and constitute the most complete record of the legitimate Broadway stage as seen by its critics, during the intervening years.

The published books by outstanding dramatic critics should form part of every high school library. Significant volumes have been written by John Mason Brown, the late George Jean Nathan, the late Ward Morehouse, Harold Clurman, the late John Gassner, Eric Bentley and Walter Kerr, to mention but a few.

The opportunities for knowing the best plays are numerous. The late Leslie Howard stated at a meeting of the Theatrical Alliance in New York City in the 1930's that a whole generation of young folks was growing up ignorant of the drama. This need not be so. Those who have ears to hear, eyes to see, and the desire to read can know many of the great plays.

Notes

1. In addition to Joe Franklin's Classics of the Silent Screen New York: Citadel, 1959, the teacher and student interested in films made from great stories or plays will find the following books extremely interesting:
    Daniel Blum, A Pictorial History of the Silent Screen New York: Putnam, 1953.
    Daniel Blum, A Pictorial History of the Talkies New York: Grossett & Dunlap.
    Ray Stuart, Immortals of the Screen (Los Angeles: Sherbourne, 1965.
    Deems Taylor, Marcelene Peterson, and Bryant Hale, A Pictorial History of the Movies New York: Simon & Schuster, 1943.
    For annual volumes, consult Screen World, which Dan-

iel Blum began editing in 1950 and which has been
edited since his death in 1965 by John Willis.

2. The address of the Film Board of National Organizations
   (1968) is 522 Fifth Avenue, New York, N. Y., 10036.

3. For a list of authors and plays in the Burns Mantle annual volumes from 1899-1950, see Index to the Best
   Plays Series, 1899-1950 (New York, 1950). A sub-
   sequent volume carrying the Index on from 1950-1960
   was published in 1961 (New York: Dodd, Mead).

4. Published by Joan Marloe and Betty Blake and may be obtained on subscription from 150 East 35th Street, New
   York, N. Y., 10016. No high school or college library should be without this valuable reference, which
   goes back to 1940.

Bibliography

Bibliography on Drama

Gohdes, Clarence Bibliographical Guide to the Study of the
    Literature of the U.S.A., ed. 2, revised and en-
    larged. Durham, North Carolina: Duke University
    Press, 1963, p. 64-68.
Hartnoll, Phyllis, ed. The Oxford Companion to the Theatre
    Oxford: Oxford University Press, 1951.
Jones, Howard Mumford and Richard M. Ludwig Guide to
    American Literature and Its Backgrounds Since 1890
    ed. 3, revised and enlarged. Cambridge: Harvard
    University Press, 1964. p. 79-81; 158-160; 180-183.
Stallings, Roy and Paul Myers A Guide to Theatre Reading
    New York: National Theatre Conference, 1949.
Vowles, Richard B. comp. Dramatic Theory, A Bibliography
    New York: New York Public Library, 1956.

Plot Summaries of Plays

Drury, F. K. W. Drury's Guide to Best Plays Metuchen,
    New Jersey: Scarecrow, 1953.
Shank, Theodore J. ed. A Digest of 500 Plays (plot outlines
    and production notes). New York: Crowell-Collier,
    1963.
Lovell, John, Jr. Digests of Great American Plays New
    York: Thomas Y. Crowell, 1961.
Cartmell, Van H., ed. Plot Outlines of 100 Famous Plays
    Philadelphia: Blakiston, 1945.

Mersand, Joseph, ed. Guide to Play Selection ed. 2, New
    York: Appleton-Century-Crofts, 1958.
Shipley, Joseph T. Guide to Great Plays Washington, D. C.:
    Public Affairs Press, 1956.
Sobel, Bernard, ed. The New Theatre Handbook and Digest
    of Plays New York: Crown, 1959.

Lists of Full Length Plays
Thomson, Ruth Gibbons Index to Full Length Plays 1895-
    1925 Boston: F. W. Faxon, 1956.
Thomson, Ruth Gibbons Index to Full Length Plays, 1926-
    1944 Boston: F. W. Faxon, 1946.
Ireland, Norma Olin Index to Full Length Plays, 1944-1964
    Boston: F. W. Faxon, 1965.
Santaniello, A. E. Theatre Books in Print New York: The
    Drama Book Shop, 1963.

Lists of One-Act Plays
Shay, Frank, comp. One Thousand and One Plays for the
    Little Theatre Cincinnati: Stewart Kidd, 1923.
Johnson, Gertrude E. Choosing a Play revised and enlarged,
    New York: Century, 1920, p. 123-164.
Mersand, Joseph Index to Plays (with suggestions for teach-
    ing) Metuchen, New Jersey: Scarecrow, 1966.
Ottemiller, John H. Index to Plays in Collections (An author
    and title index of plays appearing in collections pub-
    lished between 1900 and 1962.) ed. 4, Metuchen, New
    Jersey: Scarecrow, 1964.
Religious Drama Project Play List. Washington, D. C.:
    American Educational Theatre Association, n.d.
Play List Revision Committee of the Secondary School Thea-
    tre Conference Plays Recommended for High Schools
    rev. Washington, D. C.: American Educational
    Theatre Association, 1967.

Pictorial Histories of Stage, Screen and Opera
Blum, Daniel A Pictorial History of the Talkies New York:
    Grosset and Dunlap, 1958.
Blum, Daniel A Pictorial History of Opera in America New
    York: Greenberg, 1954.
Blum, Daniel A Pictorial History of the Silent Screen New
    York: G. P. Putnam's Sons, 1953.
Blum, Daniel A Pictorial History of the American Theatre,
    1900-1950 New York: Greenberg, 1950.
Blum, Daniel A Pictorial History of the American Theatre
    100 years, 1860-1960 New York: Chilton--Book Div.,
    1960.

Blum, Daniel Great Stars of the American Stage New York: Greenberg, 1952.

Franklin, Joe Classics of the Silent Screen New York: Citadel, 1959.

Prideaux, Tom World Theatre in Pictures New York: Greenberg, 1953.

Sobel, Bernard A Pictorial History of Vaudeville New York: Citadel, 1961.

Stuart, Ray, comp. and ed. Immortals of the Screen Los Angeles: Sherbourne Press, 1965.

Taylor, Deems, Marcelene Peterson and Bryant Hale A Pictorial History of the Movies New York: Simon and Schuster, 1943.

Chapter III

What Makes Great Dramas Great

The late A. E. Housman, one of the most accomplished poetic artists that ever lived, makes this illuminating remark in his little book, The Name and Nature of Poetry:

> Experience has taught me, when I am shaving of a morning, to keep watch over my thoughts, because, if a line of poetry strays into my memory my skin bristles so that the razor ceases to act. This particular symptom is accompanied by a shiver down the spine; there is another which consists in a constriction of the throat and a precipitation of water to the eyes; and there is a third which I can only describe by borrowing a phrase from one of Keats' last letters, where he says, speaking of Fanny Browne, 'everything that reminds me of her goes through me like a spear.' [1]

How convenient it would be for all of us if we, too, reacted in some definite, physical way to great poetry, great drama, music, architecture, and other manifestations of the human soul seeking to express its aspirations through concrete media! It would be simple indeed for all teachers and sincere students of the drama to apply such a "litmus-paper" type of test to plays. "Great play? It turns the paper red." "Mediocre or bad? The paper remains unchanged in color." The hair does not stand on edge; the heart does not palpitate; the cheeks do not become flushed.

Perhaps there are drama-lovers who react to great drama as Housman reacted to poetry. Most of us, however, are not in that category. Often we read or see a play which we thought was "simply grand" or "marvelous" or "tops," only to discover that the critics cared little for it and the public even less. Nor are we alone in our dilemma. The great producers who invest hundreds of thousands of dollars in a new play--they, too, cannot be certain that their theatrical venture will meet with critical and popular approval. It

120

is true that some very successful Broadway producers who
have one success after another attached to their names, have
an uncanny way of gauging a play's popular appeal. The late
Edna Ferber, in her autobiography, A Peculiar Treasure,
relates the opinion of the extremely successful producer, S.
H. Harris, of her play $1200 A Year. The try-out in Bal-
timore lasted a week, and Harris was asked to explain its
failure.

> "No evening clothes," he replied tersely.
> "What?" asked Miss Ferber.
> "No evening clothes. All about poor college profes-
> sors and mill workers. No evening clothes. People
> won't like it." [2]

Perhaps the tastes of audiences have changed in the
three decades since this opinion was expressed. Since the
depression of 1929 theatre-goers have applauded and sup-
ported scores of plays about millworkers and every other
kind of worker.

Yet inquisitive minds throughout the last two millen-
nia have tried to formulate the reasons for considering plays
great and the principles of dramatic effectiveness generally.
The first of these in time and perhaps still the first in excellence was Aristotle's Poetics. Two thousand years of
scholarship have been devoted to consideration of Aristotle's
theories and the final word will probably never be said as
long as each generation of drama students wishes to interpret
life and the dramatists' representations of life according to
its own standards. For the earnest student of the aesthetics
of the drama, a study of the Poetics is indispensable; and
fortunately S. H. Butcher's Aristotle's Theory of Poetry and
Fine Art (1911) and F. L. Lucas's Tragedy (1928) contain
excellent discussions and explanations of the master's principles. More recent studies of tragedy are Elder Olson's
Tragedy and the Theory of Drama (1961) and William G.
McCollom's Tragedy (1957). Excellent essays on tragedy may
be found in George Oppenheimer's The Passionate Playgoer
(1958) and in Theatre Arts Anthology (1950).

Another indispensable book for those who wish to study
the various theories of dramatic criticism throughout the ages
is Barrett H. Clark's, European Theories of the Drama. [3]
Studying the criticisms of the greatest dramatic critics, including Horace, Donatus, Dante, Daniello, Minturno, Scaliger,
Castelvetro, Sebillet, De La Taille, Cervantes, Lope de Vega,

Ben Jonson, Corneille, Molière, and many others, one will
be amazed at the different standards of judgments formulated
and various excellences critics looked for in the masterpieces
of dramatic literature.

In our own day any number of critics and scholars attempt to discern greatness in the new plays as they are produced and to reinterpret the classics in the light of their
present theories.

The question will naturally be asked: Do these plays
represent the best in American and current world drama during the past few decades? Will they all live? Are they
"Great"? How do the critics judge their greatness? How one
wishes there were answers to all of these questions or to
even one of them! Who can tell what the next generation of
playgoers will think of all of them? Perhaps they will all
be forgotten. Of the thousands of plays produced in that
truly glamorous Era of Queen Elizabeth only about five hundred
are preserved. Of these, Shakespeare's plays, with an occasional play by Ben Jonson, (Volpone), or Thomas Dekker,
(The Shoemaker's Holiday), are the active survivors. Only
rarely does Broadway see a Restoration drama like Wycherley's The Country Wife (1965). With the exception of Sheridan's The Rivals and The School for Scandal, and Goldsmith's
She Stoops to Conquer, the English drama of the Eighteenth
Century is practically nonexistent, as far as contemporary
productions are concerned. When a success of the Victorian
drama is revived in recent times, like After Dark (1929) or
Dion Boucicault's, The Streets of New York (1931), the playgoers do not take it seriously and come rather to laugh at
the theatrical fare of yesteryear than really to enjoy it. Recently the British Broadcasting Company has produced excellent versions of late 19th century and early 20th century plays,
which were rebroadcast in America by National Educational
Television (NET).

Yet each of these plays and hundreds more were considered masterpieces in their own day. It is platitudinous, of
course, to lament over the cruel hand of time, or the merciless
judgment of posterity. We must admit, nevertheless, that the
critics of all ages have erred in their judgments. Can we be certain that our own standards are less fallible?

In spite of all that, we still search for the touchstone
which will assure us that this or that play which we are enjoying is really an excellent example of dramatic art and not
a shoddy imitation. We want so much to be certain that what

we like is the right thing to like. We are so afraid that our
taste may be poor and that we may either fail to appreciate
the best or, what is worse, we may take delight in what is
positively inferior.

Are there any touchstones? If one reads enough contemporary dramatic criticism one will be amazed at the di-
versity of opinions. What is Walter Kerr's theatrical caviar
may be John Mason Brown's or Robert Brustein's poison.
When you read their excellent books like Two on the Aisle,
The Art of Playgoing, Upstage: The American Theatre in
Performance, you will be struck by their frank admission of
personal fallibility and personal standards. What is the young
lover of the drama to do? Should he read all the books by
drama critics past and present, digest them, systematize
their principles and thus have a series of touchstones?

Shall he simply go to many plays, develop his own
taste and then proudly say that "I know what I like and that's
all I care about?" Many thousands of playgoers have no better standard of judging than the personal pleasure derived
from the play. Perhaps a good case might be made for them.
When the tired business-man has paid for a seat to the comic
extravaganza and has enjoyed it, it is useless to argue with
him about taste. If he remembers a smattering of Latin, he
may even hurl at you the expression De gustibus non dispu-
tandum est, "about tastes there is no argument."

What is the bewildered young dévotée of the theatre
to do? Complicated and confusing as the picture just presented may be, the fact remains that it is a picture faced
by every person of good taste and judgment since drama began. We all have had our doubts about what is best, and if
we had remained doubtful and afraid to take a definite position there would never have been an Aristotle, a Matthew
Arnold, a Coleridge, a Walter Pater or an Anatole France.
Anatole France, in his oft-quoted definition, speaks of the
good critic as one who "relates the adventures of his soul
among masterpieces." Two conditions are stipulated in that
fascinating journey: the reaction of the soul and the presence
of the masterpieces. So many people in the presence of
masterpieces react with anything but their souls. Some of
the most amusing, yet truthful, episodes in Thomas Wolfe's
Of Time and the River describe the shallow observations of
American tourists in the presence of the mighty monuments
of European art. The critical observer sees more, retains
more, and judges more intelligently than the superficial gazer.

He who wishes to know what makes a play great can
discover for himself--and only by himself. No teacher, no
matter how ecstatic he or she may be over Shakespeare, can
make a student feel the grandeur, the humanity, the supreme
understanding of that man unless the student feels these things

himself. No amount of coaxing, threats, or blandishments
can enable a student to perceive the greatness of the Bard
of Avon, before he has been impressed by personal contact,
either through attendance at his plays or through imaginative
reading.

The teacher therefore must impress upon his students
to begin to recognize the "greatness" in great drama by recognizing the special, the unique merits of Shakespeare. About
Shakespeare's preeminence in the drama of the world, there
is hardly any dispute today, Tolstoy and Bernard Shaw's
negative criticisms notwithstanding. It seems logical to assume that the works which have been stirring audiences all
over the world for three centuries must have some meaning
for students today. Let him try to discover why at least one
play of Shakespeare is produced every year on hard-boiled
Broadway, not to mention the scores of productions in reper-
tory, college, and community theatres all across the United
States. Review the past few years of Shakespearean production with your students, for the number of different plays
produced is a revelation of the versatility of the dramatist.

It may safely be said that he who likes the plays of
Shakespeare, knows fairly well why he likes them, and will
have formulated good standards for judging the new plays as
he sees them for the first time. A few of the qualities of
Shakespeare's plays (as well as great plays of other dramatists), can now be listed. They may seem simple to the
point of obviousness, but the genuine principles of dramatic
criticism, as of all criticism, are simple, rather than com-
plex.

Great plays will possess the following:

1.   Universality of appeal in time as well as space. It
        is not surprising that every year for the past few
        decades, during the summer months, Hamlet is pro-
        duced in Elsinore Castle, Denmark, to enthralled
        audiences. Whether the production is in English, or
        in a Danish or German translation, the play has an
        immediacy of appeal found in few examples of world
        drama.

        Another instance of universal appeal, though perhaps
        on a less exalted plane, is the success of the operet-
        tas of Gilbert and Sullivan. It has been estimated that
        not a single day passes without some production of the
        Mikado somewhere in the world. Only a visit to this

operetta and the others in the series will make one
feel the joy and novelty which have enchanted playgoers for over eighty years.   Have students ask this
question: Why can they revive the Gilbert and Sullivan operettas year after year, and invariably succeed, while only a handful of more recent operettas
like Show Boat, The Merry Widow, The Student Prince,
Blossom Time, Porgy and Bess, Oklahoma, West
Side Story and South Pacific can hold their own today
in a revival?

It is not necessary to discuss the meaning of universality of appeal, since the playgoer can demon-
strate it for himself by attending (if he is fortunate
enough to be living where it is possible to do so)
these universally appealing plays.   Let him trust in
their power to enchant and stir him emotionally.
Surely what held the illiterate groundlings of the Globe
Theatre spellbound in Shakespeare's day will have a
meaning for our more sophisticated youth of today.

2.   Creation of living characters in convincing situations.
Artistic creation is the nearest approach to the creation of Man, since the artist fashions a new world
where one did not exist before.   It is a concept that
amazes the student once he grasps it.   Let him remember the lines of Hamlet, commenting on the Player's weeping over Hecuba:

> "What's Hecuba to him or he to Hecuba,
> That he should weep for her?"

The historical Hecuba or Lucrece or Agamemnon may
mean nothing to us, but once they appear before us on
the stage, they become alive.   We suffer as they suffer.   We laugh with Falstaff as we see the good-
natured old rascal succeed in his escapades.   We
sympathize with the imprisoned spirit of Nora Helmar
in A Doll's House and fight with Dr. Stockman in his
courageous opposition to the dishonest townspeople in
An Enemy of the People.   Can one help marveling at
this phenomenon?   We come to a theatre, utterly un-
aware of whom we shall see on the stage and after
two hours we leave knowing half a dozen characters
who refuse to leave us.   We sometimes know them
better than our friends or relatives.   Sometimes we
use their names to describe a living person.   Thus
Sinclair Lewis's Babbitt has gone into the dictionary
to describe a definite type of person.   So have

Dickens's Micawber and Pecksniff, and W. Somerset
Maugham's Sadie Thompson.

Dramatists who reveal the secrets of their art invariably emphasize the difficulties which they encount-
ered in creating their characters. Good plots are
relatively easy to formulate. Dialogue with crispness,
even brilliance, may flow quite easily from the pens
of relatively young playwrights, but the presentation and
projection of characters who will speak the dialogue
and participate in the plot in a manner to convince the
audience--these require the touch of the master. It
may be safe to generalize thus: the play that can
be revived successfully, long after it was written, will
have characters who are as alive for us as they were
for the audiences which first listened to them. For
example, one of the most successful plays of the New
York 1930-1931 season was Aristophanes' Lysistrata,
a play almost 2,500 years old. In 1924 there was
presented Shudraka's, The Little Clay Cart, an ancient Hindu drama over 5,000 years old. In the season of 1938-1939 the Theatre Guild offered Stefan
Zweig's, Jeremiah, a dramatization of an episode from
the Bible. Who can forget Marc Connelly's, The
Green Pastures, originally done in 1929?

If the characters live, the play will have meaning for
present and future generations.

3.   The play must stir, move, enrich, or transform the
spectator or reader. Scientists tell us that the cells
of the human body are continually dying and renewing
themselves, and that every seven years the body is
completely changed. We are never exactly the same
physically on Monday as we were on Sunday. Great
art should affect our spiritual nature the same way.
In the presence of a great play, we are affected in
a way that may influence us for our lifetime. A
young boy or girl may be made to love Shakespeare's
plays for the rest of his life if his or her first experience with them is fortunate. Likewise he may
take such a dislike to them that he will never turn
to them for pleasure, knowledge or emotional enrichment. An interesting anthology could and should be
compiled of the statements of famous people who re-
collect their first experiences in a theatre, and the
effects upon their later lives. Edna Ferber tells us
that she became stage-struck for life. Marcel Proust

in Swann's Way has one of the most revealing expo-
sitions of the effect of a great actress (Sarah Bernhardt) upon a young, sensitive boy. Scores of writers
--Goethe, Coleridge, Hebbel, Grillparzer, Lamb--to
mention but a few--have emphasized the prolonged
effect of their first plays upon their lives.

Even in later years, after one has seen many plays,
he is still affected by the play long after the final
curtain has come down. The figure of the pebble
thrown into the lake and of the ever-larger concentric
waves arising as a result of the small stone is appropriate here. Thus a play in its entirety or only
some character, some bit of dialogue or situation may
so stir up ever larger and larger waves as to strongly
influence one's entire life.

When drama first began in Greece it was performed
in massive amphitheatres, in the open daylight, before many thousands of spectators as is still done today at Epidaurus and other Greek theatres. There
was a solemnity about the subject matter, the acting,
and even the entire occasion. The plays were given
in cycles of three, and they were submitted to a con-
test, the winner of which was richly rewarded. Only
a people that was deeply moved and affected, stirred
and changed by the plays could have esteemed the
playwrights so highly.

The greatest playwrights of all ages have moved their
auditors. Whether it was Voltaire, the fighter for
freedom of thought; Lessing, the noble defender of
justice; or Shaw, or similar titans of dramatic literature, they have all recreated their audiences. Think
what the Abbey Theatre has meant for the New Ireland!
When the spectator has left a play bursting with the
desire to tell someone about it, argue about it, to
read other plays by the same author, to read other
plays on the same subject, to read the play itself out
loud, then that play possessed the power of stimula-
tion, so necessary in great drama.

4.   The other qualities may be mentioned briefly. It is
obvious that the language of a great play is superior
to one that is inferior. This does not mean that
Marlowe's "mighty line" or Shakespeare's blank verse
is the only vehicle for great drama. Sometimes a
Maxwell Anderson or Christopher Fry or T. S. Eliot
can prove that blank verse is still an effective medium

for certain types of plays--a medium which was used
in Elizabeth the Queen, Mary of Scotland, Winterset
and The Masque of Kings. Sometimes the language
may have poetry and beauty all its own, such as we
find in J. M. Synge's, Riders to the Sea and others.
The language may be charged with pungent wit as
we observe in the plays of Oscar Wilde, Bernard
Shaw, Noel Coward, and S. N. Behrman. Exposure
to these plays cannot do otherwise than enrich one's
capacity for enjoying the English language and for
using it.

5.   Great plays, in common with great literature of all
varieties, will teach the student about life, how people
think, act, and should strengthen his own hand in
facing his own life problems. For a long time, in
the rich history of the English drama, a type of play
called the morality was most popular. Everyman, the
best known of them all, is still produced to this day.
These plays aimed to teach how to live. Although we
would not care very much for moralizing tacked on to
plays, the great plays indirectly, by presenting life
problems and situations, cannot fail to elucidate some
of our own difficulties.

Notes

1.   Housman, A. E. , The Name and Nature of Poetry (New
     York, Macmillan, 1933), p. 46.

2.   Ferber, Edna A Peculiar Treasure (New York, Doubleday,
     1939), p. 249-250.

3.   A newly revised edition by Henry Popkin appeared in
     1965 (New York: Crown, 1965).

Bibliography

Sources of Critical Reviews of Plays
Adelman, Irving and Rita Dworkin Modern Drama (A check-
     list of Critical Literature on 20th Century Plays).
     Metuchen, N. J.: Scarecrow, 1967.
Salem, James M. A Guide to Critical Reviews, Part I,
     American Drama from O'Neill to Albee. Metuchen,
     N. J.: Scarecrow, 1966.

Stratman, Carl J. Bibliography of the American Theatre (excluding New York City) Chicago: Loyola University Press, 1965.

Palmer, Helen H. and Anne Jane Dyson, compilers. European Drama Criticism Hamden, Conn.: Shoe String Press, 1968.

Plamer, Helen H. and Jane Anne Dyson, compilers. American Drama Criticism (Interpretations, 1890-1965 inclusive of American Drama Since the First Play Produced in America) Hamden, Conn.: Shoe String Press, 1967.

European Dramatic Criticism

Lessing, G. E. Selected Prose Works (Laokoon, How the Ancients Represented Death, Dramatic Notes) New Edition, Revised. London: George Bell and Sons, 1890.

Sainte-Beuve Selected Essays Translated and edited by Francis Steegmuller and Norbert Guterman. Garden City: Doubleday, 1963.

Schlegel, Augustus William A Course of Lectures on Dramatic Art and Literature Tr. by John Black. London: Bell and Daldy, 1871.

Modern and Contemporary American Dramatic Critisism

Anderson, Maxwell Box Office New York: William Sloane, 1947.

Atkinson, Brooks Brief Chronicles New York: Coward McCann, 1966.

Atkinson, Brooks Broadway Scrapbook New York: Theatre Arts, 1947.

Atkinson, Brooks. Tuesday and Fridays New York: New York: Random House, 1960.

Bentley, Eric In Search of Theatre New York: Alfred A. Knopf, 1953.

Bentley, Eric The Dramatic Event Boston: Beacon Press, 1954.

Bentley, Eric What Is Theatre? A Query in Chronicle Form Boston: Beacon Press, 1956.

Broun, Heywood Seeing Things at Night New York: Harcourt, Brace, 1921.

Brown, John Mason Dramatis Personae New York: Viking Press, 1963.

Brown, John Mason The Modern Theatre in Revolt New York: W. W. Norton, 1929.

Brown, John Mason Upstage. The American Theatre in Performance New York: W. W. Norton, 1930.

Brown, John Mason Two On the Aisle Ten Years of the American Theatre in Performance New York: W. W.

Norton, 1938.
Brown, John Mason Broadway in Review New York: W. W.
    Norton, 1940.
Brown, John Mason Seeing Things New York: McGraw-Hill,
    1946.
Brown, John Mason Seeing More Things New York: McGraw-
    Hill, 1948.
Brown, John Mason Still Seeing Things New York: McGraw-
    Hill, 1950.
Brown, John Mason As They Appear New York: McGraw-
    Hill, 1952.
Eaton, Walter Prichard The American Stage of Today Boston:
    Small, Maynard, 1908.
Eaton, Walter Pritchard Leaves from a Critic's Scrapbook
    New York: Stewart and Kidd, 1916.
Gassner, John Dramatic Soundings New York: Crown, 1968.
Gibbs, Wolcott More in Sorrow New York: Henry Holt, 1958.
Green, Paul Dramatic Heritage New York: Samuel French,
    1953.
Hamilton, Clayton Problems of the Playwright New York:
    Henry Holt, 1917.
Hamilton, Clayton Seen On the Stage New York: Henry Holt,
    1920.
Hamilton, Clayton Studies in Stagecraft New York: Henry
    Holt, 1914.
Hamilton, Clayton The Theory of the Theatre and Other
    Principles of Dramatic Criticism New York: Henry
    Holt, 1910.
Hammond, Percy But Is It Art? Garden City, New York:
    Doubleday, Page, 1927.
Isaacs, Edith J. R. Theatre: Essays on the Arts of the
    Theatre Boston: Little, Brown, 1927.
Kerr, Walter The Decline of Pleasure New York: Simon
    and Schuster, 1962.
Kerr, Walter The Theatre in Spite of Itself New York: Simon
    and Schuster, 1963.
Kerr, Walter Tragedy and Comedy New York: Simon and
    Schuster, 1967.
McCarthy, Mary Sights and Spectacles, 1937-1956. New York:
    Farrar, Straus and Cudahy, 1956.
Miller, Jordan Y. Playwright's Progress: O'Neill and the
    Critics. Chicago: Scott, Foresman, 1965. PB
Morehouse, Ward Forty-Five Minutes Past Eight New York:
    Dial Press, 1939.
Moses, Montrose J. and John Mason Brown, eds. The Amer-
    ican Theatre As Seen by Its Critics 1752-1934. New
    York: W. W. Norton, 1934.

Oppenheimer, George The Passionate Playgoer New York:
    Viking Press, 1958.
Putman, Palmer G. ed. Nonsensorship New York: George P.
    Putnam's Sons, 1922.
Walkley, A. B. Still More Prejudice New York: Alfred A.
    Knopf, 1925.
Walkley, A. B. Pastiche and Prejudice London: William
    Heinemann, 1921.
William, Winter Shadows of the Stage First and Second Series.
    New York and London: Macmillan, 1892-1893.
Woolcott, Alexander Shouts and Murmurs New York: The
    Century Co., 1922.
Woolcott, Alexander Enchanted Aisles New York: George P.
    Putnam's Sons, 1924.
Woolcott, Alexander While Rome Burns New York: Viking
    Press, 1934.
Young, Stark Glamour--Essays on The Art of the Theatre
    New York: Charles Scribner's Sons, 1925.
Young, Stark Immortal Shadows--A Book of Dramatic Criti-
    cism New York: Charles Scribner's Sons, 1948.

English Dramatic Criticism Before 1890
Adams, Henry Hitch and Baxter Hathaway Dramatic Essays
    of the Neoclassic Age New York: Columbia University
    Press, 1950.
Dryden, John Dramatic Essays London: J. M. Dent and Sons,
    New York: E. P. Dutton, 1912.
Fuller, Edward The Dramatic Year, 1887-1888 London:
    Sampson Low, Marston, Searle and Rivington, 1888.

British Dramatic Criticism Since 1890
Agate, James Alarums and Excursions New York: George H.
    Doran, 1922.
Agate, James Essays of Today and Yesterday London: George
    G. Harrap, 1926.
Agate, James Immoment Toys A Survey of Light Entertain-
    ment on the London Stage, 1920-1943. London:
    Jonathan Cape, 1945.
Beerbohm, Max Around Theatres 2 vols. New York: Alfred
    A. Knopf, 1930.
Darlington, W. A. Literature in the Theatre and Other Essays
    New York: Henry Holt.
Darlington, W. A. Through the Fourth Wall New York: Bren-
    tano's, London: Chapman and Hall.
Dent, Alan Preludes and Studies London: Macmillan and Co.,
    1942.
Dutton, Cook A Book of the Play 2 vols. London: Sampson,
    Low, Marston, Searle and Rivington, 1876.

Dutton, Cook Nights at the Play A view of the English Stage
    2 vols. London: Chatto and Windus, 1883.
Grein, J. T. Premieres of the Year London: John MacQueen,
    1900.
Lumley, Frederic, ed. Theatre in Review Edinburgh: Richard
    Patterson, 1936.
Montague, C. E. Dramatic Values Garden City: Doubleday,
    Page, 1925.
Morgan, A. E. Tendencies in Modern English Drama London:
    Constable, 1924.
Scott, Clement The Drama of Yesterday and Today 2 vols.
    London: Macmillan, 1899.
Shaw, Bernard Dramatic Opinions and Essays With an
    Apology 2 vols. New York: Brentano's, 1928.
Trewin, J. C. We'll Hear a Play London: Carroll and
    Nicholson, 1949.
Walbrook, H. M. Nights at the Play London: W. J. Ham-
    Smith, 1911.
Williamson, Audrey Theatre of Two Decades New York:
    Macmillan, 1951.
Worsley, T. C. The Fugitive Art Dramatic Commentaries,
    1947-1951. London: John Lehmann, 1952.

Chapter IV

Specific Techniques for Teaching the One-Act Play

Although Shakespeare and an occasional modern dramatist have been studied in American Secondary schools for almost one hundred years, it was not until 1920 that the first
collection of one-act plays specially for high school was pub-
lished--Alice M. Smith's, Short Plays by Representative
Authors, (Macmillan). The demand for these plays was so
great that the following year [1921] three more collections appeared.

Helene Louise Cohen's, One-Act Plays by Modern Authors
    (Harcourt, Brace)
Edward Van B. Knickerbocker's, Plays for Classroom Inter-
    pretation (Henry Holt)
Sterling Andrus Leonard's, The Atlantic Book of Modern Plays
    (Little, Brown)

Since that time there have been at least thirty collections especially edited for high school use. In addition,
almost every anthology of literature for junior or senior high
school contains one or more one-act plays, with excellent
introductions, teaching aids, and bibliographies. The aim of
the following chapters is to supply for the English teacher in
junior and senior high school the necessary background about
the history and the various forms of the one-act play to enable him to teach this interesting genre with confidence.

Introducing the One-Act Play

New Interest in the One-Act Play

In the last few decades we have witnessed an astonishing revival of power on the part of dramatists specializing in
one-act plays and a strengthening of interest on the part of
the playgoing public in that art-form. Probably never in the
history of the one-act play did a single play merit the dis-
tinction of being performed at the same time in over three
hundred theatres, as was the experience in 1935 of Waiting

for Lefty by the late Clifford Odets. Never before in the
history of modern British drama did an outstanding dramatist
devote himself entirely to writing and acting in one-act plays,
as did Noel Coward in 1935. Great Britain was the bene-
ficiary of his literary and histrionic versatility in 1935, and
one of the major events of the New York theatrical season of
1936 was Noel Coward's To-night at 8:30. Some of these plays
were made into films and may occasionally be seen on television.

Eugene O'Neill, who won the Nobel Prize for literature in 1936, and was probably America's greatest dramatist,
came down to Provincetown, Massachusetts, in the summer of
1916 with a trunkful of one-act plays. Thrice winner of the
Pulitzer Prize (for Beyond the Horizon [1920], Anna Christie
[1922], and Strange Interlude [1928]), he remains the best
known American dramatist. His posthumously published works,
A Touch of the Poet and Long Day's Journey into Night added
further testimony to his dramatic genius. To many of his
admirers, his one-act plays collected in The Moon of the
Caribbees,[1] will always be effective. In 1929 the Provincetown Players presented these short plays under the title of
S. S. Glencairn. In 1940 they were combined into the motion
picture, The Long Voyage Home, which is sometimes shown
on television. In these one-act plays "one detects the first
sprigs of a talent," that rapidly came to flower in the longer
plays, as the eminent critic George Jean Nathan expressed it.

As one scans the theatrical programs of recent sea-
sons, one sees many names of dramatists who began as writers in the one-act form. Thornton Wilder, whose first dramatic efforts were in one act and who won the Pulitzer Prize
for his Our Town, began as a writer of one-acters collected
in The Angel That Troubled the Waters (Coward-McCann,
1928) and The Long Christmas Dinner (Coward-McCann, 1931).
Tennessee Williams, perhaps the most original dramatist of
the 1950's, and 1960's, began by writing one-acters. A
casual inspection of Margaret Mayorga's annual Best One-
Act Plays, published from 1937 to 1961, will reveal how many
of our best dramatists began with that form.

On television, many short plays become the fore-
runners of more notable full-length successes, the most notable in recent years being Paddy Chayefsky's Marty.

New York, to be sure, is not America, and many
things that happen on Times Square and Broadway are un-

known to Main Street, U. S. A. In the case of the one-act
play the priority has often been in the other direction.
Hundreds of one-act plays which never were intended for
metropolitan consumption, and which were of decided merit,
have been performed in small towns and cities. Many a Zen-
ith and many a Gopher Prairie bred and nourished dramatists
who were well known before they came to New York.

This state of affairs is most unusual in the history of
dramatic literature. It was always the capital to which the
young writer had to come to earn his bread and to struggle
for his hard-won recognition. In England it was London to
which the young Shakespeare had to come to present his plays;
in America it is New York to which aspiring dramatists
come. The peculiar nature of the one-act play has been fruitful in developing dramatists in all sections of the country.
In America, Paul Green has remained in North Carolina, with
no great loss to his dramatic powers. E. P. Conkle has
remained in Iowa and has written some outstanding plays.
England has developed first-rate writers in Manchester and
in Birmingham. Ireland has her own fruitful sons who were
nourished by the Abbey and Gate Theatres of Dublin.

The history of the one-act play will explain this unusual circumstance. It did not begin, as many people have
stated, in the 1890's as a curtain raiser to fill in the gap
between the opening of the theatre and the arrival of the late
diners. In medieval Japan, one-act plays, called Noh Plays,
were very popular.

When the director of the Federal Theatre Project in
the United States in 1935-1936 decided to send actors out to
perform in large vans in parks and suburbs, he was reviving
a custom of dramatic presentation that goes back[2] to medieval times with their miracle and mystery plays. Playing
to people packed closely on either side of the road or seated
on medieval equivalents of "bleacher" stands, actors performed
on large wagons one-act plays of biblical episodes. These
were grouped into series so that one might spend an entire
day seeing them all. Some of these plays are fascinating to
us today. They have humor, characterization, and unity of
plot.

Everyman is a one-act play which is older than Shakespeare's Hamlet and like the latter has been revived with success time and time again, most recently (1968) on television
by the British Broadcasting Company.

In the dramatic literature before Shakespeare's day, there were one-act plays, of which John Heywood's The Four P's is an outstanding example. The one-act play in our modern revues has ancestors which go back generations. The "ad-libbing" on vaudeville stages may seem typical products of the "Jazz Age," but in Italy and France in the sixteenth century there were similar improvisations in the commedia dell' arte. The child who stares with amazement at a one-act puppet show may not realize that some of the short plays have been handed on, father to son, by the puppeteers for centuries.

It was long a custom for amateurs to gather and present plays in the Christmas season. Thomas Hardy's novel The Return of the Native, published in 1878, represents his heroine Eustacia Vye participating in one of these one-act plays.

Thus one must traverse century after century, country after country in his search for the origin of our modern one-act play. Of course, the purposes of the one-act have changed much in the course of centuries. Formerly they were instructive, as in the medieval days in England when illiterate folk saw dramatized the Bible stories they had formerly heard about. Today the modern short play may be purely entertaining, may be thought-provoking, a character study, or a powerful instrument in sustaining morale.

Serious Study in Perfecting the Form of the One-Act Play

Before the last decade of the nineteenth century, however, the one-act play was hardly considered worthy of discussion as a special form of art. Before 1890, a one-act play was dashed off, as it were, between "tea and dinner," with no particular attention to perfection of its form. It is true that masterpieces might be created precisely in such ways, but the likelihood was slim. Lord Dunsany, author of one of the classic one-act plays, A Night at an Inn admitted that it "was written between tea and dinner in a single sitting." Such instances are rare, and the modern young writer with ambitions for success in dramatic writing, has at his disposal a number of excellent books on the technique of writing this kind of play.

The plays of our time are more polished in form. They show skill in the use of dialogue, in the manipulation of the plot, and in economy of means. The author of a short

drama realizes that he has only a limited amount of time to
get his message across the footlights, or to present his
character, or to create his mood. He must secure the best
means of achieving each of these ends.

It must not be assumed from what has just been written that studying a textbook on dramatic technique will make
one a dramatist. One will need a knowledge of life, a love
of words, a richly emotional character, and an all-seeing
eye before one can interest an audience in his works. Granted
all these attributes, the young writer can avoid many of the
mistakes and pitfalls of hundreds of his predecessors if he
studies their mistakes.

The greatest of dramatists have probably thrown into
the waste-basket more plays than they have sent to the producer. It is unfortunate that we do not possess the notebooks
of William Shakespeare, but fortunately we do possess the
scrapbooks of Henrik Ibsen, one of the greatest dramatists
since Shakespeare. From a perusal of these interesting
discarded scraps of dialogue and character-drawing we can
learn what is dramatic and what is merely words, what will
hold an audience and what will close a play after a single performance. Every dramatist has had his trials and errors.
Some of them have expressed their experiences in writing.
These many fascinating trials and mistakes have been collected and constitute the material of a text-book on one-act
plays. There is in addition the observation of perfect one-
act plays. Many a student in a course in short-story writing
has used Maupassant's "Necklace" as a model for his own
initial efforts, and many a fledgling dramatist has profited
from a study of the almost perfect construction of Where the
Cross Is Made by Eugene O'Neill.

Characteristics of the One-Act Play

It is always helpful to define one's terms in discussing
any form of literature. The one-act play has been defined
by many; but probably the clearest and most often quoted
definition is Clayton Hamilton's: "The one-act play is admirable in itself, as a medium of art. It shows the same relation to the full-length play as the short-story shows to the
novel."[3] These words, written in 1914, are applicable without any modification to the one-act plays of today.

A good idea of the conciseness of the one-act play is
Thornton Wilder's, The Message and Jehanne.[4]

The interior of a goldsmith's shop in the Paris of
the Renaissance. The tops of the windows are just
above the level of the street and through them we
see the procession of shoes, any one of them a
novel or a play or a poem. In the workshop one
finds not only medals and salad forks for prelates,
but unexpected things, a viola d'amore and folios
ruled for music.

(TULLIO, the apprentice, enters from the street
and confronts his master, CHARLES of Benicet.
TULLIO stands with his back to the door and lets
his breath out slowly, as one who has just accomplished a great work.)

CHARLES

(Rubbing his hands.)
So you delivered the rings?

TULLIO

Yes, master.

CHARLES

And what did my little brown Jacquenetta say?

TULLIO

She read twice the verse you had written in the
ring. Then she looked at me. Then she looked at
the ring. "It is too cold," she said.

CHARLES

Too cold?

TULLIO

She said: "But..but I suppose it's what must go
inside a ring." Then she kissed the ring and bade
me tell you she loved it.

CHARLES

(Arrested and puzzled.)

Too cold, the verse! - but I'll make her another.
We forget how they love us. And the other ring.
Did you deliver the Graf's ring to the Lady Jehanne
herself?

TULLIO

Yes, master. Into her very own hand. Her house
is very old and in a bad part of the city. As I
crossed the court and stood in the hall a great
German with fierce eyebrows and everything came
in from the street with me.

CHARLES

Yes, that's the one she's to marry.

TULLIO

He asked me loudly what I had there. And I said
a box for the Lady Jehanne and that it was for her
hand alone and I ran to the landing on the stairs.
Then she came out herself. He cried out upon her:
'What gift was she receiving' and 'was it from a
certain English student at Padua?' And she said:
'No, Baron, it is the wedding ring you have sent
me.' And when I gave it to her she went in, very
white, and without speaking to him. Then I went
to Jacquenetta's with the other ring and she gave
me some supper.

CHARLES

Too cold, the verse! - Start putting up the shutters.
I must go and see her.

(It has been gowing darker. Suddenly a pair of
shoes, poem these, decends from the crowd and
TULLIO opens the door to a knock. A beautiful
lady gives Christian greeting and a seat is made for
her among the littered chairs. She sits in silence
until TULLIO has lighted the candles and retired.)

JEHANNE

You are Charles of Benicet, master in precious
metals?

CHARLES

Carolus Benizentius auto argentoque magister and
composer of Music to God and such men whose
ears He chooses to open.

JEHANNE

You are a composer too?

CHARLES

They are callings like two sisters who have ever
their arms about the other's neck.   When I have
made a wedding ring I compose a motet thereto.
The boy who calls to see if the candlesticks are
done, takes back with him a Mass.

JEHANNE

(Without a breath.)

Ah.

CHARLES

Can I serve you with music or with metals?

JEHANNE

You have served me to-day.   I am the Lady Jehanne.

CHARLES

Ah, yes.   The ring was unsatisfactory?   I can
make another one to-night.   I shall set about it at
once...

JEHANNE

No, master.   The ring is very beautiful.

CHARLES

(After a pause, pretending to be embarrassed.)
I am overjoyed that it pleases you.

JEHANNE

(Suddenly)
The verses that you put in the rings, - where do
you find them?

CHARLES

Unless there is a special request, my lady, I put
in nothing but the traditional legend: fidelitas carior
vita.

JEHANNE

(Without reproach.)
But there are liberties you allow yourself?   Master
what meant you when you wrote within my ring?

CHARLES

My lady!

JEHANNE

(Giving him the ring.)
Graf Klaus addresses me thus.

CHARLES

(Reading around the inside of the ring.)
'As the hermit his twilight, the countryman his
holiday, the worshiper his peace, so do I love
thee.' It was the wrong ring that was delivered
to you, my lady.

JEHANNE

It has broken my will. I am in flight for Padua.
My family are truly become nothing but sparrows
and God will feed them.

One cannot help admiring the astonishing power of
compression. In two pages one feels the terror of the impending tragedy. One could with little difficulty imagine
Jehanne, the Baron, Tullio, and her student-lover of Padua.

The consummate art of the great one-act playwrights

rests in their ability to capture critical moments in a few lines and render them unforgettable. They are ever ready to intrigue readers and spectators who possess the proper understanding.

Expressing Mr. Hamilton's thoughts in more definite terms, we conclude that the one-act play usually:

1.   Is economical in construction, saying nothing that does not develop the plot, reveal character, or produce the intended effect.

2.   Confines itself to one central theme which is defined as the basic idea.

3.   Presents few characters and usually confines itself to one prominent character.

4.   Does not offer ordinary events of the day such as comments about the weather, eating, or working, but emphasizes something out of the ordinary, something more significant, more critical.

Life may have many crises. A great decision between one's duty and one's selfish interest will be a critical decision. A one-act play most often has such a high-pitched moment of excitement known as the climax of the play. It is the moment when the tongue becomes parched, when the breath comes more rapidly, when the heart's beating may be heard. After it is over, one can almost feel the relaxation. Members of the audience sigh with relief; and they change into less tense positions. The crisis has been passed. To repeat, a one-act play deals with such a critical event in people's lives.

5.   A play which will be over in fifteen minutes or twenty minutes must begin its action with no delay. The dramatist cannot waste precious minutes with comments on the furniture or the weather, but must present the complication immediately. The attention at the good one-act play is caught at once and held throughout the performance.

6.   The ending must be final. The play must definitely be over when the curtain falls. One must be able to say "Now, that's finished." After the first act of a full-length play the spectator, with sufficient reason, in-

quires, "What's next, I wonder?" Finality in one-act plays is so important that one never or seldom hears of sequels to such works.

7.   The characters must be presented with directness, brevity, swiftness, and careful observation.

Possibilities of the One-Act Play

These are some of the things a one-act play may be able to do.

1.   To select some outstanding experience and show its causes and results.

2.   To discover the reasons for some action. The almost perfect example is Susan Glaspell's Trifles, in which one learns the reason for murdering a husband by the subtle indications given here and there in the course of the action.

3.   To focus the attention upon one outstanding person of a group.

4.   To recount an enthralling story briefly but memorably.

5.   To portray some peculiar characteristic of a person.

6.   To present some significant idea.

What is Dramatic?

A dramatic situation arises when two strong desires conflict and the spectator wonders which will win. In this way drama is different from the other forms of literature studied. Wordsworth wrote a well-known poem about daffodils. There was no struggle in his soul, nor in that of the reader; therefore the poem is not dramatic. Coleridge wrote about the strange experiences of the Ancient Mariner. There are passages of vivid description, there are others of pure narration, but here and there dramatic passages occur because there is a struggle of different desires, wills, or personalities. Every one-act play or full-length play one will read will have such a conflict. It will stir one's feelings because it stirs the feelings of the characters of the play.

Let the student observe these clashes of temperament

or of will as he studies plays. Let him note how soon the
dramatist introduces the conflict, how he builds it up until
the moment of highest suspense. The greater the dramatist,
the more convincing will his conflicts be.

It is always helpful to compare definitions of the same
thing by different critics. The truth is not given by divine
inspiration to one person, and it may often be found between
two extremes. The greatest French critic of the nineteenth
century, Saint-Beuve, defined drama thus:

> A representation of the will of man in conflict
> and the mysterious powers or natural forces which
> limit and belittle us; it is one of thrown living
> upon the stage, there to struggle against fatality,
> against social law, against one of his fellow-mortals,
> against himself, if need be, against the ambitions,
> the interests, the prejudices, the folly, the malevo-
> lence of those who surround us. [5]

Gustav Freytag, great German dramatist as well as
student of the technique of the drama, wrote:

> What the drama presents is always a struggle which,
> with strong perturbation of soul, the hero wages
> against opposing forces. The essential nature of
> the drama is conflict and suspense. [6]

Ferdinand Brunetiere, another outstanding French
critic of the nineteenth century, stated: "Drama is essentially a struggle." in The Law of the Drama. [7]

Henry Arthur Jones, whose plays are among the few
English plays of the late nineteenth century still readable,
stated, "No adequate obstacle, no drama."[8]

George Bernard Shaw, perhaps the greatest dramatist
and dramatic critic of modern times, stated: "Drama is the
resistance of fact and law to human being."[9]

A violent struggle is not necessary. That may be the
way of the Hollywood "Westerns," which require that there
be plenty of bullets flying as well as physical struggles. As
one develops in taste, he learns to appreciate the more subtle
type of struggle, the inward conflict of emotions which may
never be expressed in a loud tone.

How Does the Dramatist Differ from Other People?

A dramatist differs from other members of the literary profession in his manner of looking at things. The historian likes to record things that have already happened; the lyric poet expresses his feelings of joy or sorrow. The novelist describes people and things and relates a story. The dramatist, however, sees things as they happen. His people are caught in the act. He has the power to create life. Things and people live for us behind the footlights.

The dramatist can show events happening because he creates characters who take part in these events. If they are stuffed figures they die there and then, but if they truly live and suffer and go through crises, then the spectator too suffers and feels emotionally aroused.

Why We Go to Plays

Let us be frank about it. Plays were meant to be seen and heard. Shakespeare never intended to have his plays printed as books to be studied scene by scene by students who had to look up hundreds of strange words in the dictionary. The Bard of Avon wanted his plays performed on the stage, so that the mighty music of his words could be heard, and his living characters might appear in flesh and blood. If it were possible to introduce every student to Shakespeare by a good production on the stage, he might become a Shakespeare lover for life. But since facilities for production are not available in all the thousands of towns and cities in which Shakespeare is studied, his plays must be read.

One-act plays, too, must be seen or heard to be appreciated fully. No dramatist would dream of writing plays merely to make up a book. A dramatist thinks in terms of the theatre, in terms of living actors and a living, alert audience. Readers must imagine themselves as spectators. They should put living actors into the speaking parts. They should see these men and women as living human beings, and they will feel what the dramatist strove so hard to make them feel.

Let the student imagine himself in a theatre seeing a perfect performance of a great play. What would it do for him?

I.   His emotions would be aroused.

A student may read about Napoleon's achievements, memorizing all the dates of his many battles. But

he may not feel anything until he witnesses a play
about Napoleon. Likewise the name of Elizabeth Barrett
meant nothing to millions of people until Rudolf Besier
wrote his play, The Barretts of Wimpole Street, in
1930 in which Katherine Cornell and Brian Ahearne
acted so well in New York and in which Norma Shearer
appeared later in the motion picture.

The student may ask: How does the play succeed in
arousing emotions in us, total strangers to the characters portrayed?   When some one dear to us dies, it
is natural to be grief-stricken; but the death of an utter stranger on the stage or screen seems to have the
same effect on us, emotionally. The student knows
very well that the actor who dies in the last act will
get up as soon as the curtain falls and will repeat the
same death and resurrection night after night; but
while the play is on, the spectator is willing to believe that the actor is not merely acting but is really
suffering. So he suffers with him and cries over his
misfortunes.

How do the characters manage to bring about belief in
their reality?

    a.   The characters themselves appear to be suffer-
          ing, and consequently the spectators suffer with
          them.

    b.   The characters must appear true to life. The
          story is told of Robert Louis Stevenson that he
          once rushed out of his study and broke into a
          fit of weeping because the hero in the book which
          he had been writing had just died. So real to
          him were his creatures of pen and ink. We all
          know certain characters in fiction as if they
          were our own friends. Sometimes a character
          from a novel or play is so lifelike that people
          try to imitate his or her clothes, manner and
          voice. The student can easily supply from his
          own experience instances of performances of
          actors who seemed so alive that he would have
          known them in the street. These characters
          in the plays, movies, and novels have become
          living beings, suffering powerful emotions which
          we experience indirectly. Think of how many
          people imitated Bonnie and Clyde in 1967-68!

II.   Vivid Experiences will be Provided For the Spectator.
        The sight of a midshipman studying at Annapolis or
        reading a newspaper would hardly arouse any emotion
        in us. To arouse emotion the writer must place his
        characters in such situations as will cause them to
        react with spirit or violence. As a result we too are
        touched. Can anyone help admiring Captain Bligh of
        Mutiny on The Bounty for persevering in his small
        boat to the very end until he sights land? Who can
        help being moved by the unfortunate miscalculations
        and misunderstandings in Romeo and Juliet? The
        circumstances in which these characters are placed
        have been made exciting or painful, and we are con-
        sequently moved by them. James Dyke in The Valiant
        is placed in the difficult position of expressing his
        love for his sister and saving his mother the humilia-
        tion of knowing that her son is a murderer. The
        agony he goes through before making his decision is
        also felt by the members of the audience. Maurya,
        the grief-stricken mother in J. M. Synge's Riders to
        the Sea feels the loss of her sons, and no one sensitive
        to great tragedy can help being moved by her sorrow.

III.   Incidents Will be Presented in Orderly Arrangement.
        Emotional experience by itself would not be a sufficient
        indication that we were feeling the effect of great
        drama. Visitors to a hospital or a battlefield might
        feel strong emotions but they would not be seeing
        plays. For a play does not merely present vivid, ex-
        citing, painful, or joyous moments of life, but presents
        them in an orderly manner. Art in general implies
        an orderly arrangement of the materials of the artist.
        An orderly bricklayer may know how to lay bricks,
        but the architect plans a structure in an orderly, ar-
        tistic way and we behold the Parthenon of Athens,
        Notre Dame Cathedral in Paris, or Radio City in New
        York. The dramatist, too, plans his play. He knows
        how to place incident after incident so that the climax
        has the maximum effect. He knows what his characters
        will say and how their words will make the plot more
        complicated; will reveal their past lives, or will in-
        dicate their future. If the student learns to appreciate
        the orderly relation of the arts he will observe that
        the Navajo Indian designing his blanket, Beethoven
        building a theme around the opening chords of his Fifth
        Symphony, and Marc Chagall designing the famous

Jerusalem glass windows are all giving orderly representations of life.

Value of Plays

An orderly representation of life which arouses our emotions will have other values to us.

1.   The play will increase our knowledge of life.

    a.   It will show other parts of the world. A play about India such as King Shudraka's The Little Clay Cart, or China such as Tairov's Roar China, will bring home to us the individual characteristics of the country more vividly than will other types of writing.

         One-act plays of American life have dealt with practically every section of the country and have contributed to a deeper understanding of the peculiarities of the different sections of the various states.

    b.   It will make events and characters of history seem real. Many plays, both one-act and full-length, have dealt with real persons who once lived, ate, fought like the rest of us, but who have now become historical. To see such a play is sometimes more illuminating than reading several biographies.

    c.   It will increase the student's power to think and understand ideas. A frequent question of young listeners to a lecturer or a public speaker or a debater is "What is he talking about; what's his idea?" It is simple enough to understand an action like a murder or the pinning on of a medal, but getting the idea behind the murder or the award is a more difficult task. Seeing and reading many plays will enrich the student's treasury of ideas. He will understand more of the world around him and enrich his conversation and writing with more maturely expressed ideas.

    d.   It will help him to understand real people. The poet Alexander Pope said, "The proper study of mankind is man." Everybody wants to understand human nature, for various reasons. It is necessary for success in one's business or professional life. It is necessary in order to get along with

people, to be outstanding in a crowd, to make a
favorable impression before strangers. Plays can
supply one with many facts about human nature,
for in a play one usually sees human beings as
they actually exist. In crises men and women
thrust aside their pretenses and affectations and
reveal their real natures. Plays should reveal
the souls and hearts of men and women.

2.   A play may be enjoyed merely for its entertainment
value through:

a.   Its wit and humor.

b.   Its novelty of treatment.

c.   Its beauty. Many of the plays of Shakespeare,
Richard Brinsley Sheridan, Oscar Wilde, Bernard
Shaw, Noel Coward and George S. Kaufman are
interesting only because of their wit. Many an
audience goes to the theatre with the clear intention of being amused. The spectators don't
want to learn anything; they don't want to reflect;
they want to laugh. It would be dishonest to say
that humorous plays do not have their place. What
are Shakespeare's As You Like It and Taming of
the Shrew but sources of amusement, pure and
simple?

d.   Novelty of treatment. As was mentioned earlier,
a book has been written with the title The Thirty-
Six Dramatic Situations to prove that there existed
no more than that number of dramatic situations.
A dramatist would soon exhaust his possibilities
unless he could think of unusual arrangements.
The contemplation of just this novelty gives one
pleasure.

Why Study One-Act Plays?

Plays are meant to be presented on the stage and to
be enjoyed by the audience. Enjoying a play and saying, "I
like it" is not enough. That is the way of young, immature
students. We should be able to give reasons for our likes or
dislikes. We must know why the play is effective or ineffec-
tive. This leads us to an analysis of the parts that make up
the one-act play.

It may be destroying some illusions to analyze the re-

action to a play; but such an analysis will deepen one's appreciation when one can apply the same procedure to any other
play.

Surely a person who has studied music and understands
its technique will appreciate a Beethoven symphony more
deeply than will one who knows nothing about this form of art.
That is why so many orchestra conductors and patrons of
music during the last few decades have provided symphony concerts for children, with analyses of the various compositions
and facts about the composers' intentions. It can safely be
said that these children's concerts have done much to increase the appreciation of music in America. Leonard
Bernstein, Conductor of the New York Philharmonic Orchestra, conducted such concerts for children in 1965 and 1966.

Observe a listener who knows nothing about the meaning of melody, harmony, counterpoint or rhythm. When the
composition is ended, he may remark, "Now, wasn't that
sweet?", a comment that could have applied with equal appropriateness to candy, a baby's antics, or a motion picture
actress. When one listens to the comments of a real student
of music one will be amazed by how much more he has heard
than a mere succession of sounds. He understands the technique of music and he enjoys it ten times as much as the
listener who is uninformed, or misinformed.

The same might be said of those who have studied art.
They derive the real joy out of contemplating this artist's
use of shade and light, out of this man's subtle contrast of
colors, of that artist's unique sense of design, out of Van
Gogh's riotous display of brilliant color, or out of Rembrant's
pictures of the human soul. To such a person a portrait is
not merely a piece of canvas 36" by 24" bound by a frame,
but a living thing, headed for immortality.

The person who would truly enjoy the one-act play
should study its constituent elements. He will be able to
perceive why he is affected in a special way. A list of
questions will help the student in formulating his reactions:

1.   Has it a good plot?

2.   Are the characters alive?

3.   Is the dialogue helpful?

4.   What is the idea of the play?

5.   What is the atmosphere?

6.   Does the setting contribute much?

7.   Are the situations effective?

8.   Is the language suitable?

To illustrate how a one-act play may be taught creatively and effectively, The Valiant by Hall and Middlemas has been chosen because it has been studied and produced in secondary schools since 1921, and can still move audiences of our own day and age.

Notes

1.   Nathan, George Jean editor, The Moon of the Caribbees (New York, 1923), p. vii.

2.   Mathews, Jane De Hart The Federal Theatre, 1935-1939 Plays, Relief and Politics (Princeton, 1967).

3.   Hamilton, Clayton Studies in Stagecraft (New York, 1914), p. 254-255.

4.   "The Message and Jehanne," reprinted from The Angel That Troubled the Waters by Thornton Wilder. Copyright, 1928, by Coward-McCann, Inc., Reprinted by permission of Brandt and Brandt.

5.   Sainte-Beuve, Charles-Augustine Etudes Critiques, vol. vii (Paris, 1865), p. 207.

6.   Freytag, Gustav Technique of the Drama, translated by E. J. MacEwan (Chicago, 1895), p. 21.

7.   Brunetiere, Ferdinand The Law of the Drama, translated by Philip M. Hayden (New York, 1914). For a generous excerpt see Barrett H. Clark, European Theories of the Drama, newly revised by Henry Popkin (New York, 1965), p. 380-386.

8.   Jones, Henry Arthur The Renaissance of the Drama (London, 1895).

9.   Shaw, George Bernard Dramatic Opinions and Essays (London, 1907).

Bibliography

Teaching Drama
Barnes, Grace and Mary Jean Sutcliffe On Stage, Everyone
    New York: Macmillan, 1954.
Hilliard, Evelyne, Theodora McCormick, and Kate Oglebay
    Amateur and Educational Dramatics New York: Mac-
    millan, 1917.
Ommaney, Katharine Anne The Stage and the School ed. 3.
    St. Louis: Webster Division, McGraw-Hill, 1960.
Overton, Grace Sloan Drama in Education Theory and Tech-
    nique New York: Century, 1926.

Play Production
Cartmell, Van H. The Amateur Theatre Handbook Garden
    City, N. Y.: Blue Ribbon Books, 1945.
Chekhov, Michael, compiled and written by Charles Leonard
    To the Director and Playwright New York and Evans-
    ton: Harper and Row, 1962.
Clark, Barrett H. How to Produce Amateur Plays--A Prac-
    tical Manual Boston: Little, Brown, 1917.
Cole, Toby and Helen Krich Chinoy, eds. Directing the Play
    Indianapolis and New York: Bobbs-Merrill, 1953.
Crafton, Allen Play Directing New York: Prentice-Hall, 1938.
Dolman, John, Jr. The Art of Play Production Harper and
    Bros. , 1928.
Gardner, Horace J. and Bonneviere Arnaud. The Book of
    Original Plays and How to Give Them New York: A.
    S. Barnes, 1945.
Gassner, John Producing the Play New York: Dryden Press,
    1941. With Philip Barber, New Scene Technician's
    Handbook.
Miller, Helen Louise Pointers on Producing the School Play
    Boston: Plays, Inc. , 1960.
Stratton, Clarence Producing in Little Theaters New York:
    Henry Holt, 1921.
Stratton, Clarence. To Read and to Act New York and London:
    McGraw-Hill, 1938.

Chapter V

How to Teach The Valiant Creatively

Nobody who ever saw the late Bert Lytell act James
Dyke on the stage or who saw Paul Muni on the screen in
this part can forget the powerful effect this little prison drama
has. It belongs to a series of great plays of prison life in
which should be included John Galsworthy's, Justice, John
Wexley's, The Last Mile and They Shall Not Die.

The part of Dyke is evnied by every young actor. It
would not be exaggerating to say that The Valiant is probably
played somewhere in the United States every single day of the
year. It is an excellent model for classroom acting, reading, and analyzing. Its construction is remarkably good and
a close study of it will give many valuable hints to the future
playwright.

A performance of The Valiant by a capable cast is the
best introduction to the play, but the serious student should
not stop at that. He should live through the experience of
the play itself if he should create the play for himself. It is
not very difficult and one does not have to be a Barrymore
to accomplish this. The procedure follows:

The following suggestions are designed to be used by
the teacher as if he were instructing his or her class. In
essence, here is a series of lesson plans on how to teach the
The Valiant, one of the most frequently anthologized one-act
plays. It is left to the individual teacher as to the number
and nature of assignments to be given for studying this play.

Notice briefly the cast of characters. Now concentrate carefully and build up before you the setting with the
words of the authors. They were probably describing some
prison-office which they had actually seen. It is not difficult to picture the warden's office. The floor is bare; the
walls are whitewashed, staring. In the centre is the flat-
topped desk and swivel chair. To the right of the desk is
the water-cooler. Above the desk is an eight-day clock.

So much for visualizing the room. You might try to
draw a sketch of it. That is an excellent practice for any
setting. Now visualize the appearance of the characters,
their faces, stature, voices, or mannerisms. In this play
the descriptions are very clear and should easily be understood. Try to recall someone whom you know in real life
who resembles these people. Perhaps you can recall some
actor of the screen whom you would put into this very office.
Develop the practice of immediately translating the author's
descriptive words into a picture.

Now read the opening lines of the play. Masters of
dramatic craftsmanship reveal themselves in the first ten
sentences. Here more than anywhere else does a play differ
from life. Suppose that you (i. e. the student) could record
the opening lines of each class in school, or of each dinner
hour. You would discover that they are monotonously the
same, day in, day out. The teacher might begin by calling
the roll and asking for the day's assignment. There is
nothing in such a beginning to hold your attention, arouse suspense, and cause emotional response in you.

Study the average conversation of two school friends
meeting in the corridor or on the street. Isn't it very often
something like this?

John: Hahya, Pete?

Peter: High!

John: Whaddyouknow?

Peter: All the news that's fit to print.

John: Ja' go to the game Saturday?

Peter: Sure, jou?

John: Say that was one sweet pass Bruce threw to
Stanton.

Peter: Gee, wasn't that? And that fifty-yard run in
the first five minutes. Say, that's playin'!

And so on, ad infinitum.

The above dialogue is no exaggeration. It is true to

life. Notice how it differs from the language of a play. You
will recall that a dramatist has only a limited amount of time
in which to tell his story. Naturally, the play must open
near the climax of the story, since a one-act play is usually
less than a half-hour long. The dramatist must, therefore,
present pertinent facts about what has already happened so
that you are prepared to understand the actual happenings.
Now the second-rate dramatist will present the past (or exposition as it technically is called) in an artificial way. Two
servants may be dragged in to discuss the curse on the house
from which the master is dying. The skilled playwright is
able to do three things at the same time. Using the characters who play important roles (not "extras" like servants or
members of a mob) he

a. develops the past
b. leads up to the present
c. reveals the personalities of the speakers

How far have the authors of The Valiant succeeded in
this most difficult task?

The Warden is smoking his cigar. He is not at ease
because he inspects his cigar critically and drums on his
desk. Immediately we are aroused by his own nervousness.
What is troubling him? His first words are spoken roughly,

"Has it started to rain?"

"Yes"

"It would rain tonight."

In three short sentences you know that something is
going to happen tonight, which is a source of displeasure to
the Warden. The presence or Father Daly ought to tell you
the rest and his second speech: "It's past eleven o'clock.
We haven't much longer to wait." answers our first big
question. What is happening tonight? The answer is an execution at midnight.

The rest of the early dialogue fills out the picture.
The prisoner is mentioned. We learn immediately that he
is quite calm, he has plenty of nerve, and that he should
have made better use of his courage. All this, we are told
in the first minute. More of the past is revealed. The prisoner had sent for Father Daly, but he refused to give any indication of his identity. Our interest is aroused to a higher

pitch. Any man of mystery is a good subject for drama.

The first long speech of the Warden tells us many
facts. The man spoken about is called James Dyke. He
has been in prison four months. The motive for his crime
is unknown. He refuses to talk, probably to shield his
family.

At this point it will be helpful to analyze the means
with which the dramatist reveals the traits of the people in
his play. These are four in number.
  a. Remarks about the person.
  b. Speech of the person.
  c. Actions of the person.
  d. Reactions of others to the person.

If you remember the old adage "Actions speak louder
than words" you will have practically all the devices for revealing character which a dramatist can use: actions and
words.

So far in the play the character of Dyke has been revealed by remarks of the Warden and Father Daly about him.
We learn of his reticence, his calmness, his courage, and
his determination by the speeches of others. This device
(i. e. , revelation by other characters) is the simplest of all
for unfolding character. It is one which we ourselves employ
and encounter all the time. When we call our chum "a
regular guy" or when father says of one of your associates,
"now Thomas is not exactly the type of fellow you ought to
associate with," the character of one human being is described
by another. In the plays and novels which you will read and
the movies which you will see, you will observe such a device frequently.

At the same time the authors must present the characters of the other members of the play. The Warden now reveals that he is not the merciless guardian of the law he
may have appeared in the beginning. This "necktie party"
is bothering him more than all the others. He feels like a
criminal to execute Dyke. Here we have an example of the
dramatic moment of inward struggle. The warden is troubled
by the conflict between his duty to the state and his conscience.

The story of the $2,500 presents another fact of the
past. This will later be important. Remember that a skil-

led dramatist never introduces any information for the sake
of marking time. It must be indispensable; else it does not
belong in the play.

The playwrights are now confronted with a problem of
technique. How are they going to produce James Dyke on the
stage? There must always be a convincing reason for the
entrance or exit of every person in a play. We see two
people before us, and we hear a third described. We want
to see who this strange, mysterious person is. Obviously
the dramatists won't let the curtain down at this point and
show us Dyke in his cell. They must bring Dyke into the
Warden's office and they must have a good reason. By using
the $2,500, the dramatists have hit upon their device. A
conference must be held between the Warden and Dyke. Ordinarily it would have been held in Dyke's cell. That would
not help us very much. The Warden decides to break the
rule for the first time in twenty-eight years. The condemned
man is walking his "last mile" before the scheduled time.
You would not realize that all this was a matter of technique,
of being confronted with a dramatic problem. Having become
aware of this and other technical devices, you cannot help
appreciating the dramatist's skill. The art that conceals art
is the greatest of all arts. By making you forget his problem
and his solution, the dramatists have woven the spell of artistic magic over you, but who that has been mystified by a
magician's trick has not begged the explanation?

Father Daly replies to the Warden's unusual suggestion,
"What on earth is your idea in doing a thing like that?" and
immediately the drama takes on a tension. Here is an external struggle between the Warden and Father Daly, to be
increased immediately by the hesitation of the jailer.

We are almost prepared for Dyke now, when the telephone bell rings. The message is from the Governor who
has sent a young lady over in his own car. This adds to
our suspense, for a new complication has arisen. It may be
destroying some of the effect by indicating that the use of a
telephone message to complicate events or to add information
is another technical device. You will notice it in many plays.
One dramatist, André de Lordé, has written a terrifying play
called The Telephone, which consists almost entirely of a
telephone message a husband in Paris is receiving from his
wife in their suburban home. Burglars have entered and
strangle the wife. The vain appeals for help over the telephone terrify the helpless husband and have a similar effect

on the audience.

Another effect of the telephone message from the
Governor was to raise the hope that a reprieve might have
been granted. The degree of suspense rose a little, but we
were not entirely disappointed since the prospect of the meeting of Dyke and the young lady is rich in dramatic possibilities.

There is no reason for delaying the entrance of Dyke.
Everything has been carefully prepared. The interview cannot last very long because the execution is scheduled at midnight. The young lady is on her way and should be here soon.

Up to this point we have had a narration of past events,
a revelation of character, and a motive for bringing the hero
on the stage. The present may be said to begin here. Every
play must indicate enough of the past in order that we may
comprehend the actions of the present. With the entrance of
the hero, the events will be determined by his own personality.

There are really very few possibilities of action that
can occur to you. Dyke must die; the Governor's message
has sealed his fate. We are curious now only about two
things: the reason for murdering his victim, and his true
identity. The rest of the play will be a conflict between
Dyke's silence and the strange lady's eloquence. Here Galsworthy's aforementioned remark deserves repetition: "A
human being is the best plot there is." James Dyke will
determine the rest of the plot by his own personality. We
don't know all about him yet, since he is just appearing
before us.

The dramatic action which now ensues is the conflict
between Dyke's determination to abide by his story and the
pleas of Father Daly and Warden Holt to have him change
it. Dyke's character determines the action, which degener-
ates merely into an argument. The Warden tries various
devices: the letters, the Liberty Bonds, appeals to his
sense of decency. The only response is a stronger determination on Dyke's part to "stick to his story." His long
speeches, beginning with, "I've heard that repentance, Father,
is the sick-bed of the soul." deserve special study. They
come from a man of twenty-seven, who has done some independent thinking, who is manly enough to admit a crime
and to take the consequences unflinchingly. His speeches
reveal his strength of character, for he is no mere murderer.

He has no fear of judgment after death because he feels when
the whole truth is told--which was not told in court--he will
be given his just deserts.

The reasons for his belief in immortality show that
he is not an ignorant killer. He can reason by analogy.
When Dyke ends his discussion of the immortality of the soul
with "And that's all there is to that," the play might have
ended. Cut out the Governor's message from the play and
you will agree that the dramatists could hardly prolong the
play after that remark. Nothing will move Dyke. He fears
nobody on earth and he has no fear of the hereafter.

There is, however, the Governor's message, and a
young lady who is about to appear. Dyke might refuse to
see her, thereby ending the play at that point, but he is not
so unchivalrous. The dramatists have portrayed him as one
who is considerate of others, as one who "never struck a
man in anger in all my life." Dyke would play the part of
the gentleman to the end.

Obviously, the dramatists could not very well end
here. A one-act play or short-story should have a finality.
Occasionally as in Frank Stockton's The Lady or the Tiger,
the reader is given his choice in making his own ending. In
The Valiant, up to the arrival of Josephine Paris, we are
too deeply interested in James Dyke to let him out of our
lives so soon. We have a slight hope that he may reveal
himself to this young lady. At any rate, our interest is
aroused, and that, as you may remember, is one of the func-
tions of the master-dramatist.

Certain human traits of Dyke determine his course of
action. At first he refuses to see Miss Paris. But he
changes his mind. Superficially the reason is her long trip
of one thousand miles. Is that, however, the true reason?
May it be the first indication of a break in his stubborn resistance to all appeals? Has the call of his family been
too strong even for him? This is an interesting problem and
is well worth your reflection. Is the bond of the family so
strong that it will survive all other experiences?

The description of Josephine Paris must be read with
great care. She does not have the magazine-cover type of
face; her clothes are not of Fifth Avenue. Here a very important principle of human relationship arises. The very
first impression we give to people is often the most enduring

one. This first impression comes from a combination of our
appearance, dress, and carriage of the body. On the stage
such first impressions are more frequent because of the lim-
itation of time.

Josephine is eighteen years of age. She seems wiser
than her years. She is self-confident, reserved, and dressed
in good taste.

The Warden's questioning serves the purpose of sup-
plying necessary information. It seems natural for a Warden
to ask such questions; we accept them quite willingly. When
the interview is over we know many things about Miss Paris
which are essential for the story. Incidentally, we learn
about her missing brother. Several details seem to apply
to James Dyke.

The meeting between Dyke and Miss Paris is irresis-
tibly touching. It begins with the expected coldness of Dyke
and ends in the display of emotions on the part of both par-
ticipants. We are swept along by the rapidity of Dyke's
story, the speech with which he adds detail to detail to convince Josephine, and his final breaking out into Shakespeare's
immortal lines. After all, human contacts have conquered
when everything else has failed. We are led to the climax
when Dyke quotes the farewell speech from Romeo and Juliet.
Until that point we are not entirely certain although many hints
have been dropped. The ending of the play is on the quiet
note, as would be expected after such an emotional climax.
How appropriate that Dyke should go to his execution quoting
from Shakespeare!

Notes

Additional suggestions for teaching The Valiant will
be found in the following anthologies containing this play:

a.   Knickerbocker, Edwin Van B. editor, Short Plays (New
       York, 1931). p. 490-491.

b.   Zachar, Irwin J. and Rodney A. Kimball, editors, Plays
       as Experience (New York, 1944), p. 257-259.

c.   Knickerbocker, Edwin Van B. editor, Short Plays, re-
       vised (New York, 1949), p. 475-476.

d. Ross, Jacob M. and Blanche Jennings Thompson, editors,
   Adventures in Reading (New York, 1949), p. 593-594.

e. Thompson, Blanche Jennings, Evan Lodge, and Jacob M.
   Ross, editors, Adventures in Reading, Mercury Edition (New York, 1952), p. 358-376.

f. Lodge, Evan, Marjorie Braymer, editors, Adventures in
   Reading, Olympic Edition (New York, 1958), p. 485.

g. Bowman, Mary Rives, Evan Lodge, Marjorie Braymer,
   editors, Adventures in Reading, Laureate Edition
   (New York, 1963), p. 464-465.

Bibliography

The Appreciation of the Technique of the Drama
Caffin, Charles H., The Appreciation of the Drama New
    York: Baker and Taylor, 1908.
Cooper, Charles W. Preface to Drama New York: Ronald
    Press, 1955.
Drew, Elizabeth Discovering Drama New York: W. W. Norton,
    1937.
Evreinoff, Nicholas The Theatre in Life Edited and translated
    by Alexander I. Nazaroff New York: Brentano's, 1927.
Freytag, Gustav Technique of the Drama Translated by E. J.
    MacEwan Chicago: S. G. Griggs, 1895.
Granville-Barker, Harley The Use of the Drama Princeton:
    Princeton University Press, 1945.
Hatlen, Theodore W. Orientation to the Theatre New York:
    Appleton-Century-Crofts, 1962
Hunt, Elizabeth R. The Play of Today Studies in Play Struc-
    ture for the Student and Theatre-Goer New York:
    John Lane, 1913.
Matthews, Brander A Study of the Drama Boston: Houghton,
    Mifflin, 1910.
Marx, Milton The Enjoyment of Drama New York: F. S.
    Crofts, 1940.
Millett, Fred B. and Gerald Eades Bentley The Art of the
    Drama New York: Appleton-Century-Crofts, 1935.
Ould, Herman The Art of the Play, ed. 2, London: Sir
    Isaac Pitman and Sons, 1948.
Price, W. T. The Technique of the Drama New York:
    Brentano's, 1892.
Rowe, Kenneth Thorpe A Theatre in Your Head New York:
    Funk and Wagnalls, 1960.

Styan, J. L. The Dramatic Experience A Guide to the Reading of Plays Cambridge, England: Cambridge University Press, 1965.
Weales, Gerald A Play and Its Parts New York: Basic Books,
1964.
Woodbridge, Elisabeth The Drama--Its Law and Its Technique
Boston and Chicago: Allyn and Bacon, 1898.

Dramatic Theory
Clark, Barrett H. European Theories of the Drama Cincin-
ati: Stewart and Kidd, 1918.
Clark, Barrett, H. European Theories of the Drama with
a supplement on the American Drama New York:
Crown, 1947.
 Clark, Barrett H. European Theories of the Drama, newly re-
vised by Henry Popkin, New York: Crown, 1965.
Gassner, John and Ralph G. Allen Theatre and Drama in the
Making Boston: Houghton, Mifflin, 1964.
Polti, George The Thirty-Six Dramatic Situations Translated
by Lucile Ray Ridgewood, New Jersey: The Editor,
1916.
Tynan, Kenneth He That Plays the King A view of the theatre.
New York, Toronto and London: Longmans, Green
and Company, 1950.

Types of Drama
Bates, Katharine Lee The English Religious Drama New York:
Macmillan, 1893.
Marks, Jeanette   English Pastoral Drama From the Restora-
tion to the Date of the Publication of the "Lyrical
Ballads." London: Methuen and Co., 1908.
McCollom, William G. Tragedy New York: Macmillan, 1957.
Motter, T. H. Vail The School Drama in England London,
New York, Toronto: Longmans, Green and Co., 1929.
Olson, Elder Tragedy and the Theory of Drama Detroit:
Wayne State University Press, 1961.
Prior, Moody E. The Language of Tragedy Bloomington;
Indiana: Indiana University Press, 1947.
Williams, Raymond Modern Tragedy Essays on the idea of
tragedy in life and in the drama, and on modern
tragic writing from Ibsen to Tennessee Williams
Stanford: Stanford University Press, 1966.
Schelling, Felix E. The English Chronicle Play New York:
Macmillan, 1902.
Thorndike, Ashley H. English Comedy New York: Macmillan,
1929.
Thorndike, Ashley H. Tragedy Boston and New York: Hough-
ton, Mifflin, 1908.

THE VALIANT
A PLAY
IN ONE ACT

BY

HOLWORTHY HALL
AND
ROBERT MIDDLEMASS

CHARACTERS

WARDEN HOLT, *about* 60

FATHER DALY, *the prison chaplain*

JAMES DYKE, *the Prisoner*

JOSEPHINE PARIS, *the Girl, about* 18

DAN, *a Jailer*

AN ATTENDANT

SCENE

The Warden's office in the State's Prison at
Wethersfield, Connecticut.

TIME

About half-past eleven on a rainy night.

NOTE:

Directors wishing to bring the war references up-to-date
may make the following changes:

Page 37, line   3: omit "trench"
          line   6: change "Jerries" to Nazis
          line 11: omit "of a trench"

Page 39, line   3: omit "was at Vimy Ridge and"

THE VALIANT

The curtain rises upon the WARDEN'S *office in the
State's Prison at Wethersfield, Connecticut. It
is a large, cold, unfriendly apartment, with bare
floors and staring, whitewashed walls; it is furnished only with the* WARDEN'S *flat-topped desk,
and swivel-chair, with a few straight-backed
chairs, one beside the desk and others against the
walls, with a water-cooler and an eight-day clock.
On the* WARDEN'S *desk are a telephone instrument, a row of electric push-buttons, and a bun-
dle of forty or fifty letters. At the back of the
room are two large windows, crossed with heavy
bars; at the left there is a door to an anteroom,
and at the right there are two doors, of which the
more distant leads to the office of the deputy
warden, and the nearer is seldom used.*
WARDEN HOLT, *dressed in a dark brown sack suit,
with a negligee shirt and black string-tie, carelessly knotted in a bow, is seated at his desk,
reflectively smoking a long, thin cigar. He is
verging toward sixty, and his responsibilities have
printed themselves in italics upon his counte-
nance. His brown hair, and bushy eyebrows are
heavily shot with gray; there is a deep parenthe-*

[3]

THE VALIANT

sis of wrinkles at the corners of his mouth and innumerable fine lines about his eyes. His bearing indicates that he is accustomed to rank as a despot, and yet his expression is far from that of an unreasoning tyrant. He is no sentimentalist, but he believes that in each of us there is a constant oscillation of good and evil; and that all evil should be justly punished in this world, and that all good should be generously rewarded—in the next.

Behind the WARDEN, *the prison chaplain stands at one of the barred windows, gazing steadily out into the night.* FATHER DALY *is a slender, white-haired priest of somewhat more than middle age; he is dressed in slightly shabby clericals. His face is calm, intellectual and inspiring; but just at this moment, it gives evidence of a peculiar depression.*

The WARDEN *blows a cloud of smoke to the ceiling, inspects the cigar critically, drums on the desk, and finally peers over his shoulder at the chaplain. He clears his throat and speaks brusquely.*

THE WARDEN.　Has it started to rain?

FATHER DALY (*Answers without turning*). Yes, it has.

THE WARDEN (*Glaring at his cigar and impatiently tossing it aside*). It *would* rain tonight. (*His tone is vaguely resentful, as though the weather had added a needless fraction to his impatience.*)

[4]

THE VALIANT

FATHER DALY (*Glances at a big silver watch*). It's past eleven o'clock. (*He draws a deep breath and comes slowly to the center of the room.*) We haven't much longer to wait.

THE WARDEN. No, thank God! (*He gets up, and goes to the water-cooler; with the glass half-way to his lips he pauses.*) Was he quiet when you left him?

FATHER DALY (*A trifle abstractedly*). Yes, yes, he was perfectly calm and I believe he'll stay so to the very end.

THE WARDEN (*Finishes his drink, comes back to his desk, and lights a fresh cigar*). You've got to hand it to him, Father; I never saw such nerve in all my life. It isn't bluff, and it isn't a trance, either, like some of 'em have—it's plain nerve. You've certainly got to hand it to him. (*He shakes his head in frank admiration.*)

FATHER DALY (*Sorrowfully*). That's the pity of it—that a man with all his courage hasn't a better use for it. Even now, it's very difficult for me to reconcile his character, as I see it, with what we know he's done.

THE WARDEN (*Continues to shake his head*). He's got my goat, all right.

FATHER DALY (*With a slight grimace*). Yes, and he's got mine, too.

THE WARDEN. When he sent for you tonight, I hoped he was going to talk.

FATHER DALY. He did talk, very freely.

THE WARDEN. What about?

[5]

THE VALIANT

FATHER DALY (*Smiles faintly, and sits beside the desk*). Most everything.

THE WARDEN (*Looks up quickly*). Himself?

FATHER DALY. No. That seems to be the only subject he isn't interested in.

THE WARDEN (*Sits up to his desk, and leans upon it with both elbows*). He still won't give you any hint about who he really is?

FATHER DALY. Not the slightest. He doesn't intend to, either. He intends to die as a man of mystery to us. Sometimes I wonder if he isn't just as much of a mystery to himself.

THE WARDEN. Oh, he's trying to shield somebody, that's all. James Dyke isn't his right name—we know that; and we know all the rest of his story is a fake, too. Well, where's his motive? I'll tell you where it is. It's to keep his family and his friends, wherever they are, from knowing what's happened to him. Lots of 'em have the same idea but I never knew one to carry it as far as this, before. You've certainly got to hand it to him. All we know is that we've got a man under sentence; and we don't know who he is, or where he comes from, or anything else about him, any more than we did four months ago.

FATHER DALY. It takes moral courage for a man to shut himself away from his family and his friends like that. They would have comforted him.

THE WARDEN. Not necessarily. What time is it?

FATHER DALY. Half-past eleven.

[6]

THE VALIANT

THE WARDEN (*Rises and walks over to peer out
of one of the barred windows*). I guess I'm getting too old for this sort of thing. A necktie
party didn't use to bother me so much; but every
time one comes along nowadays, I've got the blue
devils beforehand and afterward. And this one
is just about the limit.

FATHER DALY. It certainly isn't a pleasant duty
even with the worst of them.

THE WARDEN (*Wheels back abruptly*). But what
gets *me* is why I should hate this one more than
any of the others. The boy is guilty as hell.

FATHER DALY. Yes, he killed a man. "Wilfully,
feloniously, and with malice aforethought."

THE WARDEN. And he pleaded guilty. So he deserves just what he's going to get.

FATHER DALY. That is the law. But has it ever
occurred to you, Warden, that every now and then
when a criminal behaves in a rather gentlemanly
fashion to us, we instinctively think of him as
just a little less of a criminal?

THE WARDEN. Yes, it has. But, all the same, this
front of his makes me as nervous as the devil.
He pleaded guilty all right, but he don't *act*
guilty. I feel just as if tonight I was going to
do something every bit as criminal as he did.
I can't help it. And when I get to feeling like
that, why, I guess it's pretty nearly time I sent
in my resignation.

FATHER DALY (*Reflectively*). His whole attitude
has been very remarkable. Why, only a few min-

[7]

THE VALIANT

utes ago I found myself comparing it with the
fortitude that the Christian martyrs carried to
their death, and yet—

THE WARDEN. He's no martyr.

FATHER DALY. I know it. And he's anything in
the world but a Christian. That was just what
I was going to say.

THE WARDEN. Has he got any religious streak in
him at all?

FATHER DALY. I'm afraid he hasn't. He listens
to me very attentively, but— (*He shrugs his
shoulders.*) It's only because I offer him com-
panionship. Anybody else would do quite as
well—and any other topic would suit him better.

THE WARDEN. Well, if he wants to face God as
a heathen, *we* can't force him to change his mind.

FATHER DALY (*With gentle reproach*). No, but
we can never give up trying to save his immortal
soul. And his soul tonight seems as dark and
foreboding to me as a haunted house would seem
to the small boys down in Wethersfield. But I
haven't given up hope.

THE WARDEN. No—you wouldn't.

FATHER DALY. Are you going to talk with him
again yourself?

THE WARDEN (*Opens a drawer of his desk, and
brings out a large envelope*). I'll have to. I've
still got some Liberty Bonds that belong to him.
(*He gazes at the envelope, and smiles grimly.*)
That was a funny thing—when the newspaper
syndicate offered him twenty-five hundred for his

[8]

THE VALIANT

autobiography, he jumped at it so quick I was
sure he wanted the money for something or other.
(*He slaps the envelope on the desk.*)   But now
the bonds are here, waiting for him, he won't
say what to do with 'em.   Know why?   (FATHER
DALY *shakes his head.*)   Why, of course you do!
Because the story he wrote was pure bunk from
start to finish and the only reason he jumped at
the chance of writing it was so's he could pull
the wool over everybody's head a little farther.
He don't want the bonds, but I've got to do *something* with 'em.   (*He pushes a button on the
desk.*)   And besides, I want to make one more
try at finding out who he is.

FATHER DALY.   Shall I go with you to see him or
do you want to see him alone?

THE WARDEN (*Sits deliberating with one hand
at his forehead, and the other hand tapping the
desk*).   Father, you gave me a thought—I believe I'm going to do something tonight that's
never been done before in this prison—that is to
say—not in all the twenty-eight years that *I've*
been warden.

FATHER DALY.   What's that?

THE WARDEN (*Who has evidently come to an important decision, raps the desk more forcibly with
his knuckles*).   Instead of our going to see him,
I'll have that boy brought into this office and let
him sit here with you and me until the time comes
for us all to walk through that door to the execution room.

[9]

THE VALIANT

FATHER DALY (*Startled*). What on earth is your idea in doing a thing like that?

THE WARDEN. Because maybe if he sits here awhile with just you and me, and we go at him right, he'll loosen up and tell us about himself. It'll be different from being in his cell; it'll be sort of free and easy, and maybe he'll weaken. And then, besides, if we take him to the scaffold through this passage-way, maybe I can keep the others quiet. If they don't know when the job's being done, they may behave 'emselves. I don't want any such yelling and screeching tonight as we had with that Greek. (*A* JAILER *in blue uniform enters from the deputy's room and stands waiting.*) Dan, I want you to get Dyke and bring him to me here. (*The* JAILER *stares blankly at him and the* WARDEN'S *voice takes on an added note of authority.*) Get Dyke and bring him in here to me.

THE JAILER. Yes, sir. (*He starts to obey the order but halts in the doorway and turns as the* WARDEN *speaks again. It is apparent that the* WARDEN *is a strict disciplinarian of the prison staff.*)

THE WARDEN. Oh, Dan!

THE JAILER. Yes, sir?

THE WARDEN. How nearly ready are they?

THE JAILER. They'll be all set in ten or fifteen minutes, sir. Twenty minutes at the outside.

THE WARDEN (*Very sharp and magisterial*). Now, I don't want any hitch or delay in this

[10]

THE VALIANT

thing tonight.   If there is, somebody's going to
get in awful Dutch with me.   Pass that along.
THE JAILER.   There won't be none, sir.
THE WARDEN.   When everything's ready—not a
second before—you let me know.
THE JAILER.   Yes, sir.
THE WARDEN.   I'll be right here with Dyke and
Father Daly.
THE JAILER (*Eyes widening*).   Here?
THE WARDEN (*Peremptorily*).   Yes, here!
THE JAILER (*Crushes down his astonishment*).
Yes, sir.
THE WARDEN.   When everything and everybody
is ready, you come from the execution room
through the passage— (*He gestures toward the
nearer door on the right.*) open that door quietly
and stand there.
THE JAILER.   Yes, sir.
THE WARDEN.   You don't have to say anything,
and I don't *want* you to say anything.   Just stand
there.   That all clear?
THE JAILER.   Yes, sir.
THE WARDEN.   That'll be the signal for us to start
—understand?
THE JAILER.   Yes, sir.
THE WARDEN (*Draws a deep breath*).   All right.
Now bring Dyke to me.
THE JAILER.   Yes, sir.   (*He goes out dazedly.*)
FATHER DALY.   What about the witnesses and the
reporters?
THE WARDEN.   They're having their sandwiches
[11]

THE VALIANT

and coffee now—the deputy'll have 'em seated in another ten or fifteen minutes. Let 'em wait. (*His voice becomes savage.*)   I'd like to poison the lot of 'em. Reporters! Witnesses! (*The telephone bell rings.*)   Hello—yes—yes—what's that?—Yes, yes, right here—who wants him? (*To* FATHER DALY.)   Father, it's the Governor! (*His expression is tense.*)

FATHER DALY (*His voice also gives evidence of incredulity and hope*). What! (*He walks swiftly over to the desk.*)   Is it about Dyke?

THE WARDEN. Ssh. (*He turns to the telephone.*)   Yes, this is Warden Holt speaking. Hello—oh, hello, Governor Fuller, how are you? Oh, I'm between grass and hay, thanks.   Well, this isn't my idea of a picnic exactly—yes—yes— Oh, I should say in about half an hour or so— everything's just about ready. (*His expression gradually relaxes, and* FATHER DALY, *with a little sigh and shake of the head, turns away.*) Oh, no, there won't be any slip-up—yes, we made the regular tests, one this afternoon and another at nine o'clock tonight— Oh, no, Governor, nothing can go wrong— Well, according to the law I've got to get it done as soon as possible after midnight, but you're the Governor of the state— How long?—Certainly, Governor, I can hold it off as long as you want me to— What say?—A *girl!*—You're going to send her to me?—you *have* sent her!—she ought to be here by this time?—All right, Governor, I'll ring you up

[12]

THE VALIANT

when it's over. Good-bye. (*He hangs up the receiver, mops his forehead with his handkerchief, and turns to* FATHER DALY *in great excitement.*) Did you get *that?* Some girl thinks Dyke's her long-lost brother, and she's persuaded the old man to let her come out here tonight— he wants me to hold up the job until she's had a chance to see him. She's due here any minute, he says—in his own car—escorted by his own private secretary! Can you beat it?

FATHER DALY (*Downcast*). Poor girl!

THE WARDEN (*Blots his forehead vigorously*). For a minute there I thought it was going to be a reprieve at the very least. Whew!

FATHER DALY. So did I.

(*The door from the deputy's room is opened, and* DYKE *comes in, followed immediately by the* JAILER. DYKE *halts just inside the door and waits passively to be told what to do next. He has a lean, pale face, with a high forehead, good eyes, and a strong chin; his mouth is ruled in a firm straight line. His wavy hair is prematurely gray. His figure has the elasticity of youth, but he might pass among strangers either as a man of forty, or as a man of twenty-five, depending upon the mobility of his features at a given moment. He is dressed in a dark shirt open at the throat, dark trousers without belt or suspenders, and soft slippers. The* JAILER *receives a nod from the* WARDEN, *and goes out promptly, closing the door behind him.*)

[13]

THE VALIANT

THE WARDEN (*Swings half-way around in his swivel-chair*). Sit down, Dyke. (*He points to the chair at the right of his desk.*)

DYKE. Thanks. (*He goes directly to the chair and sits down.*)

THE WARDEN (*Leans back, and surveys him thoughtfully.* FATHER DALY *remains in the background*). Dyke, you've been here under my charge for nearly four months and I want to tell you that from first to last you've behaved yourself like a gentleman.

DYKE (*His manner is vaguely cynical without being in the least impertinent*). Why should I make you any trouble?

THE WARDEN. Well, you *haven't* made me any trouble, and I've tried to show what I think about it. I've made you every bit as comfortable as the law would let me.

DYKE. You've been very kind to me. (*He glances over his shoulder at the chaplain.*) And you, too, Father.

THE WARDEN. I've had you brought in here to stay from now on. (DYKE *looks inquiringly at him.*) No, you won't have to go back to your cell again. You're to stay right here with Father Daly and me.

DYKE (*Carelessly*). All right.

THE WARDEN (*Piqued by this cool reception of the distinguished favor*). You don't seem to understand that I'm doing something a long way out of the ordinary for you.

[14]

THE VALIANT

DYKE. Oh, yes, I do, but maybe *you* don't understand why it doesn't give me much of a thrill.

FATHER DALY (*Comes forward*). My son, the
Warden is only trying to do you one more kind-
ness.

DYKE. I know he is, Father, but the Warden isn't
taking very much of a gamble. From now on,
one place is about the same as another.

THE WARDEN. What do you mean?

DYKE (*His voice is very faintly sarcastic*). Why,
I mean that I'm just as much a condemned prisoner here as when I was in my cell. That door
(*he points to it*) leads right *back* to my cell.
Outside those windows are armed guards every
few feet. You yourself can't get through the
iron door in that anteroom (*he indicates the
door to the left*) until somebody on the outside
unlocks it; and I know as well as you do where
that door (*he points to the nearer door on the
right*) leads to.

THE WARDEN (*Stiffly*). Would you rather wait
in your cell?

DYKE. Oh, no, this is a little pleasanter. Except—

THE WARDEN. Except what?

DYKE. In my cell, I could smoke.

THE WARDEN (*Shrugs his shoulders*). What do
you want—cigar or cigarette?

DYKE. A cigarette, if it's all the same.

{*The* WARDEN *opens a drawer of his desk, takes
out a box of cigarettes, removes one and hands*
[15]

THE VALIANT

it to DYKE. *The* WARDEN *striking a match,
lights* DYKE'S *cigarette, and then carefully puts
out the match.*)

DYKE (*Smiles faintly*). Thanks. You're a good
host.

THE WARDEN. Dyke, before it's too late I wish
you'd think over what Father Daly and I've said
to you so many times.

DYKE. I've thought of nothing else.

THE WARDEN. Then—as man to man—and this
is your last chance—who are you?

DYKE (*Inspects his cigarette*). Who am I?
James Dyke—a murderer.

THE WARDEN. That isn't your real name and we
know it.

DYKE. You're not going to execute a name—
you're going to execute a *man*. What difference
does it make whether you call me Dyke or something else?

THE WARDEN. You had another name once.
What was it?

DYKE. If I had, I've forgotten it.

FATHER DALY. Your mind is made up, my son?

DYKE. Yes, Father, it is.

THE WARDEN. Dyke.

DYKE. Yes, sir?

THE WARDEN. Do you see this pile of letters?
(*He places his hand over it.*)

DYKE. Yes, sir.

THE WARDEN (*Fingers them*). Every one of

[16]

THE VALIANT

these letters is about the same thing and all put
together we've got maybe four thousand of 'em.
These here are just a few samples.
DYKE. What about them?
THE WARDEN. We've had letters from every
State in the Union and every province in Canada.
We've had fifteen or twenty from England, four
or five from France, two from Australia and one
from Russia.
DYKE. Well?
THE WARDEN (*Inclines toward him*). Do you
know what every one of those letters says—
what four thousand different people are writing
to me about?
DYKE. No, sir.
THE WARDEN (*Speaks slowly and impressively*).
Who *are* you—and are you the missing son—or
brother—or husband—or sweetheart?
DYKE (*Flicks his cigarette ashes to the floor*).
Have you answered them?
THE WARDEN. No, I couldn't. I want you to.
DYKE. How's that?
THE WARDEN. I want you to tell me who you are.
(DYKE *shakes his head.*) Can't you see you
ought to do it?
DYKE. No, sir, I can't exactly see that. Suppose
you explain it to me.
THE WARDEN (*Suddenly*). You're trying to shield
somebody, aren't you?"
DYKE. Yes—no, I'm not!
[17]

THE VALIANT

THE WARDEN (*Glances at* FATHER DALY *and nods
  with elation*). Who is it? Your family?
DYKE. I said I'm not.
THE WARDEN. But first, you said you were.
DYKE. That was a slip of the tongue.
THE WARDEN (*Has grown persuasive*). Dyke,
  just listen to me a minute. Don't be narrow, look
  at this thing in a big, broad way. Suppose you
  should tell me your real name, and I publish it,
  it'll bring an awful lot of sorrow, let's say, to
  one family, *one* home, and that's your own.
  That's probably what you're thinking about.
  Am I right? You want to spare your family and
  I don't blame you. On the surface, it sure would
  look like a mighty white thing for you to do.
  But look at it *this* way: suppose you came out with
  the truth, flat-footed, why, you might put all that
  sorrow into *one* home—your own—but at the
  same time you'd be putting an immense amount of
  relief in four thousand—others. Don't you get
  that? Don't you figure you owe something to all
  these other people?
DYKE. Not a thing.
FATHER DALY (*Has been fidgeting*). My boy, the
  Warden is absolutely right. You do owe something to the other people—you owe them peace of
  mind—and for the sake of all those thousands
  of poor, distressed women, who imagine God
  knows what, I beg of you to tell us who you are.
DYKE. Father, I simply can't do it.
FATHER DALY. Think carefully, my boy, think
[18]

THE VALIANT

very carefully. We're not asking out of idle curiosity.

DYKE. I know that, but please don't let's talk about it any more. (*To the* WARDEN.) You can answer those letters whenever you want to, and you can say I'm not the man they're looking for. That'll be the truth, too. Because I haven't any mother—or father—or sister—or wife—or sweetheart. That's fair enough, isn't it?

FATHER DALY (*Sighs wearily*). As you will, my son.

THE WARDEN. Dyke, there's one more thing.

DYKE. Yes?

THE WARDEN. Here are the Liberty Bonds (*he takes up the large envelope from his desk*) that belong to you. Twenty-five hundred dollars in real money.

DYKE (*Removes the bonds and examines them*). Good-looking, aren't they?

THE WARDEN (*Casually*). What do you want me to do with them?

DYKE. Well, I can't very well take them with me, so, under the circumstances, I'd like to put them where they'll do the most good.

THE WARDEN (*More casually yet*). Who do you want me to send 'em to?

DYKE (*Laughs quietly*). Now, Warden Holt, you didn't think you were going to catch me that way, did you?

THE WARDEN (*Scowls*). Who'll I send 'em to?

THE VALIANT

I can't keep 'em here, and I can't destroy 'em.
What do you want to do with 'em?

DYKE (*Ponders diligently and tosses the envelopes to the desk*). I don't know. I'll think of something to do with them. I'll tell you in just a minute. Is there anything else?

THE WARDEN. Not unless you want to make some sort of statement.

DYKE. No, I guess I've said everything. I killed a man and I'm not sorry for it—that is, I'm not sorry I killed that particular person. I—

FATHER DALY (*Raises his hand*). Repentance—

DYKE (*Raises his own hand in turn*). I've heard that repentance, Father, is the sick bed of the soul—and mine is very well and flourishing. The man deserved to be killed; he wasn't fit to live. It was my duty to kill him, and I did it. I'd never struck a man in anger in all my life, but when I knew what that fellow had done, I knew I had to kill him, and I did it deliberately and intentionally—and carefully. I knew what I was doing, and I haven't any excuse—that is, I haven't any excuse that satisfies the law. Now, I learned pretty early in life that whatever you do in this world you have to pay for in one way or another. If you kill a man, the price you have to pay is this (*he makes a gesture which sweeps the entire room*) and that (*he points to the nearer door on the right*) and I'm going to pay it. That's all there is to that. And an hour from now, while my body is lying in there, if a couple of

[20]

THE VALIANT

angel policemen grab my soul and haul it up before God—

FATHER DALY (*Profoundly shocked*). My boy,
my boy, please—

DYKE. I beg your pardon, Father. I don't mean
to trample on anything that's sacred to you, but
what I do mean to say is this: If I've got to be
judged by God Almighty for the crime of murder, I'm not afraid, because the other fellow will
certainly be there, too, won't he? And when
God hears the whole story and both sides of it,
which *you* never heard and never will—and they
never heard it in the court room, either—why,
then, if he's any kind of a God at all, I'm willing
to take my chances with the other fellow. That's
how concerned I am about the hereafter. And,
if it'll make you feel any better, Father, why I
do rather think there's going to be a hereafter.
I read a book once that said a milligram of musk
will give out perfume for seven thousand years,
and a milligram of radium will give out light for
seventy thousand. Why shouldn't a soul—mine,
for instance—live more than twenty-seven? But
if there *isn't* any hereafter—if we just die and are
dead and that's all—why, I'm still not sorry and
I'm not afraid, because I'm quits with the other
fellow—the law is quits with me, and it's all
balanced on the books. And that's all there is
to that. (*An attendant enters from the anteroom.*)

THE WARDEN. Well? What is it?

THE VALIANT

THE ATTENDANT. Visitor to see you, sir. With
note from Governor Fuller. (*He presents it.*)
THE WARDEN (*Barely glances at the envelope*).
Oh! A young woman?
THE ATTENDANT. Yes, sir.
THE WARDEN. Is Mrs. Case there?
THE ATTENDANT. Yes, sir.
THE WARDEN. Have the girl searched, and then
take her into the anteroom and wait till I call
you.
THE ATTENDANT. Yes, sir. (*He goes out.*)
THE WARDEN. Dyke, a young woman has just
come to see you—do you want to see her?
DYKE. I don't think so. What does she want?
THE WARDEN. She thinks maybe she's your sister,
and she's come a thousand miles to find out.
DYKE. She's wrong. I haven't any sister.
THE WARDEN (*Hesitates*). Will I tell her that,
or do you want to tell it to her yourself?
DYKE. Oh, you tell her.
THE WARDEN. All right. (*He starts to rise but
resumes his seat as* DYKE *speaks.*)
DYKE. Just a second—she's come a thousand miles
to see me, did you say?
THE WARDEN. Yes, and she's got special permis-
sion from the Governor to talk to you—that is,
with my O. K.
DYKE. A year ago, nobody'd have crossed the
street to look at me, and now they come a thousand miles!
FATHER DALY. This is one of your debts to hu-
[22]

THE VALIANT

manity, my boy. It wouldn't take you two
minutes to see her, and, if you don't, after she's
made that long journey in hope and dread and
suffering—

DYKE. Where can I talk with her—here?

THE WARDEN. Yes.

DYKE. Alone? (*The* WARDEN *is doubtful.*)
Why, you don't need to be afraid. I haven't the
faintest idea who the girl is, but if she happens
to be some poor misguided sentimental fool, with
a gun or a pocket full of cyanide of potassium,
she's wasting her time. I wouldn't cheat the
sovereign state of Connecticut for anything in the
world—not even to please a young lady.

THE WARDEN. Dyke, there's something about you
that gets everybody.

DYKE. How about the jury?

THE WARDEN. You've got a sort of way with
you—

DYKE. How about that spread-eagle district at-
torney?

THE WARDEN. I'm going to let you talk with that
girl in here—alone.

DYKE. Thanks.

THE WARDEN. It's a sort of thing that's never
been done before, but if I put you on your honor—

DYKE (*Cynically*). My honor! Thank you, so
much.

FATHER DALY. Warden, are you sure it's wise?

DYKE. Father, I'm disappointed in you. Do you
imagine I'd do anything that could reflect on

THE VALIANT

Warden Holt—or you—or the young lady—
or *me?*

THE WARDEN. Father, will you take Dyke into
the deputy's room? I want to speak to the
young lady first.

FATHER DALY. Certainly. Come, my boy.
(FATHER DALY *and* DYKE *start toward the
deputy's room.*)

THE WARDEN. I'll call you in just a couple of
minutes.

DYKE. We promise not to run away. (*They go
out together.*)

THE WARDEN (*Calls*). Wilson! (*The* ATTEND-
ANT *enters from the left.*)

THE ATTENDANT. Yes, sir.

THE WARDEN. Is the girl there?

THE ATTENDANT. Yes, sir.

THE WARDEN. Frisked?

THE ATTENDANT. Yes, sir.

THE WARDEN. Everything all right?

THE ATTENDANT. Yes, sir.

THE WARDEN (*Throws away his cigar*). Bring
her in.

THE ATTENDANT. Yes, sir. (*He speaks through
the door at the left.*) Step this way, Miss.
This here's the Warden.

(*A young girl appears on the threshold, and casts
about in mingled curiosity and apprehension.
She is fresh and wholesome, and rather pretty;
but her manner betrays a certain spiritual aloof-
ness from the ultra-modern world—a certain del-*

[24]

THE VALIANT

*icate reticence of the flesh—which immediately
separates her from the metropolitan class. Indeed, she is dressed far too simply for a metropolitan girl of her age; she wears a blue tailored
suit with deep white cuffs and a starched white
sailor-collar, and a small blue hat which fits
snugly over her fluffy hair. Her costume is not
quite conservative enough to be literally old-
fashioned, but it hints at the taste and repression
of an old-fashioned home.*
*She is neither timid nor aggressive; she is self-uncon-
scious. She looks at the* WARDEN *squarely, but
not in boldness, and yet not in feminine appeal;
she has rather the fearlessness of a girl who has
lost none of her illusions about men in general.
Her expression is essentially serious; it conveys,
however, the idea that her seriousness is due
to her present mission, and that ordinarily she
takes an active joy in the mere pleasure of existence.*)
THE WARDEN (*He had expected a very different
type of visitor, so that he is somewhat taken
aback*). All right, Wilson.
THE ATTENDANT. Yes, sir. (*He goes out.*)
THE WARDEN (*With grave deference, half rises*).
Will you sit down?
THE GIRL. Why—thank you very much. (*She
sits in the chair beside the desk and regards him
trustfully.*)
THE WARDEN (*He is palpably affected by her youth
and innocence, and he is not quite sure how best*
[25]

THE VALIANT

to proceed, but eventually he makes an awkward beginning). You've had an interview with the Governor, I understand?

THE GIRL. Yes, sir. I was with him almost an hour.

THE WARDEN. And you want to see Dyke, do you?

THE GIRL. Yes, sir. I *hope* I'm not—too late.

THE WARDEN. No, you're not too late. (*He is appraising her carefully.*) But I want to ask you a few questions beforehand. (*Her reaction of uncertainty induces him to soften his tone.*) There isn't anything to get upset about. I just want to make it easier for you, not harder. Where do you live?

THE GIRL. In Ohio.

THE WARDEN (*Very kindly*). What place?

THE GIRL. In Pennington, sir. It's a little town not far from Columbus.

THE WARDEN. And you live out there with your father and mother?

THE GIRL. No, sir—just my mother and I. My father died when I was a little baby.

THE WARDEN. Why didn't your mother come here herself, instead of sending you?

THE GIRL. She couldn't. She's sick.

THE WARDEN. I see. Have you any brothers or sisters?

THE GIRL (*Slightly more at ease*). Just one brother, sir—this one. He and I were the only children. We were very fond of each other.

[26]

THE VALIANT

THE WARDEN. He was considerably older than you?

THE GIRL. Oh, yes. He's ten years older.

THE WARDEN. Why did he leave home?

THE GIRL. I don't really know, sir, except he just wanted to be in the city. Pennington's pretty small.

THE WARDEN. How long is it since you've seen him?

THE GIRL. It's eight years.

THE WARDEN (*His voice is almost paternal*). As long as that? Hm! And how old are you now?

THE GIRL. I'm almost eighteen.

THE WARDEN (*Repeats slowly*). Almost eighteen. Hm! And are you sure after all this time you'd recognize your brother if you saw him?

THE GIRL. Well—(*She looks down, as if embarrassed to make the admission.*)—of course I *think* so, but maybe I couldn't. You see, I was only a little girl when he went away—he wasn't a bad boy, sir, I don't think he could ever be really bad—but if this *is* my brother, why he's been in a great deal of trouble and you know that trouble makes people look different.

THE WARDEN. Yes, it does. But what makes you think this man Dyke may be your brother—and why didn't you think of it sooner? The case has been in the papers for the last six months.

THE GIRL. Why, it wasn't until last Tuesday that mother saw a piece in the *Journal*—that's the

[27]

THE VALIANT

Columbus paper—that he'd written all about him·
self, and there was one little part of it that sounded
so like Joe—like the funny way he used to say
things—and then there was a picture that looked
the least little *bit* like him—well, mother just
wanted me to come East and find out for sure.

THE WARDEN.   It's too bad she couldn't come herself.   She'd probably know him whether he'd
changed or not.

THE GIRL.   Yes, sir.   But I'll do the best I can.

THE WARDEN.   When was the last time you heard
from him, and where was he, and what was he
doing?

THE GIRL.   Why, it's about five or six years since
we had a letter from Joe.   He was in Seattle,
Washington.

THE WARDEN.   What doing?

THE GIRL.   I don't remember.   At home, though,
he worked in the stationery store.   He liked
books.

THE WARDEN (*Suspiciously*).   Why do you suppose he didn't write home?

THE GIRL.   I—couldn't say.   He was just—
thoughtless.

THE WARDEN.   Wasn't in trouble of any kind?

THE GIRL.   Oh, *no!* Never.   That is—unless
he's—here now.

THE WARDEN (*Deliberates*).   How are you going
to tell him?

THE GIRL.   I don't know what you mean.

THE WARDEN.   Why, you say maybe you wouldn't

[28]

THE VALIANT

know him even if you saw him—and I'll guarantee
this man Dyke won't help you out very much.
How do you think you're going to tell? Suppose
he don't want to be recognized by you or anybody else? Suppose he's so ashamed of himself
he—

THE GIRL. I'd thought of that. I'm just going
to talk to him—ask him questions—about things
he and I used to do together—I'll watch his face,
and if he's my brother, I'm sure I can tell.

THE WARDEN (*With tolerant doubt*). What did
you and your brother ever use to do that would
help you out now?

THE GIRL. He used to play games with me when
I was a little girl, and tell me stories—that's
what I'm counting on mostly—the stories.

THE WARDEN. I'm afraid—

THE GIRL. Especially Shakespeare stories.

THE WARDEN. Shakespeare!

THE GIRL. Why, yes. He used to get the plots
of the plays—all the Shakespeare plays—out of
a book by a man named Lamb, and then he'd
tell me the stories in his own words. It was
wonderful!

THE WARDEN. I'm certainly afraid he—

THE GIRL. But best of all he'd learn some of the
speeches from the plays themselves. He liked to
do it—he was sure he was going to be an actor
or something—he was in all the high school plays,
always. And then he'd teach some of the
speeches to me, and we'd say them to each other.

[29]

THE VALIANT

And one thing—every night he'd sit side of my
bed, and when I got sleepy there were two
speeches we'd always say to each other, like good-
night—two speeches out of *Romeo and Juliet,*
and then I'd go to sleep. I can see it all. (*The*
WARDEN *shakes his head.*) Why do you do
that?
THE WARDEN. This boy isn't your brother.
THE GIRL. Do you think he isn't?
THE WARDEN. I *know* he isn't.
THE GIRL. How do you?
THE WARDEN. This boy never heard of Shakespeare—much less learned him. (*He presses a
button on his desk.*) Oh, I'll let you see him for
yourself, only you might as well be prepared.
(*The* ATTENDANT *enters from the anteroom.*)
Tell Dyke and Father Daly to come in here—
they're in the deputy's room.
THE ATTENDANT. Yes, sir. (*He crosses behind
the* WARDEN, *and goes off to the right.*)
THE WARDEN. If he turns out to be your brother
—which he won't—you can have, say, an hour
with him. If he don't, you'll oblige me by cut-
ting it as short as you can.
THE GIRL. You see, I've got to tell mother something perfectly definite. She's worried so long
about him, and—and *now* the suspense is perfectly
terrible for her.
THE WARDEN. I can understand that. You're a
plucky girl.

THE VALIANT

THE GIRL. Of course, it would be awful for us
if this *is* Joe, but even that would be better for
mother than just to stay awake nights, and wonder and wonder, and never *know* what became
of him. (*The* ATTENDANT *opens the door of
the Deputy's room, and when* DYKE *and* FATHER
DALY *have come in, he crosses again behind the*
WARDEN, *and is going out at the left when the*
WARDEN *signs to him and he stops.*)
THE WARDEN (*Gets to his feet*). Dyke, this is
the young lady that's come all the way from Pennington, Ohio, to see you.
DYKE (*Who has been talking in an undertone to*
FATHER DALY, *raises his head quickly*). Yes,
sir?
THE WARDEN. I've decided you can talk with
her here—alone. (*The* GIRL *has risen, breathless, and stands fixed;* DYKE *inspects her coldly
from head to foot.*)
DYKE. Thank you. It won't take long.
THE WARDEN (*Has been scanning the girl's expression; now, as he sees that she has neither recognized* DYKE *nor failed to recognize him, he
makes a little grimace in confirmation of his own
judgment*). Father Daly and I'll stay in the
deputy's office. We'll leave the door open.
Wilson, you stand in the anteroom with the door
open.
DYKE (*Bitterly*). My honor!
THE WARDEN. What say?
[31]

THE VALIANT

DYKE. I didn't say anything.

THE WARDEN (*To the* GIRL). Will you please remember what I told you about the time?

THE GIRL. Oh, yes, sir.

THE WARDEN. Come, Father. (*They go off into the Deputy's room, and the* ATTENDANT, *at a nod from the* WARDEN, *goes off at the left.*)

(DYKE *and the* GIRL *are now facing each other;* DYKE *is well-poised and insouciant and gives the impression of complete indifference to the moment. The* GIRL, *on the other hand, is deeply agitated and her agitation is gradually increased by* DYKE's *own attitude.*)

THE GIRL (*After several efforts to speak*). Mother sent me to see you.

DYKE (*Politely callous*). Yes?

THE GIRL (*Compelled to drop her eyes*). You see, we haven't seen or heard of my brother Joe for ever so long, and mother thought—after what we read in the papers—

DYKE. That I might be your brother Joe?

THE GIRL (*Obviously relieved*). Yes, that's it.

DYKE. Well, you can easily see that I'm not your brother, can't you?

THE GIRL (*Stares at him again*). I'm not sure. You look a little like him, just as the picture in the paper did, but then again, it's so long—(*she shakes her head dubiously*) and I'd thought of Joe so differently—

DYKE (*His manner is somewhat indulgent, as though to a child*). As a matter of fact, I

[32]

THE VALIANT

couldn't be *your* brother, or anybody else's
brother, because I never had a sister. So that
rather settles it.

THE GIRL. Honestly?

DYKE. Honestly.

THE GIRL (*Unconvinced, becomes more appealing*). What's your real name?

DYKE. Dyke—James Dyke.

THE GIRL. That's sure enough your name?

DYKE. Sure enough. You don't think I'd tell a
lie at this stage of the game, do you?

THE GIRL (*Musing*). No, I don't believe you
would. Where do you come from—I mean
where were you born?

DYKE. In Canada, but I've lived all over.

THE GIRL. Didn't you ever live in Ohio?

DYKE. No. Never.

THE GIRL. What kind of work did you do—what
was your business?

DYKE. Oh, I'm sort of Jack-of-all-trades. I've
been everything a man *could* be—except a success.

THE GIRL. Do you like books?

DYKE. Books?

THE GIRL. Yes—books to read.

DYKE. I don't read when there's anything better
to do. I've read a lot here.

THE GIRL. Did you ever sell books—for a living,
I mean?

DYKE. Oh, no.

THE GIRL (*Growing confused*). I hope you don't
mind my asking so many questions. But I—

[33]

THE VALIANT

DYKE. No—go ahead, if it'll relieve your mind any.

THE GIRL. You went to school somewhere, of course,—high school?

DYKE. No, I never got that far.

THE GIRL. Did you ever want to be an actor? Or *were* you ever?

DYKE. No, just a convict.

THE GIRL (*Helplessly*). Do you know any poetry?

DYKE. Not to speak of.

THE GIRL (*Delays a moment, and then, watching him very earnestly, she recites just above her breath*).

> Thou knowst the mask of night is on my face
> Else would a maiden blush bepaint my cheek
> For that which—

(*Realizing that* DYKE'S *expression is one of utter vacuity she falters, and breaks off the quotation, but she continues to watch him unwaveringly.*) Don't you know what that is?

DYKE. No, but to tell the truth, it sounds sort of silly to *me*. Doesn't it to you?

THE GIRL (*Her intonation has become slightly forlorn, but she gathers courage, and puts him to one more test*).

> Good-night, good-night, parting is such sweet sorrow
> That I shall say good-night till it be morrow.

DYKE (*His mouth twitches in amusement*). Eh?

THE GIRL. What comes next?

[34]

THE VALIANT

DYKE. Good Lord, *I* don't know.

THE GIRL (*Gazes intently, almost imploringly, at him as though she is making a struggle to read his mind. Then she relaxes and holds out her hand*). Good-bye. You—you're *not* Joe, are you? I—had to come and find out, though. I hope I've not made you too unhappy.

DYKE (*Ignores her hand*). You're not going now?

THE GIRL (*Spiritless*). Yes. I promised the— is he the Warden? that man in there?—I said I'd go right away if you weren't my brother. And you aren't, so—

DYKE. You're going back to your mother?

THE GIRL. Yes.

DYKE. I'm surprised that she sent a girl like you on a sorry errand like this, instead of—

THE GIRL. She's very sick.

DYKE. Oh, that's too bad.

THE GIRL (*Twisting her handkerchief*). No, she's not well at all. And most of it's from worrying about Joe.

DYKE. Still, when you tell her that her son isn't a murderer—at least, that he isn't *this* one—that'll comfort her a good deal, won't it?

THE GIRL (*Reluctantly*). Yes, I think maybe it will, only—

DYKE. Only what?

THE GIRL. I don't think mother'll ever be *really* well again until she finds out for certain where Joe is and what's become of him.

[35]

THE VALIANT

DYKE (*Shakes his head compassionately*). Mothers ought not to be treated like that. I wish I'd treated *mine* better. By the way, you didn't tell me what your name is.

THE GIRL. Josephine Paris.

DYKE (*Is suddenly attentive*). Paris? That's an unusual name. I've heard it somewhere, too.

THE GIRL. Just like the name of the city—in France.

DYKE (*Knitting his brows*). And your brother's name was Joseph?

THE GIRL. Yes—they used to call us Joe and Josie—that's funny, isn't it?

DYKE (*Thoughtfully*). No, I don't think it's so very funny. I rather like it. (*He passes his hand over his forehead as if trying to coerce his memory.*)

THE GIRL. What's the matter?

DYKE (*Frowning*). I was thinking of something —now, what on earth was that boy's name! Wait a minute, don't tell me—wait a minute— I've got it! (*He punctuates his triumph with one fist in the palm of the other hand.*) Joseph Anthony Paris!

THE GIRL (*Amazed*). Why, that's his name! That's Joe! How did you ever—

DYKE (*His manner is very forcible and convincing*). Wait! Now listen carefully to what I say, and don't interrupt me, because we've only got a minute, and I want you to get this all straight, so you can tell your mother. When

[36]

THE VALIANT

ʟne war came along I enlisted and I was overseas for four years—with the Canadians. Early one morning we'd staged a big trench raid, and there was an officer who'd been wounded coming back, and was lying out there in a shell-hole under fire. The Jerries were getting ready for a raid of their own, so they were putting down a box barrage with light guns and howitzers and a few heavies. This officer was lying right in the middle of it. Well, all of a sudden a young fellow dashed out of a trench not far from where I was, and went for that officer. He had to go through a curtain of shells and, more than that, they opened on him with rifles and machine guns. The chances were just about a million to one against him, and he must have known it, but he went out just the same. He got the officer in his arms and started back, but he'd only gone a few yards when a five point nine landed right on top of the two of them. Afterward, we got what was left—the identification tag was still there— and that was the name—Joseph Anthony Paris!

THE GIRL (*Carries both hands to her breast*). Oh!

DYKE. If that was your brother's name, then you can tell your mother that he died like a brave man and a soldier, three years ago, in France.

THE GIRL. Joe—my brother Joe—is dead?

DYKE. On the field of battle. It was one of the wonderful, heroic things that went almost unnoticed, as so many of them did. If an officer

[37]

THE VALIANT

had seen it, there'd have been a decoration for your mother to keep and remember him by.

THE GIRL. And you were there—and saw it?

DYKE. I was there and saw it. It was three years ago. That's why you and your mother haven't heard from him. And if you don't believe what I've said, why, you just write up to Ottawa and get the official record. Of course (*he shrugs his shoulders contemptuously*) those records are in terribly poor shape, but at least they can tell you what battalion he fought with, when he went overseas. Only you mustn't be surprised no matter whether they say he was killed in action, or died of wounds, or is missing, or even went through the whole war with his outfit, and was honorably discharged. They really don't know what happened to half the men. But I've told you the truth. And it certainly ought to make your mother happy when she knows that her boy died as a soldier, and not as a criminal.

THE GIRL (*Is transfigured*). Yes, yes, it will!

DYKE. And does it make you happy, too?

THE GIRL (*Nods repeatedly*). Yes. So happy —after what we were both afraid of—I can't even cry—yet. (*She brushes her eyes with her handkerchief.*) I can hardly wait to take it to her.

DYKE (*Struck by a sudden inspiration*). I want to give you something else to take to her. (*He picks up from the desk the envelope containing*

[38]

THE VALIANT

the Liberty Bonds and seals it.)   I want you to
give this to your mother from me.   Tell her it's
from a man who was at Vimy Ridge and saw
your brother die, so it's a sort of memorial for
him.   (*He touches her arm as she absently begins to tear open the envelope.*)   No, don't you
open it—let *her* do it.
THE GIRL.   What is it?   Can't I know?
DYKE.   Never mind now, but give it to her.   It's
all I've got in the world and it's too late now
for me to do anything else with it.   And have
your mother buy a little gold star to wear for
her son—and you get one, too, and wear it—
here—   (*He touches his heart.*)   Will you?
THE GIRL.   Yes—I will.   And yet somehow I'll
almost feel that I'm wearing it for you, too.
DYKE (*Shakes his head soberly*).   Oh, no!   You
mustn't ever do that.   I'm not fit to be mentioned in the same breath with a boy like your
brother, and now I'm afraid it *is* time for you
to go.   I'm sorry, but—you'd better.   I'm glad
you came before it was too late, though.
THE GIRL (*Gives him her hand*).   Good-bye, and
thank you.   You've done more for me—and
mother—than I could possibly tell you.   And—
and I'm so sorry for you—so *truly sorry*—I
wish I could only do something to make you a
tiny bit happier, too.   Is there anything I could
do?
DYKE (*Stares at her and by degrees he becomes*

[39]

THE VALIANT

wistful). Why—yes, there is. Only I— (*He leaves the sentence uncompleted.*)

THE GIRL. What is it?

DYKE (*Looks away*). I can't tell you. I never should have let myself think of it.

THE GIRL. Please tell me. I want you to. For —for Joe's sake, tell me what I can do.

DYKE (*His voice is low and desolate*). Well—in all the months I've been in this hideous place, you're the first girl I've seen. I didn't ever expect to see one again. I'd forgotten how much like angels women look. I've been terribly lonesome tonight, especially, and if you really do want to do something for me—for your brother's sake—you see, you're going to leave me in just a minute and—and I haven't any sister of my own, or anybody else, to say good-bye to me—so, if you could—*really* say good-bye— (*She gazes at him for a moment understands, flushes, and then slowly moves into his outstretched arms. He holds her close to him, touches his lips to her forehead twice, and releases her.*)

DYKE (*Thickly*). Good-bye, my dear.

THE GIRL. Good night. (*She endeavors to smile, but her voice catches in her throat.*) Good-bye.

DYKE (*Impulsively*). What is it?

THE GIRL (*Shakes her head*). N-nothing.

DYKE. Nothing?

THE GIRL (*Clutches her handkerchief tight in her palm*). I was thinking—I was thinking what I used to say to my brother—for good night.

THE VALIANT

(*She very nearly breaks down*). If I *only* could have—have said it to him just once more—for good-bye.

DYKE. What was it?

THE GIRL. I—I told it to you once, and you said it was silly.

DYKE (*Softly*). Say it again.

THE GIRL (*She cannot quite control her voice*).

Good-night, good-night, parting is such sweet sorrow
That I shall say good-night till it be morrow.

(*She goes uncertainly toward the anteroom, hesitates, almost turns back, and then with a choking sob she hurries through the door and closes it behind her. For several seconds DYKE stands rigidly intent upon that door; until at length, without changing his attitude or his expression, he speaks very tenderly and reminiscently.*)

Sleep dwell upon thine eyes, peace in thy breast;
Would *I* were sleep and peace, so sweet to rest.

(*The WARDEN and FATHER DALY come in quietly from the Deputy's room; and as they behold DYKE, how rapt and unconscious of them he is, they look at each other, questioningly. The WARDEN glances at the clock and makes as though to interrupt DYKE'S solitary reflections but FATHER DALY quietly restrains him. The CHAPLAIN sits down in one of the chairs at the back wall; the WARDEN crosses on tip-toe and sits at his desk; he is excessively nervous and he*)

THE VALIANT

continually refers to the clock. DYKE *turns, as though unwillingly, from the door; there are depths in his eyes, and his thoughts are evidently far away. He sits in the chair to the right of the* WARDEN'S *desk and leans outward, his right hand on his knee. He puts his left hand to his throat as though to protect it from a sudden pain. He gazes straight ahead into the unknown and speaks in reverie.*)

Of all the wonders that I yet have heard,
It seems to me most strange that men should fear;
Seeing that death, a necessary end,
Will come when it will come.

(*He stops and muses for a time, while the* WARDEN *glances perplexedly at* FATHER DALY *to discover if the priest can interpret what* DYKE *is saying.* FATHER DALY *shakes his head. Abruptly* DYKE'S *face is illumined by a new and welcome recollection; and again he speaks, while the* WARDEN *tries in vain to comprehend him.*)

Cowards die many times before their death;
The valiant never taste of death but once.

(*He stops again and shudders a trifle; his head droops and he repeats, barely above a whisper.*)

The valiant never taste of death but once.

(*The nearer door on the right is opened noiselessly and the* JAILER, *in obedience to his instructions, steps just inside the room and stands there mute.*

[42]

THE VALIANT

FATHER DALY *and the* WARDEN *glance at the* JAILER, *and with significance at each other, and both rise, tardily. The* WARDEN'S *hand, as it rests on his desk is seen to tremble. There is a moment of dead silence; presently* DYKE *lifts his head and catches sight of the motionless* ATTEND-ANT *at the open door. With a quick intake of his breath, he starts half out of his seat and stares, fascinated; he sinks back slowly, and turns his head to gaze first at* FATHER DALY *and then at the* WARDEN. *The* WARDEN *averts his eyes, but* FATHER DALY'S *expression is of supreme pity and encouragement. Involuntarily,* DYKE'S *hand again goes creeping upward toward his throat, but he arrests it. He grasps the arms of his chair and braces himself; he rises then, and stands very erect, in almost the position of a soldier at attention.)*

THE WARDEN (*Swallows hard*). Dyke!

FATHER DALY (*Brushes past the* WARDEN, *his right hand lifted as though in benediction*). My son!

DYKE (*Regards them fixedly; his voice is low and steady*). All right, let's go.

(*He faces about, and with his head held proud and high, and his shoulders squared to the world, he moves slowly toward the open door.* FATHER DALY, *with the light of his calling in his eyes, steps in line just ahead of* DYKE. *The* WARDEN, *his mouth set hard, falls in behind. When they have all gone forward a pace or two,* FATHER

[43]

THE VALIANT

DALY *begins to speak, and* DYKE *to reply; FATHER DALY's voice is strong and sweet; and* DYKE *speaks just after him, not mechanically, but in brave and unfaltering response.*)

FATHER DALY. "I will lift up mine eyes unto the hills—"

DYKE. "The valiant never taste of death but once."

FATHER DALY. "From whence cometh my help."

DYKE. "The valiant never taste of death but once."

FATHER DALY (*Has almost reached the door; his voice rises a semi-tone, and gains in emotion*). "My help cometh from the Lord which made Heaven and earth."

DYKE. "The valiant never taste of death—but once."

(*When the* WARDEN, *whose hands are tightly clenched, has passed the threshold, the* JAILER *follows and closes the door behind him. There is a very brief pause and then*

CURTAIN

[44]

Chapter VI

Classifying Plays

One-act plays may be classified into certain definite groups. To recognize these groups, to know the meaning of such words as comedy, tragedy, farce, melodrama, to be able to classify any new play which a student may read or see are goals worthy of attainment.

A tragedy ends in the death or overthrow of the principal character. Shakespeare's, Hamlet, Othello, Macbeth, and King Lear are tragedies. The principal character engages in a struggle against powers greater than his--"the law of God or man, the doctrine of chance, the established conventions, prejudices, and inhibitions of society, or the larger influences of heredity or environment."[1]

The Greek tragedies and Shakespeare's tragedies end in the death of the heroes, but in contemporary tragedy, the downfall from high to low estate has taken the place of actual destruction. Thus in Gordon Daviot's Richard of Bordeaux and Maxwell Anderson's Mary of Scotland, the imprisonment of the central characters is their greatest misfortune. Modern playwrights believe that death is not the worst thing that can happen to a person. Mental torture, public disgrace, loss of wordly possessions are sufficient signs of personal disaster to warrant terming the play a tragedy.

It is clear that the writer of a tragedy wants his audience to feel the emotions which led the dramatist to write his play. These emotions are generally considered to be pity and terror.

A comedy ends in the success or triumph of the principal character. It is not necessarily a funny play. Most films are comedies, for a happy ending seems a necessity in a movie. One of the strangest of all the practices in Hollywood and on television is that of changing the ending of a serious play or novel so that the lovers at the end may

live happily.   Obviously this is what the millions of movie
and television fans want, since Hollywood is very sensitive
to audience demand.   Thus, Maxwell Anderson's Winterset
on the New York stage ended in the murder of Mio and
Miriamne, but in the screen version they escape the bullets
of the gangsters waiting to kill them.

It is useless to deny that a comedy is preferred by
the average theatre-goer, movie-goer or television-watcher
after a hard day's work in school, in the kitchen, or in the
office.   Unfortunately, the word tragedy has come to mean to
these comedy-lovers something morbid or depressing, when,
as a matter of fact, it is most often spiritually elevating.
It takes more power and courage to die as a hero in a tragedy
than to rise from cab-driver to Senator in the average comedy.
The development of an appreciation for serious drama is a
sign of maturity.   Children of five or six can be amused by
the antics in a slapstick comedy.   Tragedy is for the mental
grown-ups.

Comedy has several subdivisions.   Comedies may have
worthy problems, though these do not cause disaster.   When
the humor of situation or personality is predominant, the
play is called a light comedy.   When the events are so funny
as to go beyond the limits of probability, we have a farce.
Television has many examples of farces in serials that run
for long periods of time, like Hogan's Heroes.   Famous
farces from the legitimate theatre are Charley's Aunt, Pierre
Patelin, and the Pyramus and Thisbe episode from Shakespeare's Midsummer Night's Dream.   In film, Charlie Chaplin's early films, running up to his Modern Times (1929) are
among the classics in farce.

A burlesque makes fun of something taken seriously
by others.   In revues on the contemporary stage, little burlesques are written about prominent men or events.   The
audience remembers the person or event and appreciates the
fun poked at them.   Televison programs such as the Smothers
Brothers Show and the Carol Burnett Show frequently make use
of burlesque sketches.   In fact, the television comedians would
be quite lost if they did not often fall back upon burlesques.

A melodrama originally was accompanied by music
which intended to parallel the emotions in the play.   The
death of some dear character might bring forth low strains
of Hearts and Flowers, and the Burning of Rome would accompany any excitement.   Later the music was omitted from the

plays. Today such plays make excessive use of violent
physical action. Lord Dunsany's one-act A Night at An Inn
is an excellent example. At the end of the play, corpses are
lying before us on the stage and an equal number are supposed
to be outside the room. A melodrama may be comic, as in
Holland Hudson's Action. Colloquially, melodramas are called thrillers.

A minor variety is the fantasy. These plays are
usually more poetical and deal with Pierrots and Pierrettes,
with settings in lands East of the Sun and West of the Moon.
They are usually light in dialogue, often written in poetry and
have a light, delicate note throughout.

Plays on television, such as The Twilight Zone are
frequently fantasies, as are such programs such as My
Favorite Martian, Bewitched, Star Trek, Voyage to the
Bottom of the Sea, I Dream of Jeannie (1967), and The
Invaders (1967-1968).

Notes

1. Dolman, John Jr., The Art of Play Production (New York,
   1928), p. 100.

Chapter VII

The Student Playwright

Someone has said that every living person could write at least one novel of his or her life-story. Certainly, the impulse to write is strong in all of us. Nothing would be more natural than the desire to write one's own one-act plays after having read or acted in them. The problem is: how to go about it? Dramatists--good dramatists--are not necessarily born. They may begin as very poor imitators of some famous playwright of the past or present. They end as original craftsman, and even great artists.

Many books have already been written on this subject, some of them hundreds of pages long, and the best are listed at the end of this chapter. It is obvious that only the barest of outlines can be included in this book.

Consider first the fundamental ingredients of a play. They are:

1.　action

2.　character

3.　dialogue

4.　ideas

5.　setting

One may begin with any one of these ingredients. Study these words of George P. Baker's <u>Dramatic Technique</u>:

> A play may start from almost anything; a detached thought that flashes through the mind; a theory of conduct or of art which one firmly believes or wishes only to examine; a bit of dialogue overheard or imagined; a setting, real or imagined, which

creates emotion in the observer, a perfectly de-
tached scene, the antecedents and consequences of
which are as yet unknown; a figure glimpsed in a
crowd which for some reason arrests the attention
of the dramatist, or a figure closely studied; a
contrast or similarity between two people or conditions of life; a mere incident--noted in a newspaper or book, heard in idle talk, or observed; or
a story, told only in the barest outlines or with
the utmost detail.[1]

Enough has been suggested in the paragraph above to
provide material for dozens of plays. Should the student
desire to study some books on technique, the following will
prove helpful:

Andrews, Charlton, The Technique of Play Writing (Home
    Correspondence School, 1915).

Archer, Frank, How to Write a Good Play (Samuel French, n. d.)

Archer, William, Play-Making (Small, Maynard, 1912).

Baker, George P. , Dramatic Technique, (Houghton, Mifflin,
    1919).

Freytag, Gustav, The Technique of the Drama Translated
    from German by MacEwen (Scott, Foresman, 1894).

Gannon, Robert I. , S. J. The Technique of the One-Act Play
    (Fordham University Press, 1925).

Hamilton, Clayton, So You're Writing a Play (Little, Brown,
    1935).

Hennequin, Alfred, The Art of Playwriting, (Houghton,
    Mifflin, 1890).

Hopkins, Arthur, How's Your Second Act? (Goodman, 1918).

Lewis, B. Roland, The Technique of the One-Act Play,
    (Luce, 1918).

Malevinsky, M. L. , The Science of Playwriting (Brentano,
    1925).

Niggli, Josephina, Pointers on Playwriting (The Writer, 1945).

Ould, Herman, The Art of the Play (Pitman & Sons, 1938).

Price, W. T. , The Technique of the Drama (Brentano, 1892).

Ervine, St. John, How to Write a Play, (Allen and Unwin, 1928).

Van Druten, John, Playwright at Work (Harper and Brothers, 1953)

Wilde, Percival, The Craftsmanship of the One-Act Play (Crown, 1951).

Rarely does an author bequeath to the world the method by which he writes his famous works. Fortunately certain dramatists have left such records and a study of them should be very helpful.

Edward Knobloch wrote Kismet, Milestones, and many other successful plays. He was particularly successful in dramatizing novels. Fortunately, he has described his manner of working thus:

> I have found it very useful, when asked to drama-
> tize a novel, not to read it myself, but to get
> some one else to read it and tell me about it. At
> once, all the stuffing drops away, and the vital
> active part, the verb of the novel comes to the
> fore. If the story of a novel cannot be told by
> some one in a hundred words or so, there is apt
> to be no drama in it. If I were to write a play
> on Hamilton, I would look up an article in an en-
> cyclopaedia; then make a scenario; then read de-
> tailed biographies. Too much knowledge hampers.
> It is just for that reason that short stories are
> easier dramatized than long novels. The stories
> that Shakespeare chose for his plays are practi-
> cally summaries. As long as they stirred his
> imagination, that was all he asked of them. Then
> he added his magic. Once the novel has been told,
> make the scenario. Then read the novel after.
> There will be very little to alter and only a certain
> amount of touches to add. [2]

The method of the French dramatist Sardou, who wrote scores of successful plays, and who undoubtedly employed some interesting devices offers suggestions:

Whenever an idea occurred to Sardou, he immediately
made a memorandum of it. These notes he classified and filed. For example, years before the
production of Thermidor he had the thought of one
day writing such a play. Gradually the character
of Fabienne shaped itself; Labussiere was devised
later to fit Coquelin (a great French actor, ed.).
Everything that he read about the epoch of the
French Revolution, and the ideas which his reading
inspired, he wrote down in the form of rough notes.
Engravings, maps, prints, and other documents of
the time he carefully collected. Memoirs and histories he annotated and indexed, filing away the
index references in his file cases, or dossiers. At
the time of his death, Sardou had many hundreds
of these dossiers, old and new. Some of the older
ones had been worked up into plays, while the newer
ones were merely raw material for future dramas.
When the idea of a play had measurably shaped
itself in his mind, he wrote out a skeleton plot
which he placed in his dossier. There it might
lie indefinitely. In this shape Thermidor remained
for nearly twenty years, and Theodora for ten.
When he considered that the time was ripe for one
of his embryonic plays, Sardou would take out that
particular dossier, read over the material, and lay
it aside again. After it had fermented in his brain
for a time, he would, if the inspiration seized him,
write out a scenario. After this, he began the
actual writing of the play.[3]

Thornton Wilder, author of the famous novel The
Bridge of San Luis Rey (1927) and a collection of very short
plays, The Angel That Troubled the Waters (1931) Our Town,
and The Skin of our Teeth relates some of his early experiences in writing plays. He would use the margins and
the blank half-pages of his text-book in algebra to jot down
subjects for plays. Though this may indicate a lack of interest
in algebra, it manifests a praiseworthy early interest in the
drama. Robert Louis Stevenson used to have a small notebook with him all the time. This became the repository of
beautiful words and phrases Stevenson had heard or read;
ideas for essays and stories, subjects for further study.
Such a practice is heartily recommended to all future Eugene
O'Neills, Jane Kerrs, and Lillian Hellmans.

Lord Dunsany wrote many successful one-act plays.

His suggestions are valuable. His explanation of how he began to write follows:

> I begin with anything or next to nothing. Then sud-
> denly, I get started, and go through in a hurry.
> The main point is not to interrupt a mood. Writing
> is an easy thing when one is going strong and going
> fast; it becomes a hard thing only when the onward
> rush is impeded. Most of my short plays have
> been written in a sitting or two. [4]

There are certain methods of play-making especially
adapted to boys and girls in high schools. The two most
famous schools specializing in drama for children in recent
years were the Perse School in Cambridge, England, and
the King-Coit School in New York. Giving the lie to the idea
that writing plays is a task for older people, the students in
the English school began to write original plays at twelve
years of age. These plays have been published under the
title of Play Books of the Perse School, with an introduction
by the Headmaster, Dr. W. H. D. Rouse. The boys of the
Perse School studied the stories which Shakespeare used for
his masterpieces. They dramatized stories of their own
reading. Many other schools in England and America have
encouraged original dramatic efforts.

Extracting the most helpful suggestions from the various procedures described at length, we arrive at these steps.
The teacher would use the second person in addressing his
or her class in playwriting.

1.   Become interested in the possibilities of writing a
      play which have just been suggested to you by any of
      the many agencies mentioned in Baker's list.

2.   Write a scenario, which is an outline. This should
      show:

      a. The incidents of the story in their consecutive
          arrangement.

      b. The list of characters.

      c. The setting

      d. The time

      e. The type of play

      The items are usually in the form of sentences.

3.   Work on the plot.   This must be skillfully constructed,
        like the link of a chain.   Each event must be dependent
        upon the preceding one and must cause the following
        one.   The climax or moment of highest tension must
        be adequately prepared for.   It must not be so un-
        expected as to be unconvincing.   Following the climax
        the play must end with a touch of finality.

4.   Characterization.   This is the most difficult of all
        the phases of play-writing.   Since a one-act play is
        short, there cannot be much character development.
        Human nature cannot develop very much in twenty
        minutes.   The one-act playwright is more concerned
        with character revelation or character presentation.
        Certain principles of common sense will avoid em-
        barrassing criticism later.

   a.   Be consistent.   Do not make your hero a Proteus,
        with many changing personalities.   Remember that
        most people in a fifteen or twenty minute period
        reveal only a few traits of human nature.   If
        you have decided on certain characteristics, do
        not change them.   Do not have incongruities, such
        as a college professor habitually using the lingo
        of the streets or a hobo quoting Plato as if he
        were one of the Greek's personal friends.

   b.   Make your characters individuals, not types.   Un-
        fortunately, the movies have emphasized type-
        acting.   Certain movie-stars are immediately
        called for when a certain type-part has been writ-
        ten.

        Avoid such pitfalls.   Try to see the character
        as an individual who is different from any one
        else.   (In certain respects we are.)   No two
        persons have identical fingerprints.   What is
        true of physical differences is even more true of
        our mental differences.   Carry out this practice
        of individualizing, not only in writing, but in your
        reactions to the people whom you meet.   Don't
        have classes of "nice fellers," "bad eggs," "easy
        guys."   Every snowflake has its own design.   No
        two have ever been found with identical designs.
        Surely, the respect for a snowflake's individuality
        is due to a human being as well.

   c.   Make your characters novel and colorful.   Many
        books are being written today about different areas

of the United States. The main attractions of
these books are the colorful personalities. Read
Carl Carmer's Listen for a Lonesome Drum,
about the quaint men of New York State or similar
books about the varied regions of America. Stories and plays abound in which the population of
sections of the country are unique in themselves:
the Creoles in New Orleans, the Kentucky moun-
taineers, the Indians, the various immigrant popu-
lations. Remember that people prefer to see in
the theatre more colorful personalities than are
found in their daily lives.

d. Do not include too many characters. O'Neill
wrote a play with only one speaking part, Before
Breakfast. Arthur Hopkins wrote a remarkably
effective two-character play, Moonshine.[5] The
average number of speaking parts is between
three and four. Sierra's, Joint Owners in Spain,
Lady Gregory's, The Workhouse Ward, Dunsany's
Glittering Gate, and Alice Gerstenberg's, Overtones are two-character plays.

5. Dialogue. "Good dialogue," says Galsworthy again,
"is character, marshaled so as continually to stimulate interest or excitement."[6] The very best dialogue
will always do at least one and sometimes all three
of the following things:

a. It will relate the past.

b. It will reveal character.

c. It will help the plot.

In general, good dialogue should accomplish the second
purpose--action--and should, if possible, portray
character at the same time. Lines that are clever
because the dramatist wishes to show his wit are
poor lines for a play. They may serve in a humorous
monologue. Long speeches containing the author's
views on life or art or society belong on the lecture
platform and not in a play.

Your dialogue may be quite gay and brief. Complete
sentences are not always used in daily life, and more
often monosyllables make up most of our conversation. Your dialogue should be appropriate to the
characters in the play. Do not use dialect or speech
of other times unless you are perfectly at home in

them. Paul Green has written dialect plays of people
in Southern cotton fields and in other parts of the
South. His dialogue rings true because he knows the
South. Susan Glaspell's Trifles has traces of New
England dialect which she has captured perfectly. The
plays in Beulah Marie Dix's Martial Interludes often
use speech of other centuries, but she has mastered
its characteristics.

6.   Stage directions. There are two extremes in the use
       of stage directions. One is represented by dramatists
       like Shakespeare, who use only a line or two. Another
       school of dramatists, of whom Sir James M. Barrie,
       is the best example, believes in elaborate directions.

       Barrie's stage directions are often enjoyed for their
       own value because they are entertaining, whimsical,
       and well written. Unless you are a master of the
       English language, do not undertake such assignments.
       Let your stage directions be simple--monosyllabic if
       necessary--and confine them to:

       a.   action--walking, rising, entering

       b.   pantomime--in the midst of the action

       c.   setting

       d.   lighting

       e.   sound effects, wind, off-stage noises.

7.   Experience on the stage. The final suggestion for
       writing plays is the participation in the life of the
       theatre. Act in plays when you can. Go back stage
       and study the curtains, lighting equipment, and exits.
       Attend rehersals to see how a director whips a play
       into being from a script. Many dramatists began as
       press-agents and office-boys to play-producers, as
       Moss Hart relates in Act One. Through experience
       with the stage they learned many valuable secrets
       which they have employed in their best plays.

Notes

1.   Baker, George Pierce Dramatic Technique (Boston,
     1919), p. 47. Compare with William Archer, Play-
     making (Boston, 1912), p. 21.

2. Quoted in Baker, op. cit., p. 14.

3. Hart, J. A. Sardou and the Sardou Plays (Philadelphia),
    p. 125.

4. Hamilton, Clayton Seen on the Stage (New York, 1920),
    p. 239.

5. Lewis, B. Roland The Technique of the One-Act Play
    (Boston, 1918), p. 211.

6. Galsworthy, John "Some Platitudes Concerning Drama,"
    Atlantic Monthly (December, 1909).

Bibliography

How to Write Plays
Andrews, Charlton. The Technique of Play Writing. Spring-
    field, Mass.: The Home Correspondence School, 1915.
Archer, Frank. How to Write a Good Play New York and Lon-
    don: Samuel French, n.d.
Archer, William Play-Making--A Manual of Craftsmanship
    Boston: Small Maynard and Company, 1912.
Baker, George Pierce Dramatic Technique Boston: Houghton,
    Mifflin, 1919.
Ervine, St. John How to Write a Play, rev. ed. 2. London:
    George Allen and Unwin, 1929.
Gannon, Robert I. , S. J. The Technique of the One-Act
    Play--a Text-book. New York: Fordham University
    Press, 1925.
Hamilton, Clayton So You're Writing a Play! Boston: Little,
    Brown, 1935.
Hennequin, Alfred The Art of Playwriting Boston and New
    York: Houghton, Mifflin and Company, 1890.
Lawson, John Howard Theory and Technique of Playwriting
    New York: George P. Putnam's Sons, 1936.
Lawson, John Howard Theory and Technique of Playwriting
    with a new introduction. A Dramabook. New York:
    Hill and Wang, 1960.
Lewis, B. Roland The Technique of the One-Act Play--A
    Study in Dramatic Construction Boston: John W. Luce
    and Company, 1918.
Malevinsky, Moses L. The Science of Playwriting New York:
    Brentano's, 1925.
Matthews, Brander The Principles of Playmaking and Other
    Discussions of the Drama New York: Charles

Scribner's Sons, 1919.
Niggli, Josephina Pointers on Playwriting Boston: The Writer,
    Inc., 1945.
Van Druten, John Playwright at Work New York: Harper
    and Brothers, 1953.
Wilde, Percival The Craftsmanship of the One-Act Play
    Boston: Little, Brown and Company, 1923.
Wilde, Percival The Craftsmanship of the One-Act Play
    The new augmented edition, with a section on the one-
    act play for television. New York: Crown, 1951.

Chapter VIII

General Bibliography

Histories and Critical Studies of Modern and Contemporary
World Drama
Andrews, Charlton The Drama of Today Philadelphia and
London: J. B. Lippincott, 1913.
Brown, Ben W. Theatre at the Left Stagecraft in Soviet
Russia. Providence, Rhode Island: The Booke Shop,
1938.
Brustein, Robert The Theatre of Revolt Studies in modern
drama from Ibsen to Genet. Boston: Little, Brown,
1964.
Chandler, Frank Wadleigh Aspects of the Modern Drama New
York: Macmillan, 1914.
Cheney, Sheldon The New Movement in the Theatre New York:
Mitchell Kennerley, 1914.
Clark, Barrett and George Freedley, ed. A History of
Modern Drama New York and London: D. Appleton-
Century Company, 1947.
Clark, Barrett H. A Study of the Modern Drama Rev. ed. 2.
New York: D. Appleton-Century Company, 1938.
Dickinson, Thomas H. An Outline of Contemporary Drama
Boston: Houghton, Mifflin, 1927.
Gassner, John Directions in Modern Theatre and Drama
New York: Holt, Rinehart and Winston, 1966.
Gassner, John Form and Idea in Modern Theatre New York:
Holt, Rinehart and Winston, 1956.
Gassner, John Theatre at the Crossroads New York: Holt,
Rinehart and Winston, 1960.
Gassner, John The Theatre in Our Times New York: Crown
Publishers, 1954.
Goldman, Emma The Social Significance of the Modern Drama
Boston: Richard G. Badger, 1914.
Gorelik, Mordecai New Theatres for Old New York: Samuel
French, 1945.
Hale, Edward Everett, Jr. Dramatists of Today ed. 6.
Rev. and Enlarged. New York: Henry Holt, 1911.
Hamilton, Clayton Conversations on Contemporary Drama
New York: Macmillan, 1924.

220

Henderson, Archibald European Dramatists Cincinnati:
    Stewart and Kidd, 1918.
Henderson, Archibald The Changing Drama. Contributions
    and Tendencies Cincinnati: Stewart and Kidd, 1919.
Jameson, Storm Modern Drama in Europe New York:
    Harcourt, Brace and Howe, 1920.
Lewis, Allan The Contemporary Theatre The Significant
    Playwrights of Our Time New York: Crown, 1962.
Moderwell, Hiram K. The Theatre of Today New Edition.
    New York: Dodd, Mead, 1927.
Moderwell, Hiram Kelly The Theatre of Today New York
    and London: John Lane, 1914.
Morgan, A. E. Tendencies in Modern English Drama
    London: Constable, 1924.
Palmer, John The Future of the Theatre London: G. Bell,
    1913.
Phelps, William Lyon The Twentieth Century Theatre New
    York: Macmillan, 1918.
Rice, Elmer The Living Theatre New York: Harper, 1959.
Styan, J. L. The Dark Comedy The Development of Modern
    Comic Tragedy. Cambridge, England: Cambridge
    University Press, 1962.
Treadwell, Bill 50 Years of American Comedy New York:
    Exposition Press, 1951.
Vernon, Frank The Twentieth Century Theatre London:
    George G. Harrap, 1924. See Chapter IX "The Case
    of the One-Act Play" p. 87-97.
Wellwarth, George E. The Theatre of Protest and Paradox
    Developments in the Avant-Garde Drama. New York:
    New York University Press, 1965. (P. B.)

History of British Drama
Albright, Evelyn May, Dramatic Publication in England,
    1580-1640. New York: D. C. Heath, London: Oxford
    University Press. For the Modern Language As-
    sociation of America, 1927.
Bridges-Adams, W. The British Theatre Published for the
    British Council by Longmans Green, London, New
    York, Toronto, 1944.
Chambers, R. K. The Elizabethan Stage 4 vols. Oxford:
    Oxford University Press, 1923.
Chambers, R. K. The Medieval Stage 2 vols. Oxford:
    Oxford University Press, 1923.
Dickinson, Thomas H. The Contemporary Drama of England
    Boston: Little, Brown, 1917.
Dickinson, Thomas H. The Contemporary Drama of England
    Boston: Little, Brown, 1931.

Eaton, Walter Pritchard Drama in English (pamphlet) New
    York: Scribners, 1930.
Harbage, Alfred Annals of English Drama, 975-1700. Phila-
    delphia: University of Pennsylvania Press. London:
    Oxford University Press. Published in cooperation
    with the Modern Language Association of America, 1940.
Hotson, Leslie The Commonwealth and Restoration Stage
    Cambridge: Harvard University Press, 1928.
Krutch, Joseph Wood Comedy and Conscience After the
    Restoration: Rev. Ed. New York: Columbia Univer-
    sity Press, 1949.
Rubinstein, H. F. The English Drama London: Ernest Benn,
    1928.
Schelling, Felix E. Elizabethan Drama 2 vols. Boston and
    New York: Houghton, Mifflin, 1908.
Ward, Adolphus William A History of English Dramatic
    Literature to the Death of Queen Anne ed. 2. London:
    Macmillan, 1899.

Special British Theatres
Dent, Edward J. A Theatre for Everybody The story of the
    Old Vic and Sadder's Wells. London and New York:
    T. V. Boardman, 1945.
Marshall, Norman The Other Theatre London: John Lehmann,
    1948.

History of the American Theatre

    A. General
Anderson, John The American Theatre and the Motion Pic-
    ture in America New York: Dial Press, 1938.
Burton, Richard The New American Drama New York:
    Thomas Y. Crowell, 1913.
Clark, Barrett H. An Hour of American Drama Philadelphia
    and London: J. B. Lippincott, 1930.
Hewitt, Barnard Theatre U. S. A. 1668-1957. New York:
    McGraw-Hill, 1959.
Mayorga, Margaret G. A Short History of the American Drama
    New York: Dodd, Mead, 1932.
Taubman, Howard The Making of the American Theatre New
    York: Coward, McCann, 1965.
Quinn, Arthur Hobson A History of the American Drama
    from the Beginning to the Civil War New York:
    Harper, 1923.
Quinn, Arthur Hobson A History of the American Drama
    from the Civil War to the Present Day 2 vols. New
    York: F. S. Crofts, 1937.

B. Contemporary and Modern
Broussard, Louis American Drama Contemporary Allegory
    from Eugene O'Neill to Tennessee Williams Norman:
    University of Oklahoma Press, 1962.
Burton, Richard The New American Drama New York:
    Thomas Y. Crowell, 1913.
Dickinson, Thomas H. The Case of American Drama Boston
    and New York: Houghton, Mifflin, 1915.
Downer, Alan S. Fifty Years of American Drama
    Chicago: Henry Regnery, 1951.
Flexner, Eleanor American Playwrights, 1918-1938. New
    York: Simon and Schuster, 1938.
Gagey, Edmond M. Revolution in American Theatre New
    York: Columbia University Press, 1947.
Himelstein, Morgan Y. Drama Was a Weapon The Left-
    Wing Theatre in New York 1929-1941. New Brunswick,
    N. J. Rutgers University Press, 1963.
Krutch, Joseph Wood The American Drama Since 1918 An
    Informal History New York: Random House, 1939.
Lewis, Allan American Plays and Playwrights of the Con-
    temporary Theatre New York: Crown, 1965.
Morehouse, Ward Matinee Tomorrow Fifty Years of Our
    Theatre New York: McGraw-Hill, 1949.
O'Hara, Frank Hurburt Today in American Drama Chicago:
    University of Chicago Press, 1935.
Rabkin, Gerald Drama and Commitment Politics in the Amer-
    ican Theatre of the Thirties Bloomington, Indiana:
    University Press, 1964.
Sievers, W. David Freud on Broadway A History of Psy-
    choanalysis and the American Drama New York:
    Hermitage House, 1955.
Weales, Gerald American Drama Since World War II New
    York: Harcourt, Brace and World, 1962.

C. Histories of Special Theatres in America
Carter, Jean and Jess Ogden Everyman's Drama A Study of
    the Noncommercial Theatre in the United States. New
    York: American Association for Adult Education,
    1938.
Cheney, Sheldon The Art Theatre Its character as differen-
    tiated from the commerical theatre. Its ideals and
    organization; and a record of certain European and
    American examples. New York: Alfred A. Knopf,
    1925.
Clurman, Harold The Fervent Years The Story of the Group
    Theatre in the Thirties. New York: Alfred A. Knopf,
    1945.

Deutsch, Helen and Stella Hanan The Provincetown--Story
of the Theatre New York: Farrar and Rinehart, 1931.
Dickinson, Thomas H. The Insurgent Theatre New York:
B. W. Huebsch, 1917.
Eaton, Walter Prichard The Theatre Guild--The First Ten
Years New York: Brentano's, 1929.
Flanagan, Hallie Arena, An Adventure in the American
Theatre New York: Duell, Sloan and Pearce, 1940.
Lifson, David S. The Yiddish Theatre in America New York
and London: Thomas Yoseloff, 1965.
Mathews, Jane DeHart The Federal Theatre, 1935-1939.
Plays, Relief and Politics. Princeton: Princeton
University Press, 1967.
Sper, Felix From Native Roots A Panorama of Our Regional
Drama Caldwell, Idaho: The Caxton Printers, 1948.
Steinberg, Mollie B. The History of the Fourteenth Street
Theatre New York: The Dial Press, 1931.

The American Musical
Mates, Julian The American Musical Stage Before 1800.
New Brunswick, New Jersey: Rutgers University
Press, 1962.
Ewen, David Complete Book of the American Musical Theatre,
Revised New York: Henry Holt, 1959.
Green, Stanley The World of Musical Comedy New York:
Ziff-Davis, 1960.

Irish Drama
Boyd, Ernest A. The Contemporary Drama of Ireland
Boston: Little, Brown, 1917.

Special Studies in the Theatre
Isaacs, Edith J. R. , ed. The Negro in the American Theatre.
New York: Theatre Arts, 1947.
Rosenberg, Edgar From Shylock to Svengali Jewish Stereo-
types in English Fiction Stanford: Stanford University
Press, 1963.
Lelyveld, Toby Shylock on the Stage Cleveland: The Press
of Western Reserve University, 1960.

Biographical and Critical Studies of Playwrights

American and British
Behrman, S. N. The Worcester Account New York: Random
House, 1953.
Braybrooke, Patrick The Amazing Mr. Noel Coward London:
Denis Archer, 1933.

Brown, John Mason The Worlds of Robert E. Sherwood
   Mirror to His Times, 1896-1939. New York: Harper
   and Row, 1965.
Chesterton, G. K. George Bernard Shaw London and New
   York: John Lane, 1910.
Clark, Barrett H. Intimate Portraits: Maxim Gorky, Sidney
   Howard, John Galsworthy, Edward Sheldon, George
   Moore. New York: Dramatists Play Service, 1951.
Collis, J. S. Shaw New York: Alfred A. Knopf, 1924.
Davis, Owen My First Fifty Years in the Theatre Boston:
   William H. Baker, 1950.
Dickinson, Thomas H. Playwrights of the New American
   Theatre New York: Macmillan, 1925.
Jackson, Holbrook Bernard Shaw London: Grant Richards,
   1909.
James, Henry Theatre and Friendship Letters from Henry
   James to Elizabeth Robins with a commentary by
   Elizabeth Robins New York: G. P. Putnam Sons,
   1932.
Kahn, E. J., Jr. The Merry Partners--The Age and Stage
   of Harrigan and Hart New York: Random House, 1955.
Mantle, Burns American Playwrights of Today New York:
   Dodd, Mead, 1929.
Mantle, Burns Contemporary American Playwrights New York:
   Dodd, Mead, 1938.
Morley, Robert and Sewell Stokes Robert Morley--a Reluctant
   Autobiography New York: Simon and Schuster, 1966.
Moses, Montrose J. The American Dramatist Boston: Little,
   Brown, 1925.
Williams, Emlyn George. An Early Autobiography New York:
   Random House, 1961.
Winsten, Stephen Days with Bernard Shaw New York: The
   Vanguard Press, 1949.

Biographies and Autobiographies of Theatre Personalities

A. American

Abbott, George "Mister Abbott" New York: Random House,
   1963.
Barrymore, Ethel Memories: An Autobiography London:
   Hulton Press, 1956.
Brady, William A. Showman New York: E. P. Dutton, 1937.
Lockridge, Richard Darling of Misfortune Edwin Booth:
   1833-1893. New York and London: Century, 1932.
Enters, Agna Artist's Life New York: Coward, McCann, Inc.
Gaige, Crosby Footlights and Highlights New York: E. P.
   Dutton, 1948.
Hayes, Helen A Gift of Joy New York: M. Evans, 1965.

Golden, John and Viola Brothers Shore Stage-Struck John
    Golden New York, London and Los Angeles: Samuel
    French, 1930.
Helburn, Theresa A Wayward Quest An Autobiography Boston
    and Toronto: Little, Brown, 1960.
Hopper, Hedda and James Brough The Whole Truth and
    Nothing But Garden City, New York: Doubleday, 1963.
Langner, Lawrence The Magic Curtain The story of a life
    in two fields, theatre and invention by the Founder
    of the Theatre Guild New York: E. P. Dutton, 1951.
Morris, Clara The Life of a Star New York: McClure,
    Phillips, 1906.
Nugent, Elliott Events Leading Up to the Comedy An auto-
    biography New York: Trident Press, 1965.
Reed, Joseph Verner The Curtain Falls New York: Harcourt,
    Brace, 1935.
Zolotow, Maurice Stagestruck--The Romance of Alfred Lunt
    and Lynn Fontanne New York: Harcourt, Brace, 1965.

    B. British
Bablet, Denis Edward Gordon Craig Translated by Daphne
    Woodward New York: Theatre Arts Books, 66.
Brown, Ivor The Way of My World London: Collins, 1954.
Brown, John Mason Letters from Greenroom Ghosts New
    York: The Viking Press, 1934.
Cochran, Charles B. Secrets of a Showman London: William
    Heinemann, 1925.
Forbes-Robertson, Sir Johnston A Player Under Three Reigns
    Boston: Little, Brown, 1925.
Gielgud, John Early Stages London: Macmillan, 1935.
Gielgud, John Stage Directions London: Heinemann, 1963.
Pearson, Hesketh The Last Actor-Managers London:
    Methuen, 1950.
Stoddart, James H. Recollections of a Player New York:
    Century, 1902.

    C. European
Skinner, Cornelia Otis Madame Sarah Boston: Houghton,
    Mifflin, 1966.

Shakespearean Studies
Boas, Frederick S. Shakespeare and His Predecessors
    New York: Charles Scribner's Sons, 1910.
Boardman, George Nye Shakespeare--Five Lectures Chicago:
    Fleming H. Revell, 1908.
Dunn, Esther Cloudman Shakespeare in America New York:
    Macmillan, 1939.

Hazlitt, William Lectures on the Literature of the Age of
    Elizabeth London: George Bell, 1869.
Holmes, Nathaniel The Authorship of Shakespeare 2 vols.
    Boston and New York: Houghton, Mifflin, 1887.

Design in the Theatre
Leeper, Janet Edward Gordon Craig Designs for the Theatre
    London: Penguin Books, 1948.
Simonson, Lee The Stage Is Set New York: Dover, 1946.
    Originally published by New York: Harcourt, Brace,
    1926.

Anthologies of One-Act Plays
Ansorge, Elizabeth and Others, eds. (Text) Prose and Poetry
    for Appreciation (They Fly Through the Air, Spread-
    ing the News, The American Way, Never Come
    Monday, Cartwheel) Syracuse, New York: Singer,
    1942.
Baker, George Pierce, ed. Harvard Plays, Volume I (Three
    Pills in a Bottle, The Good Men Do, Two Crooks
    and a Lady, Free Speech) New York: Brentano's,
    1918.
Baker, George Pierce, ed. Harvard Plays, Volume II (The
    Florist Shop, The Bank Account, The Rescue, America
    Passes By) New York: Brentano's, 1920.
Baker, George Pierce, ed. Harvard Plays, Volume III
    (Garafelia's Husband, The Four-Flushers, The Harbor
    of Lost Ships, Scales and the Sword) New York:
    Brentano's, 1922.
Baker, George Pierce, ed. Harvard Plays, Volume IV
    (The Playroom, The Flitch of Bacon, Cooks and
    Cardinals, Torches) New York: Brentano's, 1923.
Baker, George Pierce, ed. Yale One-Act Plays (The Mistress,
    Hans Bulow's Last Puppet, Immersion, Yella, Minnie
    Field, "L") New York: Samuel French, 1930.
Barnes, John R. and Others, eds. Prose and Poetry of the
    World (Where the Cross Is Made, Riders to the Sea)
    Syracuse: L. W. Singer, 1941.
Barnouw, Erik, ed. Radio Drama in Action (Columbus Day,
    Will The Earth Hold?, The Battle of the Warsaw
    Ghetto, Mr. Ledford and the TVA, Open Letter on
    Race Hatred, Button Woods, The Last Day of the War,
    A Child Is Born, The Halls of Congress, Radioman
    Jack Cooper, Cornering the Red Army, Inside a Kid's
    Head, London by Clipper, Japanese-Americans, The
    Lonesome Train, The Boise, Grandpa and the Statue,
    Booker T. Washington in Atlanta, North Atlantic

Testament, Typhus, Pacific Task Force, Against the
    Storm, The Negro Domestic, Japan's Advance Base:
    The Bonin Islands, The House I Live In) New York:
    Rinehart, 1945.
Barrie, James Matthew Plays (The Will, The Twelve-Pound
    Look, The Old Lady Shows Her Medals) New York:
    Scribner's, 1952.
Blair, Walter and John C. Gerber, eds. Better Reading,
    Volume 2 (A Night at an Inn) Chicago: Scotts, Fores-
    man, 1949.
Boyd, James, ed. (Radio Plays) The Free Company Presents
    (The People With Light Coming Out of them, The Mole
    On Lincoln's Cheek, An American Crusader, One More
    Free Man, Freedom's a Hard-bought Thing, His Honor,
    The Mayor, A Start in Life, The States Talking, The
    Miracle of States Talking, "Above Suspicion.") New
    York: Dodd, Mead, 1942.
Brown, Leonard Stanley and Porter, Perrin, eds. A Quarto
    of Modern Literature (In the Zone) New York:
    Scribner's, 1935.
Canfield, Curtis, ed. Plays of the Irish Renaissance
    (Deirdre, Hyacinth Halvey, The Twisting of the Rope,
    Riders to the Sea) New York: Ives Washburn, 1929.
Carpenter, Bruce, ed. A Book of Dramas (A Minuet, Miss
    Julia, The Intruder) New York: Prentice-Hall, 1929.
Carpenter, Bruce, ed. A Book of Dramas: Revised Edition
    (The Intruder, The Long Voyage Home, Riders to the
    Sea) New York: Prentice-Hall, 1949.
Cassidy, Frederic G. ed. Modern American Plays (Waiting
    for Lefty) New York and London: Longmans, Green,
    1949.
Cerf, Bennett and Van H. Cartwell, ed. Thirty Famous One-
    Act Plays (The Man Who Married a Dumb Wife, Miss
    Julie, Salome, The Rising of the Moon, The Boor,
    The Twelve Pound Look, The Green Cuckatoo, A
    Miracle of St. Antony, The Monkey's Paw, The Little
    Man, Riders to the Sea, A Sunny Morning, A Night
    at an Inn, The Dear Departed, The Drums of Oude,
    Helena's Husband, Suppressed Desires, The Game of
    Chess, Lithuania, The Valiant, In the Zone, If Men
    Played Cards as Women Do, Another Way Out, The
    Clod, Aria da Capo, Overtones, Fumed Oak, Waiting
    for Lefty, Hello Out There, Bury the Dead) Garden
    City, New York: Garden City Publishing Co., 1943. New
    York: The Modern Library, 1949.
Chayefsky, Paddy Television Plays (Holiday Song, Printer's
    Measure, The Big Deal, Marty, The Mother, The

Bachelor) New York: Simon and Schuster, 1955.
Church, Virginia Woodson, ed. Curtain! (What Men Live By,
    The Lost Silk Hat, The Man Who Died at Twelve
    O'Clock, Napoleon Crossing the Rockies, Aria da
    Capo, Good Theatre, The Angel on the Shop) New
    York: Harper and Brothers, 1932.
Clark, Barrett H. ed. Representative Plays by British and
    Irish Authors (The Widow of Wasdale Head, The Goal,
    Salome, The Man in the Stalls, 'Op o' Me-Thumb,
    The Impertinence of the Creature, The Stepmother,
    Rococo, James and John, The Snow Man, Fancy Free,
    Lonesome-Like, Miss Tassey, Makeshifts, The Maker
    of Dreams, The Land of Heart's Desire, Riders to
    the Sea, Spreading the News, The Magnanimous Lover,
    The Golden Doom) Boston: Little, Brown, 1921.
Clark, Barrett H. and Thomas R. Cook, eds. One-Act Plays
    (Sparkin', The Kelly Kid, Knives from Syria, Ile,
    Saved, The Resignation of Bill Snyder, The No 'Count
    Boy, The Organ, Bargains in Cathay, Money, Back-
    stage, The Song of Solomon) Boston: D. C. Heath,
    1929.
Clark, Barrett H. and Kenyon Nicholson, eds. The American
    Scene (Greasy Luck, Bound East for Cardiff, Chuck,
    The Quarry, Blood o' Kings, The Last Straw, Money,
    No Cause for Complaint, Wanderlust, The Girl in
    the Coffin, Town, The No 'Count Boy, Lijah, The Tie
    That Binds, Bumblepuppy, The Medicine Show, The
    Cow with Wings, The Trysting Place, The Eldest,
    The Feast of the Holy Innocents, The Barbarians,
    Bread, Trifles, Minnie Field, The Cajun, Addio, The
    Resignation of Bill Snyder, Reckless, Across the Bor-
    der, The Organ, Last Day for Grouse, The End of the
    Trail, Day's End, Good Vintage) New York: D. Apple-
    ton, 1930.
Clements, Colin Campbell, ed. Sea-Plays (The Ship Comes In,
    The Brink of Silence, Just Two Men, The Magic Sea-
    Shell, The Outside, The Rusty Door, Second Best,
    Sintram of Skagerrak, Will-o'-the Wisp, The Wonder-
    ship) New York: Dodd, Mead, 1925.
Coffman, George R. , ed. A Book of Modern Plays (Riders
    to the Sea, The Workhouse Ward, Where the Cross
    Is Made) Chicago: Scott, Foresman, 1925.
Cohen, Helen Louise, ed. One-Act Plays by Modern Authors
    (Beauty and the Jacobin, Pierrot of the Minute, The
    Maker of Dreams, Gettysburg, Wurzel-Flummery,
    Maid of France, Spreading the News, Welsh Honeymoon,
    The Boy Will, Riders to the Sea, A Night at an Inn,

The Twilight Saint, The Masque of Two, Strangers,
The Intruder, Fortune and Men's Eyes, The Little
Man) New York: Harcourt, Brace, 1921.
Cohen, Helen Louise, ed. More One-Act Plays by Modern
Authors (Night of "Mr. H." The Last of the Lowries
Hearts Enduring, Pearls, The Dear Departed, The
Poor House, The Siege, The Change-House, The Little
Father of the Wilderness, The Artist, Good Theatre,
The Carved Woman, Where the Cross Is Made, A Way
Out) New York: Harcourt, Brace, 1927.
Conkle, E. D. Crick Bottom Plays (Minnie Field, Sparkin',
Warter-Wucks, "lection, Things Is That-a-Way) New
York: Samuel French, 1928.
Cook, George Cram and Frank Shay, eds. Provincetown
Plays. (Suppressed Desires, Aria da Capo, Cocaine,
Night, Enemies, The Angel Intrudes, Bound East for
Cardiff, The Widow's Veil, The String of the Samisen,
Not Smart) New York: D. Appleton, 1921.
Cooper, Charles W., ed. A Preface to Drama (Fumed Oak,
The Long Voyage Home, "A Good Lesson," The Happy
Journey to Trenton and Camden). New York: The
Ronald Book Company, 1955.
Corwin, Norman (Radio Plays) Thirteen by Corwin (The
Odyssey of Runyon Jones, Radio Primer, They Fly
Through the Air with the Greatest of Ease, The Plot
to Overthrow Christmas, Daybreak, Old Salt, A
Soliloquy to Balance the Diet, Ann Rutledge, Seems
Radio Is Here to Stay, Tim at Twenty, My Client
Curly, Appointment, The Oracle of Philadelphia)
New York: Henry Holt, 1942.
Corwin, Norman (Radio Plays) More by Corwin (Mary and
the Fairy, Coomer, We Hold These Truths, Descent
of the Gods, The Long Name None Could Spell, Good
Heavens, Psalm for a Dark Year, A Man with a
Platform, Samson, Anatomy of Sound, Excerpts from
"This Is War," Murder in Studio One, Between
Americans, A Moment of the Nation's Time, Double
Concerto, Program to Be Opened in a Hundred Years)
New York: Henry Holt, 1944.
Corwin, Norman Untitled and Other Radio Dramas (The Un-
decided Molecule, Untitled, El Capitan and the Cor-
poral, Savage Encounter, London by Clipper, Home
Is Where You Hang Your Helmet, An Anglo-American
Angle, Clipper Home, You Can Dream, Inc., The
Moat Farm Murder, N.Y.: A Tapestry for Radio,
Tel Aviv, Moscow, There Will Be Time Later, On
a Note of Triumph, 14 August, Set Your Clock at

U 235, Critical Reception) New York: Henry Holt,
1947.
Davenport, William H., Lowry C. Wimberly and Harry Shaw,
eds. Dominant Types in British and American Litera-
ture: Vol. I. (The Twelve-Pound Look, Riders to the
Sea) New York: Harper and Brothers, 1949.
Dickinson, Thomas H., ed. Chief Contemporary Dramatists,
1st Series. (Riders to the Sea, The Hour Glass, The
Rising of the Moon, Scarecrow, The Truth) Boston
and New York: Houghton, Mifflin, 1915.
Dickinson, Thomas H. ed. Chief Contemporary Dramatists,
2nd Series (Mixed Marriage, King Argimenes and the
Unknown Warrier, Moral, Living Hours, The Concert)
Boston and New York: Houghton, Mifflin, 1921.
Dickinson, Thomas H., ed. Chief Contemporary Dramatists,
3rd Series. (Such is Life, Naked, Eyvind of the Hills)
Boston and New York: Houghton, Mifflin, 1930.
Dunsany, Lord, Five Plays (The Gods of the Mountain, The
Golden Doom, King Argimenes and the Unknown
Warrior, The Glittering Gate, The Lost Silk Hat)
Boston: Little, Brown, 1914.
Dunsany, Lord, Seven Modern Comedies (Atlanta in Wimbledon,
The Raffle, The Journey of the Soul, In Holy Russia,
His Sainted Grandmother, The Hopeless Passion of
Mr. Bunyon, The Jest of Hahalaba) New York: G. P.
Putnam, 1928.
Durham, Willard Higley and Dobbs, John W., eds., British
and American Plays, 1830-1945 (Waiting for Lefty,
Cathleen ni Houlihan) New York and London: Oxford
University Press, 1947.
Eaton, Walter Prichard, ed. Twelve One-Act Plays (The
Valiant, Romance of the Willow Pattern, The Grill,
The Last Straw, Thank You, Doctor, Copy, The Trap,
Good Medicine, God Winks, A Woman of Character,
Jazz and Minuet, The Most Foolish Virgin) New York:
Longmans, Green, 1926.
Edades, Jean, and Fosdick, Carolyn F., eds, Drama of East
and West (A Sunny Morning, Educating Josefina, A
Portrait of the Artist as Filipino) Manila: Bookman,
1956.
Eliot, Samuel A. Jr., ed. Little Theatre Classics (Bushido,
The Old Wife's Tale, The Duchess of Pavy, Pericles)
Boston: Little, Brown, 1921.
Feigenbaum, Lawrence, ed. Radio and Television Plays (Plays
from Radio: Sorry, Wrong Number, The Melody Man,
The Word, A Medal for Miss Walker; Plays from
Television: She Walks in Beauty, One in Twelve,

U. F. O. , Daniel Webster) New York: Globe Book Co. , 1956.

Finch, Robert, Plays of the American West (Miracle at Dublin Gulch, The Desert Shall Rejoice, The Old Grad, Summer Comes to Diamond O, Murder in the Snow, From Paradise to Butte, Western Night, Good-bye to the Lazy K, Johnny, Ghost Town, Rodeo, The Return, Gone Today, Near Closing Time, The Day They All Come Back) New York: Greenberg, 1947.

Flavin, Martin, Brains and Other One-Act Plays (Brains, Casualties, An Emergency Case, The Blind Man, A Question of Principle, Caleb Stone's Death Watch) New York: Samuel French, 1926.

Foote, Horton, Harrison Texas: Eight Television Plays (A Young Lady of Property, John Turner Davis, The Tears of My Sister, The Death of the Old Man, Ex-pectant Relations, The Midnight Caller, The Dancers, The Trip to Bountiful) New York: Harcourt, Brace and World, 1956.

Freier, Robert, Lazarus, Arnold Leslie, and Potell, Herbert, eds. Adventures in Modern Literature ed 4. (Trifles, The End of the Beginning) New York: Harcourt, Brace and World, 1956.

Galbraith, Ester R. , ed. Plays Without Footlights (This Bull Ate Nutmeg, Flittermouse, The Bishop's Candlesticks, Tails Up, The People with Light Coming out of Them, Fun after Supper, The Master Salesman, The Happy Journey to Trenton and Camden) New York: Harcourt, Brace and World, 1945.

Galsworthy, John, Plays (Six Short Plays: The First and Last, The Little Man, Hall-Marked Deceit, The Sun, Punch and Go) New York: Scribner's, 1928.

Gassner, John, ed. Twenty-five Best Plays of the Modern American Theatre (The Clod, Trifles, Aria da Capo, Poor Aubrey, White Dresses, Minnie Field) New York: Crown, 1949.

Gassner, John, ed. A Treasury of the Theatre (There Are Crimes and Crimes, Riders to the Sea, The Tenor) New York: Simon and Schuster, 1950.

Gerstenberg, Alice, Ten One-Act Plays (He Said and She Said, Overtones, The Unseen, The Buffer, Attuned, The Pot Boiler, Hearts, Beyond, Fourteen, The Illuminati in Drama Libre) New York: Brentano, 1928.

Goldberg, Isaac, Translator, Plays of the Italian Theatre (Sicilian Limes) Boston: John Luce, 1921.

Goldstone, George A. , ed. One-Act Plays (The Diabolical

Circle, Figureheads, The Romancers, The King's
English, The Lost Silk Hat, The Thrice-Promised
Bride, The Boor, The Unseen, Sham, Confessional,
Dust of the Road, Ile, The God of Quiet, The White
Hawk, The Workhouse Ward) Chicago and New York:
Allyn and Bacon, 1926.

Goodman, Kenneth Sawyer, Quick Curtains (Dust of the Road,
The Game of Chess, Ephraim and the Winged Bear,
Back of the Yards, Dancing Dolls, A Man Can Only
Do His Best) Chicago: Stage Guild, 1915.

Gordon, Dudley, King, Vernon R., and Lyman, William W.,
eds. Today's Literature (The Workhouse Ward, Where
the Cross Is Made, Knives From Syria, Moonshine,
Lars Killed His Son, Amaco, Youth Must Be Served)
New York: American Book Company, 1935.

Green, Paul, The House of Connelly and Other Plays (Potter's
Field, Tread the Green Grass) New York: Samuel
French, 1931.

Green, Paul In the Valley and Other One-Act Plays (In the
Valley, No 'Count Boy, In Aunt Mahaly's Cabin, Man
on the House, Supper for the Dead, Quare Medicine,
The Goodbye, The Picnic, Unto Such Glory, A Satur-
day Night, The Man Who Died at Twelve O'Clock)
New York: Samuel French, 1928.

Green, Paul The Lord's Will and Other Carolina Plays (The
Lord's Will, Blackbeard, Old Wash Lucas: the Miser,
The No 'Count Boy, The Old Man of Edmonton, The
Last of the Lowries) New York: Henry Holt, 1925.

Gregory, Lady, Seven Short Plays (Spreading the News,
Hyacinth Halvey, The Rising of the Moon, The Jack-
daw, The Workhouse Ward, The Travelling Man, The
Gaol Gate) Dublin: Maunsel, 1909.

Griffith, Francis J., and Mersand, Joseph, eds. Modern
One-Act Plays (The Will, The Doctor from Dunmore,
The Adventures of Mr. Bean, A Sunny Morning, The
Happy Journey to Trenton and Camden, God and Texas,
Franklin and the King, The Stolen Prince, The Golden
Doom, The Other Side, The Far-Distant Shore, Finders-
Keepers, Emergency, Stand By!, The Bottle Imp, My
Client Curley, The Nosebag) New York: Harcourt,
Brace and World, 1950.

Griffith, Francis J., and Mersand, Joseph, eds. One-Act
Plays for Today (The Farce of the Worthy Master
Pierre Patelin, Fright, The Gooseberry Mandarin,
The No 'Count Boy, The Boy: What Will He Become?,
Blood of the Martyrs, Movie Mother, Dark Glasses,
Cartwheel, Meridian 7-1212, Air Raid, The End of

the Trail, The Curtain) New York: Globe Book
Company, 1945.
Halline, Allan Gates, ed. American Plays (Superstition,
The Field God, The Danites in the Sierras) New York:
American Book Company, 1935.
Hampden, John, ed. Ten Modern Plays (Thirty Minutes in a
Street, The House with the Twisty Windows, Columbine,
Moonshine, The New Wing at Elsinore, Mrs. Adis,
Tickless Time, X=O: A Night of the Trojan War,
Elizabeth Refuses, Brother Wolf) London: Nelson,
1928.
Hildreth, William Henry, and Dumble, Wilson Randle, eds.
Five Contemporary American Plays (Waiting For Lefty)
New York: Harper and Brothers, 1939.
Hubbell, Joy B. , and Beaty, John O. , eds. An Introduction
to Drama (The Assumption of Hannele, The Goal, The
Land of Heart's Desire, Riders to the Sea, A Night
at an Inn, The Intruder, The Boor, Overtones, Trifles,
Peggy) New York: Macmillan, 1927.
Hughes, Glenn, ed. Short Plays for Modern Players (The
Ambush, Uncle Jimmy, The Man with the Iron Jaw,
What Never Dies, The Calf That Laid the Golden Eggs,
A Small Down Payment, Under the Oak, Three Cans
of Beans, A Duel about Nothing, Five Minutes from
the Station, Gilt-Edged, Really My Dear) New York:
D. Appleton and Co. , 1931.
Inglis, Rewey Belle, and Gehlman, John Bowman, eds. Ad-
ventures in American Literature, ed. 3. (Textiles,
Where the Cross Is Made) New York: Harcourt,
Brace and World, 1941.
Inglis, Rewey Belle, Cooper, Alice Cecilia, Oppenheimer,
Celia, and Foerster, Norman, eds. Adventures in
English Literature, ed. 4. (The Old Lady Shows Her
Medals, Riders to the Sea) New York: Harcourt, Brace
and World, 1946.
Isaacs, Edith J. R. , ed. Plays of American Life and Fantasy
(Moonshine, The Dreamy Kid, Bumblepuppy, Blockade,
The End of the Trail, Charivari, Kills-with-Her-Man,
Brother Bill, Rapunzel, The No 'Count Boy, Rose
Windows, Spring Sluicing, Zombi, The Portrait of
Tiero, Trap Doors, The Queen of Sheba, The Auto-
crat of the Coffee-Stall, The Gooseberry Mandarin)
New York: Coward-McCann, 1929.
Jagendorf, Moritz, ed. Twenty Non-Royalty Plays (Mystery
at the Depot, The Rime of the Ancient Mariner, The
Late Mr. Scarface, Terrible Night, The Shadow of
Screecham Isle, Her Highness, the Cook, Heavenly

Mystery, Snowbound, Mysterious-Yellow Moon, Clear-
Silver Moon, Fog on the Bay, The Great Meatloaf
Mystery, Shadow-een, It's About Time, End of the
Rainbow, His Wonders to Perform, False Alarm!,
Cheating Cheaters, Chost to Ghost, The Family Tree,
The Mummy's Foot) New York: Greenberg, 1945.

Johnson, Theodore, ed. Miniature Plays for Stage and Study
(Bargains, Dispatch Goes Home, Early Frost, The
Fifth Commandment, The Final Refuge, La Carota,
For Distinguished Service, The Lost Saint, Love and
Lather, The Singapore Spider, The Greek Vase)
Boston: Walter H. Baker, 1930.

Johnson, Theodore, ed. Plays in Miniature (The Baggage,
It Sometimes Happens, Catherine Parr or Alexander's
House, Wrong Numbers, Square Pegs, At the Sign of
the Cleft Heart, Fluerette and Company, The Umbrella Duologue, On the Way Home, Outwitted, Confessions) Boston: Walter H. Baker, 1928.

Johnson, Theodore, ed. More Plays in Miniature (His Only
Way, Spring, Famine and the Ghost, Xanthippe and
Socrates, The Other Voice, Secrets of the Heart,
The Drawback, The Marriage of Dotty, Double Dummy,
A Vicious Circle, Yes and No, Come Here, At the
Ferry, Au Revoir, Just advertise, The Wooden Leg)
Boston: Walter H. Baker, 1932.

Johnson, Theodore, ed. Ten Fantasies For Stage and Study
(The Apothecary, The Crown of St. Felice, The
Golden Arrow, In Arcady, Is Romance Dead?, The
Man of the Moment, The Passing of Galatea, St.
Anselm Only Carved One Soul, Twilight of the Moon,
The Workers at the Looms) Boston: Walter H. Baker,
1932.

Johnson, Theodore, and Phillips, Leroy, eds. Types of
Dramatic Composition. (The Kelly Kid, The Dweller
in the Darkness, Wanderlust, Grandma Pulls the
Strings, Gabbages and Kings, A Fool of a Man, Dawn,
Bethlehem,   Maurice's Own Idea, The Crumbs that
Fall, 'Lijah, Meredew's Right Hand, Trifles, Peggy,
Uncle Jimmy, The Closet, The Killer, The Lean
Years, Pierrot, Before the Seven Doors, Daggers
and Diamonds) Boston: Walter H. Baker, 1927.

Kelly, George, The Flattering Word, and Other One-Act
Plays (The Flattering Word, Smarty's Party, The
Weak Spot, Poor Aubrey) Boston: Little, Brown, 1925.

Knickerbocker, Edwin Van B., ed. Short Plays (The Florist
Shop, The Game of Chess, The Man Who Married a
Dumb Wife, Two Crooks and a Lady, Torches, Poor

Maddalena, A Wedding, The Valiant, The Gods of
the Mountain, Pyramus and Thisbe, On Vengeance
Height, The Noble Lord, The Stepmother, Where the
Cross Is Made, Ulysses) New York: Henry Holt, 1931.
Knickerbocker, Edwin Van B. , ed. Twelve Plays (Where but
in America?, The Forfeit, Poor Maddalena, Playing
With Fire, The Stepmother, On Vengeance Height,
The Marriage Proposal, The Pipe of Peace, Enter
the Hero, The Pot Boiler, Over the Hills, A Game
of Chess) New York: Henry Holt, 1924.
Koch, Frederick H. , ed. Carolina Folk Plays 1st Series
(When Witches Ride, Peggy, Dod Gad Ye Both, Off
Nags Head, The Last of the Lowries) New York:
Henry Holt, 1922.
Koch, Frederick H. , ed. Carolina Folk Plays, 2nd Series
(Trista, The Return of Buck Gavin, Gaius and Gaius
Jr. , Fixin's, The Beaded Buckle) New York: Henry
Holt, 1926.
Koch, Frederick H. , ed. Carolina Folk Plays, 3rd Series
(The Scuffletown, Outlaws, Job's Kinfolks, In Dixon's
Kitchen, A Shotgun Splicin', Lighted Candles, Quare
Medicine) New York: Henry Holt, 1928.
Koch, Frederick H. , ed. Carolina Folk Comedies, 4th Series
of Carolina Folk Plays (Cloey, Magnolia's Man, Com-
panion-Mate Maggie, Ever' Snitch, Agatha, Dogwood
Bushes, The Lie, The New Moon) New York: Henry
Holt, 1931.
Kozlenko, William, ed. The Best Short Plays of the Social
Theatre (The Dog Beneath the Skin, Plant in the Sun,
The Cradle Will Rock, Hymn to the Rising Sun, This
Earth of Ours, Private Hicks, Waiting for Lefty,
Bury the Dead, Give All Thy Terrors to the Wind,
Running Dogs) New York: Random House, 1939.
Kozlenko, William, ed. One-Hundred Non-Royalty, One Act
Plays (Women in Council, Do Unto Others, And No
Birds Sing, Title Go, The Long Retreat, Second Honey-
moon, Goodbye to the Lazy K, Death Comes to My
Friends, The Man in the Fur Cap, Best Friend Grad-
uates, Mildred Is My Name, The Fallen Bough, Who
Stand and Wait, Escape, Day for Truants, Souls at
Sea, Calling Mr. and Mrs. America, Lo, the Gaunt
Wolf, Library Open Hours, Indian Summer, The Other
Mother, The Darkest Night, In the Merry Month of
May, The Jeweled Toad, The Master's Touch, The
Last One, The Third Plate, Jade, Even Exchange,
Saturday Supplement, Mind over Matter, Primary Day,
Quarantine, Bitter Wine, The Parrot, An Empty

Gesture, The First Margaret, Morgan's Raid, Phoebe
Louise, Pierrot, Poltram, Jilted, Company House, The
Byronic, Escape by Moonlight, Night Call, Progress
in the Air, Babylon, Greece, The World, The Bird
on Nellie's Hat, Rehearsal, The Desire of All Nations-
Egypt, The Nativity, Halves!, Unto Bethlehem Oh,
Say, Can You Sing!, Too Many Hands on a Watch,
Youth Adds a Dash of Pepper, Low Bridge, The
Ghost of Green Mansion, Yesterday's Rations, David,
Sixteen, Fortune Is a Cowboy, Mama Goes to the Con-
vention, This Lad George, Virginia Creeper, Vaca-
tion Memories, The Kingdom of Happiness, Our
Country, The Floating Branch, Tempest over a Tea-
Cup, The Pied Piper of Healthy Town, Danger over
Dumpling, Zelda, The Elves and the Shoemaker, The
Fate of Greedy Gus, The Gift Perfect, King Cole's
Court, Rainbow Gold, The Truth Fairy and the Magic
Ink, Exit the Queen, Marybell, The Discovery of Amer-
ica, Red Riding Hood, Flopodopolus, Bumpingjump
Steps into Legend, The Easter Rabbit, Hansel and
Gretel, A Christmas Miracle, Where the Cross Was
Made, The Declaration of Independence, The Winning
of Ohio, Braddock's Defeat, The Luck of Roaring
Camp, The Autocrat of the Breakfast Table, The Fall
of the House of Usher, The Legend of Sleepy Hollow,
When Lincoln Came to Pittsburgh, Typee) New York:
Greenberg, 1940.
Kozlenko, William, ed. One-Hundred Non-Royalty Radio
Plays (A Special Announcement, Two Bottles of Relish,
Luck, The Pussycat and the Expert Plumber Who Was
a Man, Red Head Baker, All You Need Is One Good
Break, A Matter of Life and Death, Moon Watch,
Arena, The League of Animals, Royal March, Three
Strikes You're Out, The "Americas" Cup, Sherril,
Boy Waiting, The Man Who Broke Bingo, The Long
Hour, Telegram from Heaven, John Wiffle Concentrates,
Back to 1960!, Prague is Quiet, Derricks on a Hill,
Frontier Fighters, I Wyatt Erp, II Wild Bill Hickok,
The Rebel Saint, Unidentified, The University Today,
Virginia's Letter to Santa Claus, Widows Shouldn't
Weep, Hunk Is a Punk, Alabama Fables, The Black
Death, Panic in Salem, A Blot on the Landscape,
High Water, Unfinished Symphony, The Girl from
Kavalla, The Past Is Present, Banting: Discoverer
of Insulin, What's in a Word?, The Rights of Man,
1. The Exile, 2. Racial Freedom, 3. Cultural Free-
dom, 4. The Right to Organize, Independence Hall,

And the Gods Play, William Ireland's Confession,
Mount Vernon Interlude, The Devil's Flower, The
Last Word, The Odyssey of Homer, The Affidavit,
Gardenias: Ten Cents, Revolt in Orthoepy, The Christ-
mas Story, The Story of Silent Night, My Mother,
These Honored Dead, Give Me Wings, Brother, His
Name Shall Be: Remember, Dvorak's Song of the New
World, Ask Aunt Mary, Facing Westward, Delayed
Glory, Going Home, This Obscene Pomp, The Ladder
Under the Maple Tree, What We Defend, The March
on Chumley Hollow, Nancy Clare, The Soldiers of
Fortune, Speak o' the Devil, Even the Blind, The
Lion Roars, Legend of Dust, The Magic Git-Flip,
Cask of Amontillado, What Time Is It?, Handsome Is,
Peace on Earth, The Old Oaken Bucket, The Key,
Story in Dogtown Common, Visitation, What Men Live
By, Murder among Psychologists, Who Called You
Here, Away from It All, Henry Hudson, What's Your
Name, Dear?, Prometheus in Granada, The Bottle
Imp, The Comeback, The Silver Coronet, $100,000
for a Wife, The Quality of Mercy). New York: Green-
berg, 1949.

Kozlenko, William, ed. Twenty-Five Non-Royalty One-Act
American Comedies (From Paradise to Butte, Cupid's
Bow, The Reign of Minnie Belle, The More the
Merrier, The Man of the House, Freedom's Bird,
The Package for Ponsomby, Man of Arts, Bargain
Rack, Over Fourteen and Single, Mary's Cerise Heart,
Yankee Nickels, Two Birds with One Stone, Quimby
Comes Across, For Better or Worse, Keep Me a
Woman Grown, Triflin', Jennie Knows, Moonlight to
Match, What's in a Name?, Outbound for Romance,
For a Rainy Day, Annie's Man, Remember Your Dia-
phragm, Psychologically Speaking) New York: Green-
berg, 1943.

Kreymborg, Alfred, ed. Poetic Drama (Aria da Capo)
Modern Age Books (Out of Business)

Kreymborg, Alfred, ed. Puppet Plays (When the Willow Nods,
Blue and Green, Manikin and Minikin, Jack's House,
Lima Beans, People Who Die, Pianissimo) London:
Martin Secker and Warburg, 1923.

Lass, A. H., McGill, E. L., and Axelrod, Donald, eds.
Plays from Radio (Sorry, Wrong Number, My Client
Curley, The Signal Man, The Ghost of Benjamine Sweet,
The Test, The Clinic, A Trip to Czardis, One Special
for Doc, Read Death, One More Free Man, Grandpa
and the Statue, Little Johnny Appleseed, The Devil

and Daniel Webster, Many a Watchful Night) Boston:
Houghton, Mifflin, 1948.
Law, Frederick Houk, ed. Modern Plays, Long and Short
(What Men Live By, Masks, Just Neighborly, Bushido,
Benjamin Franklin, Journeyman, Off Nags Head, The
Pioneers, The Maid Who Wouldn't Be Proper) New
York: Appleton-Century-Crofts, 1924.
Leonard, Sterling Andrus, ed. The Atlantic Book of Monthly
Plays (The Philosopher of Butterbiggens, Spreading
the News, The Beggar and the King, Tides, Ile,
Campbell of Kilmhor, The Sun, The Knave of Hearts,
Fame and the Poet, The Captain of the Gate, Gettys-
burg, Lonesome-Like, Riders to the Sea, The Land
of Heart's Desire, The Riding to Lithend) Boston:
Atlantic Monthly Press, 1921.
Leverton, Garrett Hasty, ed. Plays for the College Theatre
(The Man Who Married a Dumb Wife, Lima Beans,
The Moon of the Caribbes, The Drums of Oude, The
Lord's Will, "L") New York: Samuel French, 1932.
Lewis, B. Roland, ed. Contemporary One-Act Plays (The
Twelve-Pound Look, Tradition, The Exchange, Sam
Average, Hyacinth Halvey, The Gazing Globe, The
Boor, The Last Straw, Manikan and Manikin, White
Dresses, Moonshine, Modesty, The Deacon's Hat,
Where but in America, A Dollar, The Diabolical
Circle, The Far-Away Princess, The Stronger) New
York: Charles Scribner's, 1922.
Lewis, B. Roland, ed. University of Utah Plays (The Ex-
change, The Gray Switch, The Boomer, Sara, the
Turkey Girl, And the Devil Laughs, A Man of Temper-
ament) Boston: Walter H. Baker, 1928.
Locke, Alan Le Roy and Montgomery, Gregory, ed. Plays of
Negro Life (Sahdji, an African Ballet, Rackey, The
Death Dance, The No 'Count Boy, White Dresses,
Plumes, 'Cruiter, The Dreamy Kid, The Broken
Banjo, The Flight of the Natives, Judge Lynch, The
Starter, Balo, The Dance Calinda, Granny Maumee,
The Rider of Dreams, The Bird Child, Sugar Cane)
New York: Harper, 1927.
Loomis, Roger Sherman and Clark, Donald Leman, eds.
Modern English Readings (The Moon of the Caribbees)
New York: Farrar and Rinehart, 1934.
Loomis, Roger Sherman and Clark, Donald Leman, eds.
Modern English Readings, ed. 3. (Riders to the Sea)
New York: Farrar and Rinehart, 1939.
Loomis, Roger Sherman and Clark, Donald Leman, eds.
Modern English Readings, ed. 4. (Riders to the Sea)

New York: Farrar and Rinehart, 1942.
Loomis, Roger Sherman and Clark, Donald Leman, eds.
Modern English Readings, ed. 5. (Riders to the Sea)
New York: Rinehart and Co., 1946
Lucas, Harriet Marcelia and others, eds. Prose and Poetry
for Appreciation ed. 4. (The Odyssey of Runyon Jones,
Trifles) New York: L. W. Singer, 1950.
Mackay, Constance D'Arcy, ed. Patriotic Plays and Pageants
for Young People (Abraham Lincoln: Rail-Splitter,
Benjamin Franklin: Journeyman, The Boston Tea
Party, Daniel Boone: Patriot, George Washington's
Fortune, In Witchcraft Days, Merrymount, Princess
Pocahontas) New York: Henry Holt, 1912.
Mantle, Burns and Gassner, John, eds. A Treasury of the
Theatre, Rev. and Adapted for Colleges by Philo M.
Buck, Jr., John Gassner, and H. S. Albertson,
Vol I. (Riders to the Sea) New York: Simon and
Schuster, 1940.
Mantle, Burns and Gassner, John, eds. A Treasury of the
Theatre, ed. 3. (Riders to the Sea) New York: Simon
and Schuster, 1955.
Marks, Jeanette, ed. The Merry Merry Cuckoo and Other
Welsh Plays (The Merry Merry Cuckoo, The Deacon's
Hat, Welsh Honeymoon, A Tress of Hair, Love Let-
ters, Steppin' Westward, Look to the End) New York:
Appleton-Century-Crofts, 1927.
Marriott, J. W., ed. The Best One-Act Plays of 1931.
(Mrs. Noah Gives the Sign, Women Do Things like
That, Vindication, Poet's Corner, Smoke-Screens,
The Bride, The Hoose o' the Hill, The Annual Jumble
Sale, Exit, Shanghai, The Perfect Marriage, Back
Home) London: George G. Harrap, 1932.
Marriott, J. W., ed. One-Act Plays of Today, 1st Series
(Boy Comes Home, Followers, The Stepmother, The
Maker of Dreams, The Little Man, A Night at an
Inn, Campbell of Kilmhor, The Grand Cham's Dia-
mond, Thread o' Scarlet, Becky Sharp, X=O: A Night
of the Trojan War) London: George G. Harrap, 1924;
New York: Dodd, Mead, 1929.
Marriott, J. W., ed. One-Act Plays of Today, 2nd Series.
(Riders to the Sea, Waterloo, It's the Poor That
'Elps the Poor, A Marriage Has Been Arranged,
Lonesome-Like, The Rising of the Moon, The King's
Waistcoat, The Dear Departed, 'Op-o'-Me-Thumb,
The Monkey's Paw, Night Watches, The Child in
Flanders) London: George G. Harrap, 1925; New
York: Dodd, Mead, 1929.

Marriott, J. W. , ed. One-Act Plays of Today, 3rd Series
    (The Dumb and the Blind, How the Weather Is Made,
    The Golden Doom, Rory Aforesaid, The Master of the
    House, Friends, Mimi, The Bishop's Candlesticks,
    Between the Soup and the Savory, Master Wayfarer,
    The Pot of Broth, A King's Hard Bargain) London:
    George G. Harrap, 1926.
Marriott, J. W. , ed. One-Act Plays of Today, 4th Series
    (The Prince Who Was a Piper, Square Pegs, The Man
    in the Bowler Hat, The Betrayal, The Flight of the
    Queen, St. Simeon Stylites, The Patchwork Quilt, Five
    Birds in a Cage, Paddly Pools, The Poacher, The
    Constant Lover) London: George G. Harrap, 1928.
Marriott, J. W. ed. One-Act Plays of Today, 5th Series
    (The Stoker, Birds of a Feather, The Invisible Duke,
    Old Boyhood, The Spartan Girl, The King of Barven-
    der, The Lovely Miracle, The Mousetrap, The Scare-
    crow, The Pathfinder, Aucassin and Nicolette) London:
    George G. Harrap, 1931.
Mayorga, Margaret, ed. Best One-Act Plays of 1937 (A
    Husband for Breakfast, Soldadera, Devil Take a
    Whittler, The Foundling, If the Shoe Pinches, Twenty-
    Five Cents, The Maker of Laws, Tobacco Alley, This
    Earth Is Ours, Debt Takes a Holiday, The Fall of
    the City, Goodnight Please!) New York: Dodd, Mead,
    1938.
Mayorga, Margaret, ed. Best One-Act Plays of 1938.
    (Mañana Bandits, Farewell to Love, The Feast of
    Ortolans, Hawk A-Flyin', Ballad of Youth, Never No
    Third Degree, Cloud over Breakshin, Alma Mater,
    Dust, Resurrection Ezra, This Is Villa, Goodnight,
    Caroline) New York: Dodd, Mead, 1939.
Mayorga, Margaret, ed. Best One-Act Plays of 1939 (Air
    Raid, A World Elsewhere, That's Hollywood, God Is
    Where you Don't Find It, The Hungerers, The
    Captains and the Kings, Hospital Scene, Haunted
    Water, The Devil Is a Good Man, One-Car Wedding,
    Of Time and the Blizzard, Days End) New York:
    Dodd, Mead, 1940.
Mayorga, Margaret, ed. Best Plays of 1940 (Mr. F. Moony's
    Kid Don't Cry, Summer Comes to the Diamond O,
    Subway Circus, Rainbows in Heaven, According to
    Law, Farmer Brown's Pig, Danbury Fair, Sleeping
    Dogs, Parting at Imsdorf) New York: Dodd, Mead,
    1941.
Mayorga, Margaret, ed. The Best One-Act Plays of 1941
    (The States Talking, Until Charlot Comes Home, All-

American Ape, Equinox, The Lady of Larkspur
Lotion, The Miracle of the Danube, The Love of An-
nuziata, The Doctor from Dunmore, Hello Out There,
It's Fun to Be Free) New York: Dodd, Mead, 1942.
Mayorga, Margaret, ed. The Best One-Act Plays of 1942
(The Last of My Solid Gold Watches, House Divided,
The Courting of Marie Jenvrin, City Symphony, The
Strangest Feeling, We Refuse to Die, We Hold These
Truths, Memo to Berchtesgaden, They Burned the
Books, So Long, Son) New York: Dodd, Mead, 1943.
Mayorga, Margaret, ed. The Best One-Act Plays of 1943
(Letter to Jackie, God and Texas, Quiet-Facing the
Park, A Tribute to Gallantry, Where E're We Go,
Mid-Passage, The Death of Aunt Aggie, Murder Is
Fun!, They Asked for It, Journey for an Unknown
Soldier, The Bridegroom Waits) New York: Dodd,
Mead, 1944.
Mayorga, Margaret, ed. The Best One-Act Plays of 1944.
(The Picnic, It Ain't Brooklyn, District of Columbia,
That They May Win, Miracle on the Pullman, Con-
cerning the Red Army, Ship Ahoy!!, On the Way Home,
Strange Rain, 27 Wagons Full of Cotton, The Ad-
miral) New York: Dodd, Mead, 1945.
Mayorga, Margaret, ed. The Best One-Act Plays of 1945
(Atomic Bombs, A Note of Triumph, The Face, To
the American People, A Bunyan Yard, Summer Fury,
The Devil's Foot, The Unsatisfactory Supper, The
Fisherman, Silver Nails, The Far-Distant Shore)
New York: Dodd, Mead, 1946.
Mayorga, Margaret, ed. The Best One-Act Plays of 1946-
1947 (How They Knocked the Devil out of Uncle Ezra,
Freight, Making the Bear, Transition in India, Skele-
tons, Bride-Ship, The Lord and Hawksaw Sadie (Play
with Music), Open Secret, The Soldier Who Became
a Great Dane, The Eagle (Television Script) New
York: Dodd, Mead, 1947.
Mayorga, Margaret, ed. The Best One-Act Plays of 1947-
1948 (On This Green Bank, The Sunny Side of the
Atom, Suffer the Little Children, Who Are the
Weavers, A Woman's Privilege, Frankie and Albert,
Easter Eve, Through a Glass, Darkly, The Meadow,
Before the Bullfight) New York: Dodd, Mead, 1948.
Mayorga, Margaret, ed. The Best One-Act Plays of 1949-
1950 (Doctor Faustus Lights the Lights, The Camel
and I, August Heat, Going Home, The Beast, Day
Before Yesterday, Exodus, Period House, Fantasia
on an Old Familiar Theme, The Long Fall) New York:

Dodd, Mead, 1950.
Mayorga, Margaret, ed. The Best One-Act Plays of 1951-
1952 (The Least One, Paradise Inn, In Darkness,
Hugh of the Glen and His Clogs Are All One, The
Shadow of the Cathedral, Tour of Duty, Glory Day,
The Safecracker's Pride, The Happy Housewife, Sun
Deck) New York: Dodd, 1952.
Mayorga, Margaret, ed. The Best Short Plays of 1952-
1953 (Innermost I Land, The Beams of Our House,
Dope, Tunnel of Love, A Trap Is a Small Place,
Arbie, the Bug Boy, The Youngest Shall Ask, Inci-
dent at a Grave, The Changeling, The Imploring Flame)
New York: Dodd, Mead, 1953.
Mayorga, Margaret, ed. The Best Short Plays of 1953-
1954 (The Little Flaw of Ernesto Lippi, Telling of
the North Star, John Turner Davis, A Remittance from
Spain, Salt for Savor, The Forgotten Land, A Word
in Your Ear, Another Summer, Karma, The Wishful
Taw) New York: Dodd, Mead, 1954.
Mayorga, Margaret, ed. The Best Short Plays of 1954-
1955 (The Conquerer, Song for a Hero, Brewsie and
Willie, Rouge Atomique, Half-Hour, Please, The
Return of Chandra, Next-to-Last Rites, The Island,
A Medal for Julien, A Cabin by the Lake) New York:
Dodd, Mead, 1955.
Mayorga, Margaret, ed. The Best Short Plays of 1955-
1956 (Once a Thief, This Music Crept by Me upon
the Waters, Something Unspoken, Five Days, The High
School, Hangs over Thy Head, Dino, Let There Be
Farce, Three People, Blue Concerto) New York:
Dodd, Mead, 1955.
Mayorga, Margaret, ed. The Best Short Plays, 20th Anni-
versary ed. (In the Zone, In Abraham's Bosom, The
Fall of the City, Devil Take a Whittler, The Man
with the Heart in the Highlands, The Miracle of the
Danube, Summer Fury, The Fisherman, The Soldier
Who Became a Great Dane, Frankie and Albert,
Through a Glass, Darkly, The Long Fall, Fortunata
Writes a Letter, The Triumph of the Egg, A Trap
Is a Small Place, Brewsie and Willie, 27 Wagons
Full of Cotton, The Stallion) Boston: Beacon Press,
1957.
Mayorga, Margaret G., ed. Representative One-Act Plays
by American Authors (Sam Average, Six Who Pass
While the Lentils Boil, Voices, Merry Merry Cuckoo,
Sintram of Skagerrak, Wil-o'-the-Wisp, Beyond, A
Good Woman, Funiculi Funicula, Hunger, In the Zone,

The Brink of Silence, Allison's Lad, Mrs. Pat and
the Law, Lima Beans, The Wonder Hat, Suppressed
Desires, Where but in America, A Question of Moral-
ity, Martha's Mourning, Ryland, The Last Straw,
Hattie, Dregs) Boston: Little, Brown, 1919.
Mayorga, Margaret, ed. Representative One-Act Plays by
American Authors, Rev. ed. (Sam Average, A Good
Woman, Pawns, The Merry Merry Cuckoo, Ryland,
The Clod, Will o' the Wisp, Six Who Pass While the
Lentils Boil, In the Zone, Suppressed Desires, The
Last Straw, The Wonder Hat, Tuning In, Sintram of
Skagerrak, The Robbery, Poor Aubrey, Good Vintage,
Unto Such Glory, Sparkin', Reckless, The Terrible
Meek, The Last Mile, Lawd, Does You Undastan'?,
Till the Day I Die, America, America) Boston: Little,
Brown, 1937.
McGraw, H. Ward, ed. Prose and Poetry of America
(Trifles, Moonshine) New York: L. W. Singer, 1934.
McGraw, H. Ward, ed. Prose and Poetry for Appreciation
(A Night at an Inn, The Rising of the Moon, The
Grand Cham's Diamond) New York: L. W. Singer,
1934.
McGraw, H. Ward, ed. Prose and Poetry of England (The
Lost Silk Hat) New York: L. W. Singer, 1934.
Miller, Helen Louise, ed. Gold Medal Plays for Holidays
(The Greedy Goblin, A School for Scaring, The Mystery
of Turkey-Lurkey, Strictly Puritan, Thanks to Butter-
fingers, Mr. Snow White's Thanksgiving, Mary's
Invitation, Turning the Tables, The Miraculous Tea
Party, The Forgotten Hero, Vicky Gets the Vote,
The Christmas Umbrella, Softy the Snowman, the Birds'
Christmas Carol, The Santa Claus Twins, The Christ-
mas Runaways, Santa Claus for President, Mystery
at Knob Creek Farm, Melody for Lincoln, The Tree
of Hearts, Crosspatch and Cupid, The Washington
Shilling, Dolly Saves the Day, Washington's Leading
Lady, Bunnies and Bonnets, The Bashful Bunny,
Mother's Fairy Godmother, The Magic Carpetsweeper,
Lacey's Last Garland, The Talking Flag) Boston:
Plays, 1958.
Miller, Helen Louise, ed. On Stage for Teen-Agers (Party
Line, Pin-Up Pals, What's Cooking?, Snoop's Scoop,
Cupid on the Loose, Homework, Band Aid, Doctor's
Daughter, Say It with Flowers, Papa Pepper's Bomb-
shell, Horrors, Incorporated, The Rummage Rumpus,
The Softhearted Ghost, Thanksgiving Beats the Dutch,
Angel Child, Home for Christmas, The Missing Link,

Miss Lonelyheart, The Washingtons Slept Here, Nothing
to Wear, A Surprise for Mother) Boston: Plays, 1948.
Millett, Fred Benjamin, ed. Reading Drama (The Will, A
Farewell Supper, Riders to the Sea, The Long Christ-
mas Dinner, Cathleen ni Houlihan) New York: Harper,
1950.
Millett, Fred Benjamin and Bentley, Gerald Eades, eds. The
Play's the Thing (Hyacinth Halvey, The Drums of
Oude) New York: Appleton-Century-Crofts, 1936.
Moses, Montrose Jonas, ed. Representative One-Act Plays
by Continental Authors (Countess Mizzie, Death and
the Fool, The Blind, The Birthday Party, The Woman
Who Was Acquitted, Five Little Dramas, Francoise's
Luck, Morituri: Theias, The Court Singer, Sacred
Ground, An Incident, A Merry Death, By Their Words
Ye Shall Know Them, The Lover, Simoom) Boston:
Little, Brown, 1922.
Nathan, George Jean, ed. Five Great Modern Irish Plays
(Spreading the News, Riders to the Sea) New York:
Modern Library, 1941.
Nelson, John Herbert and Cargill, Oscar, eds. Contemporary
Trends: American Literature since 1900, Rev. ed.
(Bound East for Cardiff) New York: Macmillan, 1949.
Nicholson, Kenyon, ed. The Appleton Book of Short Plays,
1st Series (The Managers, Finders-Keepers, Apart-
ments to Let, One Egg, The End of the Trail, George
Washington at Delaware, Society Notes, Social Balance,
The Wedding Dress, When the Clock Strikes, Pier-
rot's Mother, The Ghost Story) New York: Appleton-
Century-Crofts, 1926.
Nicholson, Kenyon, ed. The Appleton Book of Short Plays,
2nd Series (The Eldest, Post Mortems, Samson à
La Mode, The Warrior's Husband, Ambush, The Mel-
ancholy Dame, A Cup of Tea, Gas Air and Earl,
Appearances, 'Twas Ever Thus, Prince Gabby, De-
lilah) New York: Appleton-Century-Crofts, 1927.
Oboler, Arch and Longstreet, Stephan, eds. Free World
Theatre (The People March, Your Day Is Coming,
Rip Van Dinkel of Nuremberg, I Have No Prayer,
White House Kitchen, Music for Freedom, The Fountain
of Dancing Children, Night Flight, Fiesta, U.S.S.
Middletown, China to America, Last Will and Testa-
ment of Tom Smith, My Mothers Never Weep, Something About Joe, Man with a Beard, General Arm-
chair, The Second Battle of Warsaw, In Memory of
a Hero, V-Day) New York: Random House, 1944.
Oboler, Arch, ed. Ivory Tower and Other Radio Plays (Ivory

Tower, Alter Ego, The Ugliest Man in the World)
    New York: William Targ, 1940.
Oboler, Arch, ed. Plays for Americans (Letter at Midnight,
    Hate, Ghost Story, Chicago, Germany, Paul Reverski,
    Memo To Berchtesgaden, Adolph and Mrs. Runyon,
    Miracle in 3B, The Welburns-A Confidential Report,
    Blood Story, Execution, The Last in the World,
    Johnny Quinn, U.S.N.) New York: Rinehart, 1942.
O'Neill, Eugene, Gladstone, The Long Voyage Home: Seven
    Plays of the Sea (The Moon of the Caribbees, Bound
    East for Cardiff, The Long Voyage Home, In the
    Zone, Ile, The Rope, Where the Cross Is Made)
    New York: Random House, 1946.
Parker, Kenneth T., Parker's Television Plays (A Cup of
    Tea, Shall We Dance?, Voice of the Machines, Star
    Minded, Within the Family, Cry on My Shoulder,
    Stand Up to Death, Double Identity) Minneapolis:
    Northwestern Press, 1954.
Pence, Raymond Woodbury, ed. Dramas by Present-Day
    Writers (The Slave with Two Faces, Cophetua, Trifles,
    Spreading the News, The Goal, Thursday Evening,
    Ile, A Marriage Has Been Arranged, Confessional)
    New York: Charles Scribner's, 1927.
Rickaby, Franz, ed. Dakota Playmaker Plays, First Series
    (The Diabolical Circle, John Bargrave, Gentleman,
    Another Man's Place, Dowry and Romance) Boston:
    Walter H. Baker, 1923.
Rockwell, Ethel, ed. Wisconson Rural Plays (Goose Money,
    Dreams, King Row, Sons of the Soil, Short Cut)
    Chicago: Dramatic Publishing Co., 1931.
Rose, Reginald, ed. Six Television Plays (The Remarkable
    Incident at Carson Corners, Thunder at Sycamore
    Street, Twelve Angry Men, An Almanac of Liberty,
    Crime in the Streets, The Incredible World of Horace
    Ford) New York: Simon and Schuster, 1956.
Rowe, Kenneth Thorpe, University of Michigan Plays, Vol. I.
    (Outside This Room, Passion's Progress, My Man,
    The Joiners, Puppet) Ann Arbor, Michigan: George
    Wahr, 1929.
Rowe, Kenneth Thorpe, ed. University of Michigan Plays,
    Vol. II. (Lassitude, The Day's Work, Three-a-Day,
    Many Happy Returns, Wives-in-Law, They Too) Ann
    Arbor, Michigan: George Wahr, 1930.
Ryerson, Florence and Clements, Colin, eds. All on a
    Summer's Day and Six Other Short Plays (All on a
    Summer's Day, On the Lot, Men Folk, Storm,
    Letters, A Romantic Interval, Love Is Like That) New

York: Samuel French, 1928.
Saunders, Louise, ed. Magic Lanterns (Figureheads, Our
Kind, Poor Maddalena, See-Saw, King and Commoner)
New York: Charles Scribner's, 1923.
Shaw, Bernard Selected Plays, Vol. I. (The Man of Destiny)
New York: Dodd, Mead, 1948.
Shaw, Bernard, Selected Plays, Vol. III. (Fanny's First
Play, The Dark Lady of the Sonnets) New York:
Dodd, Mead, 1948.
Shay, Frank, ed. The Appleton Book of Christmas Plays
(Dust of the Road, The Littlest Shepherd, Christmas
Eve, A Christmas Tale, A Modern Viking, The Boy
on the Meadow, Exile, The Enchanted Christmas Tree,
The Duquesne Christmas Mystery, A Christmas Carol,
The Seven Gifts) New York: Appleton-Century-Crofts,
1929.
Shay, Frank, ed. The Appleton Book of Holiday Plays (The
Pie and the Tart, Lee the Virginian, Child of the
Frontier, Young Washington at Mt. Vernon, Two Blind
Men and a Donkey, Washington and Betsy Ross, Some
There Are Who Remember, For God and Spain, Two
Plum Puddings, Columbine Madonna) New York:
Appleton-Century-Crofts, 1930.
Shay, Frank and Loving, Pierre, eds. Fifty Contemporary
One-Act Plays (Madonna Dianora, Literature, The
Intruder, Interlude, Autumn Fires, M. Lamblin,
Françoise' Luck, Altruism, The Tenor, A Good Woman,
The Little Stone House, Mary's Wedding The Pierrot
of the Minute, The Subjection of Kezia, The Constant
Lover, The Judgment of Indra, The Workhouse Ward,
Louise, The Grandmother, The Rights of the Soul,
Love of One's Neighbor, The Boor, His Widow's
Husband, A Sunny Morning, The Creditor, Brothers,
In The Morgue, The Baby Carriage, A Death in
Fever Flat, The Slave With Two Faces, The Slump,
Mansions, Trifles, The Pot Boiler, Enter the Hero,
The Shepherd in the Distance, Boccaccio's Untold
Tale, Another Way Out, Aria da Capo, Helena's
Husband, The Shadowed Star, Ile, The Nursery Maid
of Heaven, Three Travellers Watch a Sunrise, Sham,
The Medicine Show, For All Time, The Finger of
God, Night, Forgotten Souls) New York: Appleton-
Century-Crofts, 1920.
Shay, Frank, ed. Fifty More Contemporary One-Act Plays
(Liars, Marthe, Faithful Admirer, A Morality Play
for the Leisured Class, Winter's Night, Death Says
It Isn't So, Orlando Furioso, The Duchess Says Her

Prayers, Across the Border, Mountain Laurel, A
Lady and the Law, The Weather Breeder, Whose
Money?, Winners All, Two Passengers for Chelsea,
The Home for the Friendly, Bumbo the Clown, The
Vanishing Princess, The Death of Nero, Quare Medicine,
Juliet and Romeo, Jack and Jill and a Friend, The
Demands of Society, Creeds, The Unruly Member, A
Lead-Year Bride, Pottery, The Liar and the Uni-
corn, The Eve in Evelyn, A Comedy of Danger, Blue
Blood, Don Juan's Christmas Eve, The Threshold,
The Avenue, The Razor, The Marriage of Little Eva,
The Birdcatcher, The Moon of the Caribbees, Wind o'
the Moors, Escape, Brothers, The Chip Woman's
Fortune, The Veil, Bumblepuppy, The Third Angel,
Moral Courage, The Giant's Stair, The Dance Below,
A Budapest Salesman Should Not Read French Illus-
trated Magazines, The Letters) New York: Appleton-
Century-Crofts, 1928.

Shay, Frank, ed. Plays for Strolling Mummers (Dancing
Dolls, Inside Stuff, Great Moments, The Flirtation,
All on a Summer's Day, My Tailor, A Course in
Piracy, Creatures of Impulse) New York: Appleton-
Century-Crofts, 1926.

Shay, Frank, ed. Treasury of Plays for Men (Four Who
Were Blind, The Devil's Gold, Blood o' Kings, It
Isn't Done, Outclassed, The Hand of Siva, Action!,
The Alchemist, The Silent Waiter, Vote the New
Moon, The Stick-Up, The Accomplice, The Judgment
of Indra, The Beggar and the King, Just Two Men,
Freedom, Release, The Rusty Door, The Gold Circle,
Three Wishes, In Front of Potter's) Boston: Little,
Brown, 1932.

Shay, Frank, ed. Treasury of Plays for Women (The Siege,
Columbine, The Lost Pleiad, The China Pig, A
Patroness, Ever Young, For Distinguished Service,
Rocking Chairs, Manikin and Minikin, The Death of
Tintagiles, The Conflict, The Lamp and the Bell,
Rehearsal, Before Breakfast, My Lady Dreams,
Blackberryin', The Stronger Woman, Motherly Love)
Boston: Little, Brown, 1922.

Shay, Frank, ed. Twenty Contemporary One-Act Plays,
American (Mirage, Napoleon's Barber, Goat Alley,
Sweet and Twenty, Tickless Time, The Hero of Santa
Maria, All Gummed Up, Thompson's Luck, Fata
Deorum, Pearl of Dawn, Finders-Keepers, Solomon's
Song, Matinata, The Conflict, Two Slatterns and a
King, Thursday Evening, The Dreamy Kid, Forbidden

Fruit, Jezebel, Sir David Wears a Crown) New York:
Appleton-Century-Crofts, 1922.
Shay, Frank, ed. Twenty-Five Short Plays, International
(The Accomplice, The Festival of Bacchus, Interior,
Chintamani, The Witness, Pyentsa, Brother in Arms,
The Thrice-Promised Bride, When Love Dies, Eyes
That Cannot See, Pan in Pimlico, Pierre Patelin,
Jubilee, The Bridegroom, The Marriage, A Snowy
Night, The Cherry-Blossom River, The Sentence of
Death, In Confidence, On the Highway, The Street
Singer, The Disenchanted, Poverty, Joe, The Shuna-
mite) New York: Appleton- Century-Crofts, 1925.
Smith, Alice M., ed. Short Plays by Representative Authors
(The Hraun Farm, The Merry Merry Cuckoo, The
Locked Chest, The Post Office, Six Who Pass While
the Lentils Boil, The Silver Lining, By Ourselves,
The Rider of Dreams, Spreading the News, The Swan
Song, The Man on the Kerb, The Shadowed Star)
New York: Macmillan, 1922.
Smith, Betty, ed. Twenty Prize-Winning Non-Royalty One-
Act Plays (According to Law, Western Night, Give
Us Time to Sing, Franklin and the King, To the
Lovely Margaret, These Doggone Elections, The Feast
of Ortolans, Comin' for to Carry, The Ring for
General Macias, Exclusive Model, Short-Tail Boy,
Mañana Bandits, Ring Once for Central, There's a
Nation, Fires at Valley Forge, Her Husband's Consent,
Danbury Fair, Casualty South of Manila, Pot Luck,
The Levite) New York: Greenberg, 1943.
Smith, Milton, ed. Short Plays of Various Types (The Dark
of the Dawn, The Maker of Dreams, A Night at an
Inn, The Brink of Silence, The Rising of the Moon,
The Silver Lining, The Turtle Dove, The Romancers,
Pyramus and Thisbe, A Comedie Royall, The Falcon,
Where but in America) Indianapolis: Bobbs-Merrill,
1924.
Smith, Robert M. Types of Farce Comedy Vol. II, World
Drama Series (The Man Who Married a Dumb Wife)
Englewood Cliffs, N. J.: Prentice-Hall, 1928.
Sutro, Alfred, ed. Five Little Plays (The Man in the Stalls,
A Marriage Has Been Arranged, The Man on the Kerb,
The Open Door, The Bracelet) Brentano's (Out of
Business), 1912.
Thomas, Charles Swain, ed. Atlantic Book of Junior Plays
(What Men Live By, Kinfolk of Robin Hood, Nerves,
The Violin-Maker of Cremona, The Dyspeptic Ogre,
The Fifteenth Candle, The Bellman of Mons, A

250   Marriage Proposal, Jeptha's Daughter, A Minuet, The
Play of St. George, The Birthday of the Infanta, the
Christmas Guest) Boston: Atlantic Monthly Press, 1924.

Thomas, Russell Brown, ed. Plays and the Theatre (Poor
Aubrey, Master Pierre Patelin, In the Zone, The Giant's
Stair) Boston: Little, Brown, 1937.

Tucker, S. Marion, ed. Modern American and British Plays
(The Field God, Granite, The Hero, The King's
Jewry) New York: Harper and Brothers, 1931.

Tucker, S. Marion, ed. Twelve One-Act Plays for Study and
Production (The Trysting Place, A Night at an Inn,
Thursday Evening, Confessional, The Hundredth Trick,
The Aulis Difficulty, A Minuet, Where the Cross Is
Made, The Workhouse Ward, Moonshine, Back of the
Yards, The Grand Cham's Diamond) Boston: Ginn,
1929.

Tucker, S. Marion and Downer, Alan S., eds. Twenty-Five
Modern Plays, Rev. Ed. (Riders to the Sea) New
York: Harper and Brothers, 1948.

Vidal, Gore, ed. Best Television Plays (The Mother, Thun-
der on Sycamore Street, Man in the Mountaintop, A
Young Lady of Property, The Strike, The Rabbit Trap,
Visit to a Small Planet) New York: Ballantine, 1956.

Walker, Stuart, ed. Portmanteau Adaptations (The Birthday
of the Infanta, Sir David Wears a Crown, Nellijumbo)
New York: Appleton-Century-Crofts, 1921.

Walker, Stuart, ed. Portmanteau Plays (The Trimplet,
Nevertheless, The Medicine Show, Six Who Pass
While the Lentils Boil) New York: Appleton-Century-
Crofts, 1917.

Watson, Ernest Bradlee, and Pressey, Benfield, Contemporary
Drama, Vol. II, English and Irish Plays (Riders to
the Sea, Hyacinth Halvey, The Glittering Gate) New
York: Charles Scribner's, 1931.

Watson, Ernest Bradlee and Pressey, Benfield, editors, Con-
temporary Drama: European, English and Irish (The
Glittering Gate, Hyacinth Halvey, Riders to the Sea)
New York: Charles Scribner's, 1941.

Watson, Ernest Bradlee and Pressey, Benfield, eds. Contemporary Drama: Eleven Plays (The Happy Journey
to Trenton and Camden, Ways and Means, Hello Out
There) New York: Charles Scribner's, 1956.

Watt, Homer Andrew and Cargill, Oscar, eds. College
Reader (Radio Primer, Spreading the News) Englewood Cliffs, N.J.: Prentice-Hall, 1948.

Watt, Homer Andrew and Munn, James Buell, eds. Ideas
and Forms in English and American Literature, Vol.
II. (Hyacinth Halvey, Riders to the Sea, The Land
of Heart's Desire) Chicago: Scott, Foresman, 1932.

Weatherly, Edward Howell, Moffett, Harold Y., Prouty,
    Charles T., and Noyes, Henry H., eds. The English
    Heritage, Vol. II. (The Twelve-Pound Look, Riders
    to the Sea) Boston: Ginn, 1945.
Webber, J. P., and Webster, H. H., eds. One-Act Plays
    for Secondary Schools (Boy Comes Home, Followers,
    Sunny Morning, Falcon, Coming of Fair Annie, Ro-
    mancers, Lord's Prayer, Cottage on the Moor, Solemn
    Pride, X=O: A Night of the Trojan War, Rising of the
    Moon, Nevertheless, Manikin and Minikin, Beau of
    Bath, Unseen Host, Shoes That Danced, Columbine)
    Boston: Houghton, Mifflin, 1923.
Webber, J. P., and Webster H. H., eds. Short Plays for
    Junior and Senior High Schools (Prince of Stamboul,
    Toy Shop, Stolen Prince, End of the Rainbow, Prin-
    cess on the Road, "Good Night Babette", To Dust
    Returning, Travelling Man, Shuttin' o' the Door,
    Wraggle-Taggle Gypsies, Pyramus and Thisbe, Miss
    Burney at Court, John Silver Off Duty, Little Boy
    Out of the Wood, Legend of St. Dorothy, In the Good
    Green Wood, Lion's Whelp, Benjamin Franklin:
    Journeyman, Boston Tea Party, Little King) Boston:
    Houghton, Mifflin, 1925.
Webber, J. P., and Webster, H. H., eds, Typical Plays
    for Secondary Schools (The Rehearsal, A Mistake at
    the Manor, The Prince of Court Painters, Frances
    and Francis, Augustus in Search of a Father, Pharaoh's
    Daughter, The Thrice-Promised Bride, The Copper
    Pot, Sweethearts, The Gibson Upright, The Dragon)
    Boston: Houghton, Mifflin, 1929.
Weiser, Norman S., ed. The Writer's Radio Theatre (We
    Hold These Truths, Stronghold of the Buccaneers,
    Millions for Defense, The Welburns-Confidential
    Report, Native Land, The Precious Freedom, Welcome
    to Glory, Thanks to Mr. Shakespeare, Splash of
    Water, The Hollywood Doctor) New York: Harper,
    1941.
Whitman, Charles Huntington, ed. Representative Modern
    Dramas (Riders to the Sea) Boston: Houghton, Mifflin,
    1936.
Whitman, Charles Huntington, ed. Seven Contemporary Plays
    (Riders to the Sea) Boston: Houghton, Mifflin, 1931.
Wilder, Thornton, The Angel That Troubled the Waters and
    Other Plays (Nascunter Poetae, Proserpina and the
    Devil, Fanny Otcott, Brother Fire, The Penny That
    Beauty Spent, The Angel on the Ship, The Message
    and the Jehanne, Childe Roland to the Dark Tower

Came, Centaurs, Leviathan, And the Sea Shall Give
up Its Dead, Now the Servant's Name Was Malchus,
Mozart and the Gray Stewart, Has Thou Considered
My Servant Job?, The Flight into Egypt, The Angel
That Troubled the Waters) New York: Coward-
McCann, 1928.
Wilder, Thornton, The Long Christmas Dinner and Other
Plays in One Act (The Long Christmas Dinner, Queens
of France, Pullman Car Hiawatha, Love, and How
to Cure It, Such Things Only Happen in Books, The
Happy Journey to Trenton and Camden) New York:
Coward-McCann, 1931.
Williams, Tennessee, American Blues (Moony's Kid Don't
Cry, The Dark Room The Case of the Crushed
Petunias, The Long Stay Cut Short; or, the Unsatis-
factory Supper, Ten Blocks on the Camino Real) New
York: Dramatists Play Service, 1948.
Williams, Tennessee, Twenty-Seven Wagons Full of Cotton,
and Other One-Act Plays (This Property Is Condemned,
The Purification, The Last of My Solid Gold Watches,
Auto-da-Fé, The Strangest Kind of Romance, 27
Wagons Full of Cotton, The Lady of Larkspur Lotion,
Hello from Bertha, Portrait of a Madonna, Lord
Byron's Love Letters, The Long Goodbye, Something
Unspoken, Talk To Me Like the Rain, and Let Me
Listen) New York: New Directions, 1953.
Wishengrad, Morton, ed. The Eternal Light (The Tender
Grass, Moses Mendelssohn, The Battle of the Warsaw
Ghetto, The Parable of Reb Yisrael, Thomas Kennedy,
A Pity for the Living, A Sound of Music, A Rhode
Island Refuge, Schecter, The Black Death, The Micro-
scope and the Prayer Shawl, They Knocked the Devil
out of Uncle Ezra, Hunger, A Chassidic Tale, A
Second Exodus, The Death of Akiba, The Day of the
Shadow, The Broken Sabbath of Rabbi Asher Brandeis,
My Father's Talis, The Ransom of Rabbi Moir, My
Cousin Aveigdor, Rabbi Israel Salenter, My Favorite
Assassin, For a Suit of New Clothes, The Lantern
in the Inferno) New York: Crown, 1947.
Wylie, Max, ed. Best Broadcasts of 1938-1939 (Surprise for
the Boys, A Trip to Czardis, Blood of the Martyrs,
The Lighthouse Keepers, The Story of John Milton,
The Nuremberg Stove, New Horizons, Alice in Wonder-
land, The Twilight Shore, Peter Stuyvesant, The Eddie
Doll Case, The Steel Worker, Expert Opinion, Sand-
hogs, No Help Wanted, We Become a Nation, Seems
Radio Is Here to Stay, Air Raid, The Trojan Women)

New York: Whittlesey House, 1939.
Wylie, Max, ed. Best Broadcasts of 1939-1940 My Client
Curley, In the Fog, The Dark Valley, For-Richer-
For-Richer, This Lonely Heart, The Clinic) New
York: Whittesey House, 1940.
Wylie, Max Best Broadcasts of 1940-1941 (We Hold These
Truths, An American Crusader, Maudie's Dairy,
Honest Abe, Roadside, And Six Came Back, The Lit-
tle Wife, Elementals) New York: Whittesey House,
1941.
Yeats, William Butler Plays in Prose and Verse (Cathleen
ni Houlihan, The Pot of Broth, The Hour-Glass)
New York: Macmillan, 1922.
Zachar, Irwin J., and Kimball, Rodney A., eds. Plays As
Experience (Three's a Crowd, A Night at an Inn,
The Boor, The Last of the Lowries, Spreading the
News, Western Night, Bread, The Fifteenth Candle,
The Devil and Daniel Webster, The Valiant, Haven of
the Spirit, We'd Never Be Happy Otherwise, Pawns,
Suffer Little Children) New York: The Odyssey Press,
1944.

All American University One-Act Plays (Barbara Celebrates,
The Easy Way, The Family, A Half Hour Reforma-
tion, The Higher Command, If Lacking Only Truth,
LeDonne, Lita's Man, Puppets, The Scientist, Two
Pairs of Spectacles) Franklin, Ohio: Eldridge, 1931.
Book of Make-Believe, The (Told in a Chinese Garden, Robin
Hood in Sherwood, The Romancers, The Finger of
God, The Farce of the Worthy Master Pierre Patelin,
Dust of the Road, The Thrice-Promised Bride, The
Man Who Married a Dumb Wife, The White Hawk,
The Lost Silk Hat, Sham, The Boor, The God of
Quiet) Boston: Allyn and Bacon, 1932.

Eleven Short Biblical Plays (Betrayal, Cleopas, The Door,
Elisha, For His Name's Sake, The Friend of Poti-
phar's Wife, The Gift of Jehova, The Light Upon the
Way, Maunday Thursday, The Third Shepherd's Play,
The Woman from Nod) New York and Canada: Long-
mans, Green, 1929.
New Plays for Women and Girls (O Bright Flame Lifted,
For the Love of Michael, The First White Woman,
Green Eyes from Romany, I Know George Washington,
The Night-Club Girl, Mrs. Leicester's School, Up-
lifting Sadie, One of Those Days, Lady Luck, Let It
Burn, I'm Not Complaining, The Wish Shop, Lavender

and Red Pepper, The Clouds) New York: Samuel
French, 1932.
One-Act Plays for Stage and Study, 1st Series (The Man Up-
stairs, The Mayor and the Manicure, The Red Owl,
The Rector, A Flower of Yeddo, Deceivers, The Girl,
Peace Manoeuvers, Moonshine, The Dying Wife, The
Little Father of the Wilderness, The Robbery, Such
a Charming Young Man, Judge Lynch, The Widow of
Wasdale Head, Dolly's Little Bills, The Man in the
Bowler Hat, Lonesome-Like, Hanging and Wiving,
'Op-o-Me-Thumb, Phipps, Spreading the News, A
Minuet, The Ghost of Jerry Bundler, Wealth and
Wisdom) New York: Samuel French, 1924.
One-Act Plays for Stage and Study, 2nd Series (The Drums
of Oude, Young America, The Prarie Doll, The Pas-
sing of Chow-Chow, The Dickey Bird, Meet the Missus,
The Same Old Thing, Red Carnations, Saved, The Man
Who Died at Twelve O'Clock, Among Thieves, A
Question of Principle, And There Was Light, The
Corsican Lieutenant, On the Race Course, The Black
Bottle, The Knife, Claude, The Idealist, At the Tele-
phone, The Host) New York: Samuel French, 1925.
One-Act Plays for Stage and Study, 3rd Series (One of Those
Things, Napoleon Crossing the Rockies, Jane, Jean
and John, Knives from Syria, The Kite, The Eligible
Mr. Bangs, The Londonderry Air, Changing Places,
The Sundial, Youth Must Be Served, Papers, The
Voice of the Snake, Unto Such Glory, Mary Means
What She Says, Dave, The Cobbler's Den, Cupid in
Clapham, When Did They Meet Again?, Duetto, The
Weathervane Elopes, The Betrayal) New York: Samuel
French, 1927.
One-Act Plays for Stage and Study, 4th Series (Blue Thunder,
Reckless, So's Your Old Antique, In-Laws, The
Miracle of St. Martin, The Snake-Eater, The Fourth
Mrs. Phillips, The Wily One, The Witch's Daughter,
Cobweb Kings, Fortinbras in Plain Clothes, Three
Players, a Fop and a Duchess, Invitation, A Wedding,
Lenna Looks Down, A Tune of a Tune, Brother Bill,
Things Is That-a-Way, The Pipe in the Fields, Christ-
mas Eve, Cured, Love in a French Kitchen) New York:
Samuel French, 1928.
One-Act Plays for Stage and Study, 5th Series (A Diadem of
Snow, The Late Captain Crow, It's an Ill Wind, The
Stoker, The Wedding Rehearsal, No More Americans,
Art and Mrs. Palmer, Rescue, Black Oliver, Mrs.
Adis, The Widdy's Mite, Angelus, Limping Along,

Babouscka, Hot Lemonade, Jumpin' the Broom, The
Man with the Iron Jaw, The Haunted Coal Mine, Mai-
zie, Balm, Words and Music) New York: Samuel
French, 1930.
One-Act Plays for Stage and Study, 6th Series. (The Still
Alarm, Speaking Terms, Murder! Murder! Murder!,
The Moving Finger, Men, Women and Goats, Colman
and Guaire, The Willow Plate, The Woman Who Under-
stood Men, Poetry and Plaster, The Bad Penny, The
Lost Princess, The Chinese Water Wheel, The Ghosts
of Windsor Park, Traffic Signals, Babbitt's Boy,
Josephine, St. Cyprian and the Devil, The Wolf at
the Door, The Pie and the Tart, A Change of Mind,
The Snake Charmer) New York: Samuel French, 1931.
One-Act Plays for Stage and Study, 7th Series (Boy-Chinnen,
Are Men Superior?, Chatterton, Counsel's Opinion,
The Way Out, Laid Off, Grandma-Old Style, Smoke-
Screens, Some Words in Edgewise, On the Portsmouth
Road, Family, The March Heir, Funny Business,
The Tea-Pot on the Rocks, Accidents Will Happen,
Here Are Sailors, The Good and Obedient Young Man,
Knock Three Times, The Last Refuge, Moses Was
an Oyster-Man, As the Tumbrils Pass) New York:
Samuel French, 1932.
Twelve One-Act Plays (The Valiant, Romance of the Willow
Pattern, The Grill, The Last Straw, Thank You
Doctor, Copy, The Trap, Good Medicine, God Winks,
A Woman of Character, Jazz and Minuet, The Most
Foolish Virgin) New York: Longmans, Green, 1926.

Index

Abbott, George: 225
Abou Ben Adhem: 38
Abraham Lincoln: 62, 89
Action: 209
Action, plotting of: 25
Act One: 217
Adams, Henry Hitch: 131
Addison: 8
Adelman, Irving: 128
Admirable Crichton, The: 89
Adventures in American
    Literature: 234
Adventures in Modern Litera-
    ture: 232
Adventures in Reading: 161
Advise and Consent: 114
After Dark: 122
Agate, James: 111, 131
Age of Innocence, The: 113
Ahearne, Brian: 146
Alarums and Excursions: 131
Albright, Evelyn May: 221
Alcestis: 8
Aldrich, Thomas Bailey: 39
All American University One-
    Act Plays: 253
Allen, John: 112
Allen, Ralph G. : 162
"Allison's Lad": 50
All on a Summer's Day and
    Six Other Short Plays: 246
Amateur and Educational
    Dramatics: 152
Amateur Theatre Handbook,
    The: 152
Amazing Mr. Noel Coward,
    The: 224
American Blues: 252
American Drama: 223

American Drama Criticism:
    129
American Drama Since 1918,
    The: 223
American Drama Since World
    War II: 223
American Dramatist: 225
American Musical Stage Before
    1800, The: 224
American Plays: 234
American Plays and Play-
    wrights of the Contempo-
    rary Theatre: 223
American Playwrights: 223
American Playwrights of To-
    day: 225
American Scene, The: 229
American Stage of Today, The
    130
American Theatre and the Mo-
    tion Picture in America,
    The: 222
Anatomy of Drama, The: 112
Ancient Mariner, The: 109
Anderson, John: 222
Anderson, Judith: 113
Anderson, Maxwell: 127, 129,
    207, 208
Andrews, Charlton: 211, 218,
    220
Angel That Troubled the Waters
    and Other Plays, The: 251
Angel That Troubled the Waters,
    The: 134, 151, 213
Anna Christie: 134
Anna Karenina: 114
Annals of English Drama: 222
Anoulh, Jean: 114
An Outline of Contemporary
    Drama: 220

Ansorge, Elizabeth: 227
Antigone: 8
Appleton Book of Christmas
 Plays, The: 247
Appleton Book of Holiday
 Plays, The: 247
Appleton Book of Short Plays,
 The: 245
Appreciation of the Drama,
 The: 161
Archer, Frank: 211, 218
Archer, William: 211, 217,
 218
Arden Gazette: 68
Arena, An Adventure in the
 American Theatre: 224
Aristophanes: 126
Aristotle: 121, 123
Aristotle's Theory of Poetry
 and Fine Art: 121
Arliss, George: 89
Arnold, Matthew: 30, 123
Around Theatres: 131
Artist's Life: 225
Art of Judging a Play, The:
 111
Art of Playwriting, The: 211,
 218
Art of the Drama, The: 161
Art of Playgoing, The: 112,
 123
Art of Play Production, The:
 152
Art of the Play, The: 161,
 212
Art of Theatre-Going, The:
 112
Art Theatre, The: 223
Aspects of the Modern Drama:
 220
As They Appear: 130
As You like It: 8, 15, 20, 24,
 33, 37, 68, 76, 149
Atkinson, Brooks: 129
Atlantic Book of Junior Plays,
 The: 54, 249
Atlantic Book of Modern Plays,
 The: 43, 54, 133

Atlantic Book of Monthly Plays,
 The: 239
Audio-visual aids: 61, 69
Aurthur, Robert Alan: 102
Authorship of Shakespeare,
 The: 227
Axelrod, Donald: 238

Bablet, Denis: 226
Bach: 110
Baker, Franklin T.: 12, 14,
 15, 16, 20, 24, 33, 37, 73,
 214
Baker, George Pierce: 210,
 211, 217, 218, 227
Barber, Philip: 152
Barnes, Grace: 152
Barnes, John R.: 227
Barnouw, Erik: 227
Barrett, Elizabeth: 146
Barretts of Wimpole Street,
 The: 146
Barrie, James Matthew (editor)
 228
Barrie, Sir James M. (play-
 wright): 68, 89, 114, 217
Barrows, Marjorie Wescott:
 54
Barrymore: 153
Barrymore, Ethel: 225
Bates, Katharine Lee: 162
Beaty, John O.: 234
Beerbohm, Max: 152
Beethoven: 147, 150
Before Breakfast: 216
Behrman, S. N.: 114, 128, 224
Beiser, Rudolf: 146
Ben-Hur: 108
Bennett, Arnold: 62
Bentley, Eric: 116, 129
Bentley, Gerald Eades: 161,
 245
Bernard Shaw: 225
Bernhardt, Sarah: 127
Bernstein, Leonard: 150
Best Broadcasts of 1938-1939:
 252
Best Broadcasts of 1939-1940:
 253

Best Broadcasts of 1940-1941: 253
Best One-Act Plays: 115, 134
Best One-Act Plays of 1931, The: 240
Best One-Act Plays of 1937: 241
Best One-Act Plays of 1938: 241
Best One-Act Plays of 1939: 241
Best One-Act Plays of 1940: 241
Best One-Act Plays of 1941, The: 241
Best One-Act Plays of 1942, The: 242
Best One-Act Plays of 1943, The: 242
Best One-Act Plays of 1944, The: 242
Best One-Act Plays of 1945, The: 242
Best One-Act Plays of 1946-1947, The: 242
Best One-Act Plays of 1947-1948, The: 242
Best One-Act Plays of 1949-1950, The: 242
Best One-Act Plays of 1951-1952, The: 243
Best Plays of 1909-1919, The: 114
Best Short Plays, The: 243
Best Short Plays of 1952-19-53, The: 243
Best Short Plays of 1953-1954, The: 243
Best Short Plays of 1954-1955, The: 243
Best Short Plays of 1955-1956, The: 243
Best Short Plays of the Social Theatre, The: 236
Best Television Plays: 250
Better Reading, Volume 2: 228
Beulah, Marie Dix: 50
Bewitched: 209

Beyond the Horizon: 134
Bibliographical Guide to the Study of the Literature of the U.S.A.: 117
Bibliography of the American Theatre: 129
Billy Budd: 114

Blair, Walter: 228
Blaisdell, Thomas C.: 72-74, 78, 81
Blake, Betty: 117
Blakely, Gilbert Sykes: 19, 24, 33; method of teaching drama, 15, 16.
Blank verse, relation to drama: 61
Blossom Time: 125
Blue Bird, The: 62, 89
Blum, Daniel: 116-119
Boardman, George Nye: 226
Boas, Frederick S.: 226
Bolenius, Emma Miller: 34-40, 43, 60
Bonanza: 108
Bonneviere, Arnaud: 152
Bonnie and Clyde: 146
Book of Dramas, A: 228
Book of Make-Believe, The: 253
Book of Modern Plays, A: 229
Book of Original Plays and How to Give Them, The: 152
Book of the Play, A: 131
Boucicault, Dion: 122
Bowman, Mary Rives: 161
Box Office: 129
Boyd, Ernest A.: 224
Boyd, James: 228
Brady, William A.: 225
Brains and Other One-Act Plays: 232
Brandt and Brandt: 103
Braybrooke, Patrick: 224
Braymer, Marjorie: 161
Breakfast at Tiffany's: 114
Brewster, Eugene V.: 111

259

Brewster, William T. : 23-25
Bridge of San Luis Rey, The: 213
Bridges-Adams, W. : 221
Brief Chronicles: 129
British and American Plays: 231
British Broadcasting Company: 122
British Theatre, The: 221
Broadway in Review: 130
Broadway Scrapbook: 129
Bro, Marguerite: 112
Brough, James: 226
Broun, Heywood: 129
Broussard, Louis: 223
Brown, Ben W. : 220
Browne, Fanny: 120
Browning, Elizabeth Barrett
   See Barrett, Elizabeth
Brown, Ivor: 226
Brown, John Mason: 112, 116, 123, 129, 130, 225, 226
Brown, Leonard Stanley: 228
Brunetiere, Ferdinand: 144, 151
Brustein, Robert: 123, 220
Burke, Edmund: 66
Burton, Richard (actor): 113
Burton, Richard (writer): 112, 222, 223
Burning of Rome: 208
Butcher, S. H.: 121
But Is It Art?: 130

Caffin, Charles H. : 161
Candida: 113
Candide: 114
Canfield, Curtis: 228
Cannan, Gilbert: 112
Cargill, Oscar: 245, 250
Carmer, Carl: 216
Carol Burnett Show: 208
Carolina Folk Comedies: 236
Carolina Folk Plays: 236
Carpenter, Bruce: 228
Carter, Jean: 223
Cartmell, Van H.: 117, 152

Cartwell, Van H. : 228
Case of American Drama, The: 223
Cassidy, Frederic G. : 228
Castelvetro: 121
Cat on a Hot Tin Roof: 114
Cato: 8, 9
Cerf, Bennett: 228
Cervantes: 121
Chagell, Marc: 147
Chambers, R. K.: 221
Chandler, Robert Wadleigh: 220
Changing Drama, The: 220
Chantecleer: 89
Chaplin, Charlie: 208
Character, how to study: 31
Charley's Aunt: 208
Chayevsky, Paddy: 102, 134, 228
Chekhov, Anton: 114
Chekhov, Michael: 152
Cheney, Sheldon: 112, 220, 223
Cherry Orchard, The: 113
Chesterton, G. K.: 225
Chief Contemporary Dramatists: 231
Chinoy, Helen Krich: 152
Choosing a Play: 118
Christmas Carol: 64
Chubb, Percival: 9, 11, 21-23, 26, 30, 34, 40, 64, 68, 72
Churchhill, Winston: 27
Church, Virginia: 54, 229
Clark, Barrett H.: 54, 121, 151, 152, 162, 220, 222, 225, 229
Clark, Donald Leman: 239
Classic, assignments in a: 63
Classics of the Silent Screen: 116, 119
Clements, Colin Campbell: 229, 246
Clurman, Harold: 116, 223
Cochran, Charles B.: 226

260

Coffman, George R.: 229
Cohen, Helen Louise: 43-49,
  54, 56, 103, 133, 229, 230
Cole, Toby: 152
Coleridge: 109, 123, 127, 143
College Reader: 250
Commedia dell' arte: 136
Common Sense About Drama:
  112
Complete Book of the American
  Musical Theatre, Revised:
  224
Comus: 15, 23, 24, 56
Conkle, E. P.: 135, 230
Collis, J. S.: 225
Comedy and Conscience After
  the Restoration: 222
Commonwealth and Restoration
  Stage, The: 222
Connelly, Marc: 126
Contemporary American Play-
  wrights: 225
Contemporary Drama: Eleven
  Plays: 250
Contemporary Drama, English
  and Irish Plays: 250
Contemporary Drama: Euro-
  pean, English and Irish:
  250
Contemporary Drama of
  England, The: 221
Contemporary Drama of Ire-
  land, The: 224
Contemporary One-Act Plays:
  53, 239
Contemporary Theatre, The:
  221
Contemporary Trends: Ameri-
  can Literature since 1900:
  245
Conversations on Contemporary
  Drama: 220
Cook, George Cram: 230
Cook, Thomas R.: 54, 229
Cooper, Alice Cecilia: 234
Cooper, Charles W.: 161, 230
Corneille: 122
Cornell, Katherine: 89, 113,
  146

Corson, Hiram: 14
Corwin, Norman: 102, 230
Craftsmanship of the One-Act
  Play, The: 212, 219
Country Wife, The: 122
Coward, Noel: 114, 128, 134,
  149
Cowl, Jane: 89
Crafton, Allen: 152
Craig, Virginia J.: 74, 76, 77,
  85, 89
Crane, George J.: 104
Crick Bottom Plays: 230
Curtain: 54
Curtain!: 229
Curtain Falls: 226
Cyrano de Bergerac: 113

Dakin, Dorothy: 90-93
Dakota Playmaker Plays: 246
Daniello: 121
Dante: 121
Dark Comedy, The: 221
Darling of Misfortune: 225
Darlington, W. A.: 131
Davenport, William H.: 231
Daviot, Gordon: 207
Davis, Owen: 225
Days with Bernard Shaw: 225
Decker, Richard G.: 54
Decline of Pleasure, The: 130
Dekker, Thomas: 122
Delaney, Shelagh: 114
De La Taille: 121
Dent, Alan: 131
Dent, Edward J.: 222
Deutsch, Helen: 224
Dickens: 64, 108, 126
Dickinson, Thomas H.: 56,
  220, 223-225, 231
Digest of 500 Plays, A: 117
Digests of Great American
  Plays: 117
Directing the Play: 152
Directions in Modern Theatre
  and Drama: 220
Discovering Drama: 161
Dix, Beulah Marie: 217

Dobbs, John W.: 231
Doll's House, A: 125
Dolman, John, Jr.: 152, 209
Donatus: 121
Downer, Alan S.: 223, 250
Downs, Harold: 112
Drama: 47
Drama and Commitment: 223
Drama, how an English teacher
  should prepare to teach, 89;
  teaching in the 1930's, 72;
  teaching modern, 56; the
  technique of, 35.
Drama in Education: 152
Drama in English: 222
Drama: Its Law and Its Tech-
  nique, The: 25, 162
Drama of Today, The: 220
Drama of Yesterday and Today,
  The: 132
Drama I.: 54
Dramas by Present-Day Writ-
  ers: 246
Dramatic Essays: 131
Dramatic Essays of the Neo-
  classic Age: 131
Dramatic Event, The: 129
Dramatic Experience, The: 162
Dramatic Heritage: 130
Dramatic Opinions and Essays:
  151
Dramatic Opinions and Essays
  With out Apology: 132
Dramatic Presentation of
  scenes: 30, 76, 91
Dramatic Publication in
  England: 221
Dramatic Soundings: 130
Dramatics, outcomes of prop-
  erly directed work in,
  67
Dramatic Technique: 210, 211,
  217, 218
Dramatic Theory, A Bibliogra-
  phy: 117
Dramatic Values: 132
Dramatic, what is: 143

Dramatic Year, 1887-1888,
  The: 131
Dramatis Personae: 129
Dramatists of Today: 220
Drama Was a Weapon: 223
Drew, Elizabeth: 161
Drinkwater, John: 62, 89, 112
Drums of Oude, The: 110
Drury, F. K.: 117
Drury's Guide to Best Plays:
  117
Dryden, John: 131
Dumble, Wilson Randle: 234
Dunn, Esther Cloudman: 226
Dunsany, Lord: 50, 136, 209,
  213, 216, 231
Durham, Willard Higley: 231
Dutton, Cook: 131, 132
Dworkin, Rita: 128
Dyson, Anne Jane: 129
Early Stages: 226
Eaton, Walter Prichard: 130,
  222, 224, 231
Edades, Jean: 231
Edward Gordon Craig: 226
Edward Gordon Craig Designs
  for the Theatre: 227
El Cid: 114
Electra: 114
Elements of Drama, The: 112
Eleven Short Biblical Plays:
  253
Eliot, Samuel A. Jr.: 231
Eliot, T. S.: 127
Elizabethan Drama: 222
Elizabethan Stage, The: 221
Elizabeth the Queen: 113, 128
Elmer Gantry: 114
Enchanted Aisles: 131
Enemy of the People, An: 125
English Chronicle Play, The:
  162
English Comedy: 162
English Drama, The: 222
English Heritage, The: 251
English Pastoral Drama: 162

262

English Religious Drama, The: 162

Enjoying Music: 107

Enjoyment of Drama, The: 161

Enters, Agna: 225

Ervine, St. John: 212, 218

Essays of Today and Yesterday: 131

Essential Principles of Teaching Reading and Literature: 63

Eternal Light, The: 252

Etudes Critiques: 151

Euripides: 8

European Dramatists: 221

European Theories of the Drama: 121, 151, 162

Evans, Maurice: 113

Events Leading Up to the Comedy: 226

Everyman: 128, 135

Everyman's Drama: 223

Evreinoff, Nicholas: 161

Ewen, David: 224

Far Country, A: 27

Faust: 20

"Feathertop": 64

Federal Theatre, The: 224

Federal Theatre, 1935-1939, The: 151

Feigenbaum, Lawrence: 231

Ferber, Edna: 121, 126, 128

Fervent Years, The: 223

15 American One-Act Plays: 54

Fifth Symphony: 147

Fifty Contemporary One-Act Plays: 247

Fifty More Contemporary One-Act Plays: 247

50 Years of American Comedy: 221

Fifty Years of American Drama: 223

Film Reports: 114

Finch, Robert: 232

Five Little Plays: 249

Five Plays: 231

Flanagan, Hallie: 224

Flattering Word, and Other One-Act Plays, The: 235

Flavin, Martin: 232

Flexner, Eleanor: 223

Foerster, Norman: 234

Fontanne, Lynn: 113

Foote, Horton: 232

Footlights and Highlights: 225

Foot-music: 107, 108

Forbes-Robertson, Sir Johnston: 226

Form and Idea in Modern Theatre: 220

Forty-Five Minutes Past Eight: 130

Fosdick, Carolyn F.: 231

Four P's, The: 136

France, Anatole: 123

Franklin, Joe: 116, 119

Free Company Presents, The: 228

Freedley, George: 112, 220

Free World Theatre: 245

Freier, Robert: 232

French, Samuel: 103

Freud on Broadway: 223

Freytag, Gustav: 25, 31, 60, 82, 144, 151, 161, 211

Fries, Charles Carpenter: 65, 66

From Shylock to Svengali: 224

From Native Roots: 224

Fry, Christopher: 127

Fugitive Art Dramatic Commentaries, The: 132

Fuller, Edward: 131

Furness, Horace Howard: 58

Furness Variorum Edition: 80, 86

Future of the Theatre, The: 221

263

Gagey, Edmond M.: 223
Gaige, Crosby: 225
Galbraith, Ester R.: 232
Galsworthy, John: 62, 114,
    153, 158, 216, 218, 232
Gannon, Robert I.: 211, 218
Gardner, Horace J.: 152
Gassner, John: 54, 112, 114,
    116, 130, 152, 162, 220,
    232, 240
Gehlman, John Bowman: 234
George. An Early Autobiogra-
    phy: 225
George Bernard Shaw: 225
Gerber, John C.: 228
Gerstenberg, Alice: 216, 232
Gibbs, Wolcott: 130
Gielgud, John: 226
Gift of Joy, A: 225
Gilbert and Sullivan: 124
Glamour - Essays on The Art
    of the Theatre: 131
Glaspell, Susan: 143, 217
Glittering Gate: 216
Goethe: 20, 127
Gohdes, Clarence: 117
Goldberg, Isaac: 232
"Golden Doom, The": 50
Golden, John: 226
Goldman, Emma: 220
Gold Medal Plays for Holidays:
    244
Goldsmith, Oliver: 20, 37, 38,
    43, 56, 122
Goldstone, George A.: 54,
    232
Goodman, Kenneth Sawyer: 233
Good Reading for High Schools:
    80
Good-Natured Man: 20, 59
Gorboduc: 20
Gordon, Dudley: 233
Gorelik, Mordecai: 220
Gounod: 69
Granville-Barker, Harley: 161
Great Stars of the American
    Stage: 119

Greenlaw, Edwin: 66
Green, Paul: 47, 130, 135,
    217, 233
Green, Stanley: 224
Green Pastures, The: 126
Gregory, Lady: 50, 216, 233
Grein, J. T.: 132
Griffith, Francis J.: 54, 233
Grillparzer: 127
Guide to American Literature
    and Its Backgrounds Since
    1890: 117
Guide to Critical Reviews, A:
    128
Guide to Great Plays: 118
Guide to Play Selection: 118
Guide to Theatre Reading, A:
    117
Gunsmoke: 108
Guterman, Norbert: 129

Hale, Bryant: 116, 119
Hale, Edward Everett, Jr.:
    220
Hall: 151
Halline, Alan Gates: 234
Halman, Doris F.: 50
Hamilton: 212
Hamilton, Clayton: 130, 137,
    142, 151, 211, 218, 220
Hamlet: 20, 23, 37, 62, 73,
    91-93, 110, 113, 124, 135,
    207
Hammond, Percy: 130
Hampden, John: 234
Hanan, Stella: 224
Hanford, James Holly: 65
Hanson, Charles L.: 23, 24,
    25
Happy Journey to Trenton and
    Camden, The: 110
Harbage, Alfred: 222
Hardy, Thomas: 136
Harris, Julie: 113
Harris, S. H.: 121
Hart, J. A.: 218
Harrison Texas: Eight Tele-
    vision Plays: 232

264

Hart, Moss: 217
Hartnoll, Phyllis: 117
Harvard Plays: 227
Hathaway, Baxter: 131
Hatlen, Theodore: 161
Hawthorne: 38, 64
Hayden, Philip M.: 151
Hayes, Helen: 89, 113, 225
Hazlitt, William: 227
Head-music: 107, 110, 111
Heart-music: 107, 108, 109, 110
Hearts and Flowers: 208
Hebbel: 127
Helburn, Theresa: 226
Hellman, Lillian: 213
Henderson, Archibald: 221
Hennequin, Alfred: 211, 218
Henry IV: 8
Henry V: 8, 20, 24, 33, 58
Henry VI: 8
He That Plays the King: 162
Hewitt, Barnard: 222
Heywood, John: 136
Hildreth, William Henry: 234
Hilliard, Evelyne: 152
Himelstein, Morgan Y.: 223
History of English Dramatic
    Literature to the Death of
    Queen Anne: 222
History of Modern Drama, A:
    220
History of the American Dra-
    ma, A: 222
History of the Fourteenth
    Street Theatre, The: 224
History of the Theatre, A:
    112
Hogan's Heroes: 208
Holmes, Nathaniel: 227
Homer: 108
Hopkins, Arthur: 112, 211, 216
Hopper, Hedda: 226
Horace: 121
Hotson, Leslie: 222
Hour of American Drama, An:
    222

House of Connelly and Other
    Plays, The: 233
Housman, A. E.: 120, 128
Howard, Leslie: 116
How's Your Second Act?: 112, 211
How to Produce Amateur
    Plays - A Practical
    Manual: 152
How to See a Play: 112
How to Teach English Class-
    ics: 20
How to Write a Good Play:
    211, 218
How to Write a Play: 212, 218
Hubbell, Joy B.: 234
Hudson, 72, 80
Hudson: Holland: 209
Hughes, Glenn: 112, 234
Humor in drama: 31
Hunt, Elizabeth R.: 161
Ibsen, Henrik: 35, 137
Ideas and Forms in English
    and American Literature:
    250
I Dream of Jeannie: 209
Immoment Toys: 131
Immortals of the Screen: 116, 119
Index to Full Length Plays,
    1895-1925: 118
Index to Full Length Plays,
    1926-1944: 118
Index to Full Length Plays,
    1944-1964: 118
Index to Plays: 118
Index to Plays in Collections:
    118
Inglis, Rewey Belle: 234
In Search of Theatre: 129
Instruments of Darkness: 68
Insurgent Theatre, The: 224
Intimate Portraits: 225
Introducing the Theatre: 112
Introduction to Drama, An:
    234

265

Introduction to the English
    Classics, An: 23
Invaders, The: 209
Invitation to the Theatre: 112
Ireland, Norma Olin: 118
Irving: 38
Isaacs, Edith J. R.: 130, 224,
    234
Ivanhoe: 38, 108
Ivory Tower and Other Radio
    Plays: 245

Jackson, Holbrook: 225
Jagendorf, Moritz: 234
James, Henry: 225
Jameson, Storm: 221
Jeremiah: 126
Jew of Malta, The: 8
Johnson, Gertrude E.: 118
Johnson, Theodore: 235
Joint Owners in Spain: 216
Jones, Henry Arthur: 144, 151
Jones, Howard Mumford: 117
Jonson, Ben: 122
Joy of the Theatre, The: 112
Julius Caesar: 9, 11, 15, 20,
    24, 30, 32, 33, 35, 37, 38,
    58, 63, 64, 68, 88, 91
Junior Play Book, The: 45, 46
Justice: 62, 153

Kahn, E. J., Jr.: 225
Kaufman, George S.: 149
Keats: 120
Kellogg, Brainerd: 7, 9
Kelly, George: 235
Kerr, Jane: 213
Kerr, Walter: 116, 123, 130
Ketterlinus Company, The:
    115
Kimball, Rodney A.: 160, 253
King John: 8
King Lear: 20, 207
King, Vernon R.: 233
Kismet: 212
Kittredge, George Lyman: 115
Knickerbocker, Edwin Van B.:

43, 56, 133, 160, 236;
    contributions to teaching of
    one-act play, 48-53
Knoblock, Edward: 62, 212
Koch, Frederick H.: 48, 236
Konick, Marcus: 54
Kozelka, Paul: 54
Kreymborg, Alfred: 238
Krutch, Joseph Wood: 222, 223
Kozlenko, William: 236-238

La Brant, Lou: 77-80, 83, 86,
    87
Lady of the Lake, The: 38
Lady or the Tiger, The: 159
Lamb: 82, 127
Langner, Lawrence: 226
Language of Tragedy, The:
    162
Lass, Abraham H.: 104, 238
Last Actor-Managers, The:
    226
Last Mile, The: 153
Last of the Lowries, The,
    study questions on, 47-48
Law, Frederick Houk: 54, 239
Law of the Drama, The: 144,
    151
Lawson, John Howard: 218
Lazarus, Arnold Leslie: 232
Leaves from a Critic's Scrap-
    book: 130
Le Gallienne, Eva: 89
Legend of Sleepy Hollow: 38
Leonard, Charles: 152
Leonard, Sterling Andrus: 43,
    54, 63, 64, 67, 133, 239
Lessing, G. E.: 127, 129
Lewis, Allan: 221, 223
Lewis, B. Roland: 53, 211,
    218, 239
Lewis, Sinclair: 125
Lectures on the Literature of
    the Age of Elizabeth: 227
Leeper, Janet: 227
Lelyveld, Toby: 224
Letters from Greenroom
    Ghosts: 226

Leverton, Garrett Hasty: 239
Life of a Star, The: 226
Lifson, David S.: 224
Listen for a Lonesome Drum: 216
Literature and Life: 66
Literature in the Theatre and Other Essays: 131
Little Clay Cart, The: 126, 148
Little, Frederick H.: 54
Little Theatre Classics: 231
Living Stage - A History of the World Theatre, The: 112
Living Theatre, The: 221
Locke, Alan Le Roy: 239
Lockridge, Richard: 225
Lodge, Evan: 161
Long Christmas Dinner and Other Plays in One Act, The: 252
Long Day's Journey into Night: 114, 134
Longer Plays by Modern Authors: 56
Longstreet, Stephan: 245
Long Voyage Home: Seven Plays of the Sea, The: 246
Long Voyage Home, The: 134
Loomis, Roger Sherman: 239, 240
de Lorde, André: 157
Lord's Will and Other Carolina Plays, The: 233
Lord's Will, The: 48
Loving, Pierre: 247
Lowell: 38
Lucas, F. L.: 121
Lucas, Harriet Marcelia: 240
Ludwig, Richard M.: 117
Lumley, Frederic: 132
Lunt, Alfred: 113
Lyman, William W.: 233
Lysistrata: 126
Lytell, Bert: 101, 153

Macbeth: 20, 33, 62, 68, 78, 91-93, 207; characters in, 25, 26; class reading, 34; composition based on, 22-23, 34; humor in, 31; plot analysis, 25; plot of, 31; questions on, 90; scenes for class reading, 34; stimulating interest in, 27-29, 90; teaching of, 12, 15, 16, 24, 37, 63, 73.

MacEwan, E. J.: 25, 151, 161, 211
MacGowan, Kenneth: 112
Mackay, Constance D-Arcy: 240
MacKaye: 68
Madame Sarah: 226
Maeterlinck, Maurice: 35, 62, 68, 89
Magic Curtain, The: 226
Magic Lanterns: 247
Making of the American Theatre, The: 222
Malevinsky, M. L.: 211, 218
Mantle, Burns: 114, 117, 225, 240
Marks, Jeanette: 162, 240
Marloe, Joan: 117
Marlowe: 8, 61, 127
Marriott, J. W.: 240, 241
Marshall, Norman: 222
Marsh, George L.: 33, 34
Martial Interludes: 217
Marty: 134
Marx, Milton: 161
Mary of Scotland: 114, 128, 207
Masque of Kings, The: 128
Masters of European Drama: 112
Masters of the Drama: 112
Mates, Julian: 224
Mathews Jane De Hart: 151, 224
Matinee Tomorrow: 223
Matthews, Brander: 161, 218
Maugham, W. Somerset: 126
Maupassant: 137
Mayorga, Margaret: 115, 134, 222, 241-244

McCarthy, Mary: 130
McCollom, William G.: 121, 162
McCormick, Theodora: 152
McGill, E. L.: 238
McGraw, H. Ward: 244
Medea: 113
Medieval Stage, The: 221
Melnitz, William: 112
Memories: 225
Memorization of scenes: 30
Mendelssohn: 58, 69
Merchant of Venice, The: 8, 15, 20, 24, 31, 33, 35, 37-40, 65, 66, 87, 93; how to teach the reading of, 77-80
Merry Merry Cuckoo and Other Welsh Plays, The: 240
Merry Partners--The Age and Stage of Harrigan and Hart, The: 225
Merry Widow, The: 125
Mersand, Joseph: 54, 118, 233
Message and Jehanne, The: 103, 137, 151
Middlemas, Robert: 151, 163
Midsummer Night's Dream, A (Mendelssohn): 58
Midsummer Night's Dream, A (Shakespeare): 20, 24, 31, 33, 113, 208
Mikado: 124
Miles, Dudley: 67
Miles Standish, Dramatization of: 20
Milestones: 59, 62, 212
Miller, Alice Duer: 68
Miller, Helen Louise: 152, 244
Miller, Jordan Y.: 130
Millett, Fred Benjamin: 161, 245
Milton: 8, 15, 23, 66
Miniature Plays for Stage and Study: 235
Minturno: 121
Mirrielees, Lucia B.: 86-89
Miscellany: 61
"Mister Abbott": 225

Modern American and British Plays: 250
Modern American Plays: 228
Modern Drama: 128
Modern Drama in Europe: 221
Modern English Readings: 239
Modern One-Act Plays: 54, 103, 233
Modern Plays-Short and Long: 54, 239
Modern Theatre, The: 129
Modern Times: 208
Modern Tragedy: 162
Moderwell, Hiram K.: 221
Moffett, Harold Y.: 251
Molière: 122
Montague, C. E.: 132
Montgomery, Gregory: 239
Moon of the Caribbees, The: 134, 151
Moonshine: 216
More by Corwin 230
Morehouse, Ward: 116, 130, 223
More in Sorrow: 130
More One-Act Plays: 230
More One-Act Plays by Modern Authors: 45, 47
More Plays in Miniature: 235
Morgan, A. E.: 132: 221
Morley, Malcolm: 112
Morley, Robert: 225
Morris, Clara: 226
Moses, Montrose Jonas : 130, 225, 245

Muni, Paul: 153
Munn, James Buell: 250
Munro, C. K.: 112
Mutiny on the Bounty: 114, 147
Myers, Paul: 117
My Favorite Martian: 209
My First Fifty Years in the Theatre: 225

Name and Nature of Poetry, The: 120, 128

Nathan, George Jean: 116, 134, 151, 245
National Educational Television: 122
Nazaroff, Alexander I.: 161
Nazimova, Madame: 109
"Necklace": 137
Negro in the American Theatre, The: 224
Nelson, John Herbert: 245
New American Drama, The: 222, 223
New Movement in the Theatre, The: 220
New Plays for Women and Girls: 253
New Theatre Handbook and Digest of Plays, The: 118
New Theatres for Old: 220
New York Theatre Critics Reviews: 116
Nicholson, Kenyon: 245
Niggli, Josephina: 211, 219
Night at An Inn, A: 209
Nights at the Play: 132
No Exit: 114
Nonsensorship: 131
Noyes, Henry H.: 89, 251
Nugent, Elliott: 226

Oboler, Arch: 102, 245, 246
Odets, Clifford: 134
Odyssey: 108
Of Time and the River: 123
Ogden, Jess: 223
Ogleby, Kate: 152
O'Hara, Frank Hurburt: 112, 223
Oklahoma: 125
Old Lady Shows Her Medals, The: 102
Oliver, Margaret Scott: 50
Olson, Elder: 121, 162
Ommaney, Katharine Anne: 152
One-act play, characteristics of the, 137; new interest in the, 133; perfecting the

form of the, 136; techniques for teaching the, 133; why study the, 149
One-Act Plays (Barrett and Cook): 229
One-Act Plays (Clark and Cook): 54
One-Act Plays (Goldstone): 54, 232
One-Act Plays (Webber and Webber): 53
One-Act Plays by Modern Authors: 43, 54, 56, 133, 229
One-Act Plays for Secondary Schools: 251
One-Act Plays for Stage and Study: 254, 255
One-Act Plays for Study and Production: 54
One-Act Plays For Today: 54, 233
One-Act Plays of Today: 240, 241
One-Hundred Non-Royalty, One-Act Plays: 236
One-Hundred Non-Royalty Radio Plays: 237
O-Neill, Eugene: 68, 102, 114, 134, 137, 213, 216, 246
One Thousand and One Plays for the Little Theatre: 118
On-Stage - A History of Theatre: 112
On Stage, Everyone: 152
On Stage for Teen-Agers: 244
Oppenheimer, Celia: 234
Oppenheimer, George: 121, 131
Orientation to the Theatre: 161
Othello: 207
Other Theatre, The: 222
Ottemiller, John H.: 118
Overtones: 216
Ould, Herman: 161, 212
Our Town: 134, 213
Overton, Grace Sloan: 152

Oxford Companion to the Theatre, The: 117

Palmer, Helen H.: 129
Palmer, John: 221
Paperbound Books In Print: 114
Parker, Kenneth T.: 246
Parker's Television Plays: 246
Passionate Playgoer, The: 121,
131
Pastiche and Prejudice: 131
Pater, Walter: 123
Patriotic Plays and Pageants
for Young People: 240
Peabody, Josephine Preston:
62, 89
Peculiar Treasure, A: 121, 128
Pearson, Hesketh: 226
Pence, Raymond Woodbury: 246
Peter Pan: 89
Peterson, Marcelene: 116, 119
Phelps, William Lyon: 221
Phillips, Leroy: 235
Phillips, Stephen: 50, 68
Pictorial History of Opera, A:
118
Pictorial History of the Amer-
ican Theatre, 1900-1950, A:
118
Pictorial History of The Amer-
ican Theatre 100 Years,
1860-1960, A: 118
Pictorial History of the Mo-
vies, A: 116, 119
Pictorial History of the Silent
Screen, A: 116, 118
Pictorial History of the Talk-
ies, A: 116, 118
Pictorial History of Vaude-
ville, A: 119
Pierre Patelin: 208
Piper, The: 59, 62, 89
Plan of study: 7, 9
Play and Its Parts, A: 162
Play Books of the Perse
School: 214

Playboy of the Western World:
114
Player Under Three Reigns,
A: 226
Play Directing: 152
Playgoing - An Essay: 111
Play List Revision Committee
of the Secondary School
Theatre Conference: 118
Play-Making: 211, 217, 218
Play of Today, The: 161
Plays: 232
Plays and the Theatre: 250
Plays as Experience: 160,
253
Plays, classifying, 207; class-
room interpretation of one-
act, 50; how to visualize,
29; reading, 39; standards
for judging great, 124;
teaching one-act, 43; value
of, 148; vocabulary and al-
lusions in, 30; why we go
to, 145
Plays for Americans: 246
Plays for Classroom Interpre-
tation: 43, 49, 53, 56, 133
Plays for Modern Youth: 54
Plays for Our Time: 54
Plays for Strolling Mummers:
248
Plays for the College Theatre:
239
Plays from Radio: 238
Plays in Miniature: 235
Plays in Prose and Verse:
253
Plays of American Life and
Fantasy: 234
Plays of Negro Life: 239
Plays of the Irish Renaissance:
228
Plays of the Italian Theatre:
232
Plays Recommended for High
Schools: 118
Play's The Thing, The: 245

Plays Without Footlights: 232
Playwright at Work: 212, 219
Playwrights of the New Amer-
ican Theatre: 225
Playwright's Progress: O'Neill
and the Critics: 130
Playwright, the student: 210
Plot, how to study, 31, 60;
making a chart of, 39
Plot Outlines of 100 Famous
Plays: 117
Plummer, Christopher: 113
Plutarch: 11
Poetic appeal, how to
achieve: 30
Poetic Drama: 238
Poetics: 121
Pointers on Playwriting: 211,
219
Pointers on Producing the
School Play: 152
Polti, George: 110, 162
Pope, Alexander: 148
Popkin, Henry: 128, 151, 162
Porgy and Bess: 125
Porter, Harold E. : 163
Porter, Perrin: 228
Portmanteau Adaptions : 250
Portmanteau Plays: 250
Potell, Herbert: 232
Preface to Drama, A: 161,
230
Preludes and Studies: 131
Premieres of the Year: 132
Pressey, Benfield: 250
Price, W. T. : 161, 212
Prideaux, Tom: 119
Primer for Playgoers, A: 112
Princess, The: 38
Principles of Playmaking and
Other Discussions of the
Drama: 218
Prior, Moody E. : 162
Prize-Winning Non-Royalty
One-Act Plays: 249
Problems of the Playwright:
130
Procrustean model: 60

Producing in Little Theaters :
152
Producing the Play: 152
Prose and Poetry for Appreci-
ation: 227, 240, 244
Prose and Poetry of America:
244
Prose and Poetry of England:
244
Prose and Poetry of the
World: 227
Proust, Marcel: 126

Provincetown Plays: 230
Provincetown--Story of the
Theatre, The: 224
Puppet Plays: 238
Putnam, G. Palmer: 131
Pygmalion: 113, 114

Quality Street: 113
Quarto of Modern Literature,
A: 228
Quick Curtains: 233
Quinn, Arthur Hobson: 222

Rabkin, Gerald: 223
Radio and Television Plays:
231
Radio Drama in Action: 227
Ralph Roister Doister: 20
Ray, Lucile: 162
Reading Drama: 245
Recollections of a Player: 226
Reed, Joseph Verner: 226
Reeves, John L. : 112
Religious Drama Project Play
List: 118
Representative Modern Dramas:
251
Representative One-Act Plays
by American Authors: 243,
244
Representative One-Act Plays
by Continental Authors: 245
Representative Plays by
British and Irish Authors:
229

Return of Odysseus, The: 65
Revolution in American Theatre: 223
Rice, Elmer: 221
Richard of Bordeaux: 207
Richard II: 8
Reading and Staging the Play: 54
Rembrant: 150
Renaissance of the Drama, The: 151
Return of the Native, The: 136
Rickaby, Franz: 246
Riders to the Sea: 48, 128, 147
Rip Van Winkle: 38
Rivals, The: 20, 122
Roar China: 148
Robert Morley: 225
Roberts, Vera Mowry: 112
Robins, Elizabeth: 225
Rockwell, Ethel: 246
Romeo and Juliet: 20, 33, 66, 113, 147, 160
Rosenberg, Edgar: 224
Rose, Reginald: 246
Ross, Jacob M.: 161
Rostand: 35, 89
Rouse, W. H. D.: 214
Rowe, Kenneth Thorpe: 161, 246
Rubinstein, H. F.: 222
Ryerson, Florence: 246

Sainte-Beuve, Charles-Augustine: 129, 144, 151
Saint Joan: 113
Salem, James: 128
Samson Agonistes: 8
Santaniello, A. E.: 118
Sardou 212
Sardou and the Sardou Plays: 218
Sartre, Jean Paul: 114
Saunders, Louise: 247
Scaliger: 121
Schelling, Felix E.: 162, 222
Schlegel, Augustus William: 129

Scholastic Teacher: 27
School Drama in England, The: 162
School for Scandal, The: 59, 122
Schuker, Louis A.: 104
Schweitzer, John C.: 54
Science of Playwriting, The: 211, 218
Scott, Element: 132
Screen World: 116
Sea Gull, The: 113
Sea-Plays: 229
Sebillet: 121
Second Shepherd's Play, The: 20
Secrets of a Showman: 226
Seeing More Things: 130
Seeing Things: 130
Seeing Things at Night: 129
Seen on the Stage: 130, 218
Selected Essays: 129
Selected Plays: 247
Selected Prose Works: 129
Serling, Rod: 102
Seven Contemporary Plays: 251
Seven Modern Comedies: 231
Seven Short Plays: 233
Seventeen: 46
Shadows of the Stage: 131
Shakespeare and His Predecessors: 226
Shakespeare - Five Lectures: 226
Shakespeare in America: 226
Shakespeare, life and work of, 26: methods of teaching 9, 21, 23, 29, 59, 80; studying characterization in, 39; time and person of, 39
"Shakespeare--The King": 39
Shank, Theodore J.: 117
Sharp, Russell A.: 62, 63
Shaw: 225
Shaw, Bernard: 33, 35, 56, 114, 124, 127, 128, 132, 144, 149, 151, 247

272

Shaw, Harry: 231
Shay, Frank: 118, 230, 247-249
Shearer, Norma: 146
Sheridan, Richard Brinsley: 20, 122, 149
Sherman, L. A.: 14
Sherwood: 89
Sherwood, Garrett P.: 114
She Stoops to Conquer: 20, 37, 38, 43, 56, 59, 122
Shipley, Joseph T.: 118
Shoemaker's Holiday, The: 122
Shore, Viola Brothers: 226
Short, Ernest: 112
Short History of the American Drama, A: 222
Short Plays: 49, 53, 160
Short Plays by Representative Authors: 43, 133, 249
Short Plays for Junior and Senior High Schools: 54, 251
Short Plays for Modern Players: 234
Short Plays of Various Types: 54, 249
Short Plays: Revised: 49
Shouts and Murmurs: 131
Show Boat: 125
Showman: 225
Shudraka, King: 126, 148
Shylock on the Stage: 224
Sierra: 216
Sievers, W. David: 223
Sights and Spectacles: 130
Silas Marner: 38, 64
Simonson, Lee: 227
Singing Leaves: 38
Six Television Plays: 246
Skinner, Cornelia Otis: 226
Skinner, Otis: 89
Skin of our Teeth, The: 213
Smith, Alice M.: 43, 133, 249
Smith, Betty: 249
Smith, Milton M.: 54, 249
Smith, Reed: 80-85, 89
Smith, Robert M.: 249
Smothers Brothers Show: 208

Snow Image: 38
Sobel, Bernard: 118, 119
Social Significance of the Modern Drama, The: 220
"Some Platitudes Concerning Drama": 218
Sophocles: 8
South Pacific: 125
So You're Writing a Play: 211, 218
Spaeth, Sigmund: 107, 108
Sper, Felix: 224
"Spreading the News": 50
S. S. Glencairn: 134
Stage and the School, The: 152
Stage Directions: 226
Stage is Set, The: 227
Stage-Struck John Golden: 226
Stagestruck - The Romance of Alfred Lunt and Lynn Fontanne: 226
Stallings, Roy: 117
Star Trek: 209
Steegmuller, Francis: 129
Steeves, Harrison Ross: 65, 66
Steinberg, Mollie B.: 224
Stevenson, Robert Louis: 108, 146, 213
Still More Prejudice: 131
Still Seeing Things: 130
Stockton, Frank: 159
Stoddart, James H.: 226
Stokes, Sewell: 225
Story of the Theatre, The: 112
Strange Interlude: 134
Stratman, Carl J.: 129
Stratton, Clarence: 56-60, 62, 152
Streets of New York, The: 122
Streicher, Samuel: 104
Strong, L. A. G.: 112
Stuart, Ray: 116, 119
Student Prince, The: 125
Studies in Stagecraft: 130, 151
Study of the Drama, A: 161
Study of the Modern Drama, A: 220

Sutro, Alfred: 249
Styan, J. L.: 112, 162, 221
Surrey, Earl of: 61
Swann's Way: 127
Synge, J. M.: 35, 48, 114, 128, 147

Tairov: 148
Tale of Two Cities, A: 38, 108
Tales from Shakespeare: 82
Talks to Beginning Teachers of English: 90
Taming of the Shrew, The: 113, 149
Tarkington, Booth: 45, 46
Taste of Honey, A: 114
Taubman, Howard: 222
Taylor, Deems: 116, 119
Teacher's Outlines for Studies in English: 15
Teaching Composition and Literature in Junior and Senior High School: 86
Teaching English in High Schools: 62
Teaching Literature: 67
Teaching Literature in the Grammar Grades and High School: 35, 36
Teaching of English, The: 68
Teaching of English in the Elementary and Secondary School, The: 9, 12
Teaching of English in the High School: 56
Teaching of English in the Secondary School, The: 27, 67
Teaching of High School English, The: 74
Teaching of Literature, The: 65
Teaching of Literature in the High School, The: 80
Teaching of Literature in the Secondary School, The: 77
Technique of Play Writing, 211, 218

Technique of the Drama, The (Freytag): 25, 151, 161, 211
Technique of the Drama, The (Price): 212
Technique of the One-Act Play, The: 211
Technique of the One-Act Play-- a Text-book, The: 211, 218
Telephone, The: 157
Television Plays: 228
Tempest, The: 7, 20, 31, 33, 113
Tendencies in Modern English Drama: 132, 221
Ten Fantasies for Stage and Study: 235
Ten Modern Plays: 234
Ten One-Act Plays: 232
10 Short Plays: 54
Theatre and Drama in the Making: 162
Theatre and Friendship: 225
Theatre Arts Anthology: 121
Theatre Arts Books, Inc.: 115
Theatre Arts Monthly: 47
Theatre at the Crossroads: 220
Theatre at the Left: 220
Theatre Books in Print: 118
Theatre: Essays on the Arts of the Theatre: 130
Theatre for Everybody, A: 222
Theatregoing: 112
Theatre Guild Anthology, The: 114
Theatre Guild, The: 224
Theatre in Life, The: 161
Theatre in Our Times, The: 220
Theatre in Review: 132
Theatre in Spite of Itself, The: 130
Theatre in Your Head, A: 161
Theatre Magazine: 47
Theatre of Protest and Paradox, The: 221
Theatre of Revolt, The: 220

Theatre of Today, The: 221
Theatre of Two Decades: 132
Theatre, The: 112
Theatre: Three Thousand Years
  of Drama, Acting and Stage-
  craft, The: 112
Theatre, U. S. A.: 222
Theatrical Alliance: 116
Theodora: 213
Theory and Technique of Play-
  writing: 218
Theory of the Theatre, The:
  130
Thermidor: 213
They Shall Not Die: 153
Thirteen by Corwin: 230
Thirty Famous One-Act Plays:
  228
Thirty-Six Dramatic Situations,
  The: 110, 149, 162
Thomas, Charles Swain: 19-25,
  27-33, 54, 56, 60, 67, 72-
  74, 79, 83, 86, 88, 89, 249
Thomas, Russell Brown: 250
Thompson, Alan Reynolds: 112
Thompson, Blanche Jennings:
  161
Thomson, Ruth: 118
Thorndike, Ashley H.: 162
Through the Fourth Wall: 131
Today in American Drama: 223
Tolstoy: 124
Today's Literature: 233
To-night at 8:30: 134
To Read and To Act: 152
To the Director and Playwright:
  152
Tottel: 61
Touch of the Poet, A: 134
Tragedy (Lucas): 121
Tragedy (McCollom): 121, 162
Tragedy (Thorndike): 162
Tragedy and Comedy: 130
Tragedy and the Theory of
  Drama: 121, 162
Treadwell, Bill: 221
Treasure Island: 108

Treasury of Plays for Men:
  248
Treasury of Plays for Women:
  248
Treasury of the Theatre, A:
  (Burns & Gassner): 240
Treasury of the Theatre, A:
  (Gassner) 114, 232
Trent, William P.: 23, 24, 25
Trewin, J. C.: 132
Trifles: 143, 217
Trysting Place, The: 45; sug-
  gestions for study of, 46
Tucker, S. Marion: 54, 250
Tuesdays and Fridays: 129
"Turtle Dove, The": 50
Twelfth Night: 20, 24, 33, 37
$1200 a Year: 121
Twelve One-Act Plays: 231, 255
Twelve One-Act Plays for
  Study and Production: 250
Twelve Plays: 49, 52, 53, 236
Twentieth Century Theatre,
  The: (Phelps) 221
Twentieth Century Theatre,
  The: (Vernon) 221
Twenty Contemporary One-
  Act Plays, American: 248
Twenty-Five Best Plays of
  the Modern American The-
  atre: 232
Twenty-Five Modern Plays:
  250
Twenty-Five Non-Royalty One-
  Act American Comedies:
  238
Twenty-Five Short Plays,
  International: 249
Twenty Non-Royalty Plays: 234
Twenty-Seven Wagons Full of
  Cotton, and Other One-Act
  Plays: 252
Twilight Zone, The: 209
"Two Crooks and a Lady": 50
Two on the Aisle: 123, 129
Two for the Seesaw: 114
Tynan, Kenneth: 162

Types of Dramatic
  Composition: 235
Types of Farce Comedy: 249
Typical Plays for Secondary
  Schools: 251

"Ulysses": 50
University of Michigan Plays:
  246
University of Utah Plays: 239
Untitled and Other Radio
  Dramas: 230
Upstage: The American The-
  atre in Performance:123,129
Use of the Drama, The: 161

Valiant, The: 101-103, 110,
  147, 151; how to teach, 153-
  160; text of, 163-206
Van Druten, John: 212, 219
Van Gogh: 150
Variety of Plays, A: 54
Variorum Shakespeare: 58
de Vega, Lope: 121
Verdi: 69
Vernon, Frank: 221
Vidal, Gore: 102, 250
Volpone: 122
Voltaire: 114, 127

Voyage to the Bottom of the
  Sea: 209

Wagner: 110
Waiting for Lefty: 133
Walbrook, H. M.: 132
Walker, Stuart: 250
Walkley, A. B.: 131
Waltz of the Toreadors: 114
Ward, Adolphus William: 222
Watching a Play: 112
Watson, Ernest Bradlee: 250
Watt, Homer Andrew: 250
Way of the World, The: 226
Ways to Teach English: 72
Wayward Quest, A: 226
Weales, Gerald: 162, 223

Weatherly, Edward Howell:
  251
Webber, Hart Hanson: 53, 54
Webber, James Plaisted: 53,
  54, 251
Weiser, Norman S.: 251
Weiss, M. Jerry: 54
We'll Hear a Play: 132
Wellwarth, George E.: 221
West Side Story: 125
Wexley, John: 153
What Every Woman Knows: 114
What is Theatre?: 129
Where the Cross is Made: 110,
  137
While Rome Burns: 131
Whitman, Charles Huntington:
  251
Whole Truth and Nothing But,
  The: 226
Wilde, Oscar: 128, 149
Wilde, Percival: 212, 219
Wilder, Thornton: 103, 134,
  137, 213, 251, 252
Williams, Emlyn George: 225
Williams, Raymond: 162
Williams, Tennessee: 134, 252
Williamson, Audrey: 132
William, Winter: 131
Willis, John: 117
"Will o' the Wisp": 50
Wimberly, Lowry C.: 231
Wingless Victory, The: 113
Winsten, Stephen: 225
Winterset: 128, 208
Wisconsin Rural Plays: 246
Wishengrad, Morton: 252
Wolfe, Thomas: 123
Woodbridge, Elizabeth: 25, 31,
  35, 162
Woodward, Daphne: 226
Woolcott, Alexander: 131
Worcester Account, The: 224
Wordsworth: 143
Workhouse Ward, The: 216
World of Musical Comedy, The:
  224

276

Worlds of Robert E. Sherwood,
    The: 225
World Theatre in Pictures: 119
Worsley, T. C.: 132
Wright, Edward A.: 112
Writer's Radio Theatre, The:
    251
Wycherley: 122
Wylie, Max: 252, 253

Yale One-Act Plays: 227
Yeats, William Butler: 253
Young, Stark: 131

Zachar, Irwin J.: 160, 253
Zolotow, Maurice: 226
Zweig, Stefan: 126